LED BY LOVE

LED BY LOVE

Worship Resources for Year B

LAVON BAYLER

United Church Press
Cleveland, Ohio

To our three sons, David, Jonathan, and Timothy

United Church Press, Cleveland, Ohio 44115

© 1996 by United Church Press

Printed in the United States of America on acid-free paper

01 00   5 4 3

Library of Congress Cataloging-in-Publication Data

Bayler, Lavon, 1933–
    Led by love : worship resources for year B / Lavon Bayler.
        p.   cm.
    Includes index.
    ISBN 0-8298-1124-9 (alk. paper)
    1. Church year.   2. Worship programs.   I. Title.
    BV30.B384   1996
    264—dc20   95-51672
                                                                              CIP

C o n t e n t s

Introduction

The Gospel of Mark leads us through Year B of the Revised Common *Lectionary*. This earliest telling of the story of Jesus traces the actions of a vital, caring leader at whom people were "amazed and glorified God, saying, "'We have never seen anything like this!'" (2:12b).

Readings from Mark are supplemented by extensive passages from John, who noted explicitly that "God is love." In Jesus of Nazareth, the love of God took on flesh and blood. People could see and hear and experience in the depth of human encounter the spiritual realities they had sensed but only dimly understood. For those few brief years in Galilee and on the journey to Jerusalem, they were *led* by love in ways that have reverberated through the centuries. Self-giving, risk-taking witness became for many a way of life that was transforming for all who sensed its authenticity. We are invited to walk with Jesus that we, too, may be led by love to address the issues of our own day with compassionate servant leadership.

During the season of Advent through the Sundays after Epiphany, selections from throughout the Hebrew Scriptures are intended to illuminate the gospel. Second readings are drawn primarily from the letters to the Corinthians. Important narratives of faith from the Hebrew Scriptures and the Acts of the Apostles mark the days from Ash Wednesday through Pentecost. They are chosen to relate to the Gospels, while the second readings feature a semicontinuous consideration of the First Letter of John.

The *Revised Common Lectionary* provides two tracks through the Sundays after Pentecost. We are to choose and follow one of these tracks, not jump back and forth. One set of readings from the Hebrew Scriptures takes us through the stories of David and into the Wisdom literature. This is the one reflected in this book. The other track (center column in this book) presents us with random selections chosen for their relationship to the gospel of the day. During this "ordinary time," our reading of Mark's Gospel is interrupted by five Sundays spent in the sixth chapter of John. Semicontinuous selections from 2 Corinthians, Ephesians, James, and Hebrews make up the second readings. The eschatological theme at the end of the church year brings us back to where we began on the first Sunday in Advent, anticipating the coming (return) of Jesus.

It has been a privilege once again to wrestle with the scriptures to produce liturgies that weave together the experiences of our daily lives with the themes of the Bible. What is offered here is meant to spark your own creativity as you plan for worship that uplifts and inspires. For each occasion, I have provided a call to worship, invocation, call to confession, prayer of confession, assurance of pardon, collect, offertory invitation, offertory prayer, and commission and blessing.

As in previous books, the prayers are augmented by hymns based on the scriptures for the day. These are gathered together in the appendix. For each hymn, I have noted by name a tune I had in mind while writing the words. *The Hymnal* of the Evangelical and Reformed Church and *The Pilgrim Hymnal* were my primary companions as I wrote. Hymns are also designated by meter, which simply notes the number of syllables in each line. By consulting a hymnal's metrical index, you can usually find other tunes to which my words may be sung.

If you choose to print any of these resources in your worship bulletins, United Church Press requests that you also include the permission stated on the copyright page at the beginning of this volume. If you edit my work in the process, please note "adapted from."

Thanks to all of you who have written notes of appreciation that have kept me writing far longer than I originally intended. I trust that our current ecumenical lectionary will endure through the rest of my lifetime. The revisions published in 1992 led to this second series of books.

Special recognition is due Pat Kitner, who once again translated my hand-written notebooks into manuscript form. Thanks also to Bob Bayler, whose continuing support and encouragement allow me time around the fringes of our busy lives to complete these resources.

Worship Resources

THE ADVENT SEASON

Isaiah 64:1–9   1 Corinthians 1:3–9
Psalm 80:1–7, 17–19   Mark 13:24–37

CALL TO WORSHIP

Awake, people of God, and stay alert for Christ's coming.
Grace to you and peace from God who sent Jesus to us.
>*Make your ways known to us, O God.*
>*Show us once more your awesome presence.*

We are all God's people; no one is excluded.
Come together as God's family for worship and prayer.
>*Let the mountains quake before you, mighty God.*
>*Let the nations tremble in awe and reverence.*

Praise the One who grants us the gift of life.
Give thanks for God's continuing faithfulness.
>*Heaven and earth will pass away,*
>*But the Word of God is true for all times and places.*

INVOCATION

Amid threatening clouds of anger and selfish strife, come, O God, to bring light. Into our days of worry and anxiety, send a confident hope. Enrich us with spiritual gifts that transcend disappointments and spill out in generous compassion for all your suffering children. Meet us today where we are so we may be equipped for trials yet to come and for joys yet to be revealed. In Jesus' name. Amen.

CALL TO CONFESSION

As a new year begins in the church, we seek to leave behind our past unfaithfulness. We remember our doubts and neglect, the empty times when prayer is forgotten and our focus is narrowed to petty concerns. God is waiting to hear from us. Let us pray.

PRAYER OF CONFESSION

Awesome God, we confess the sin of our separation from you. We have blamed you for hiding from us, rather than admitting we have failed to see you in the thousands of ways you are revealing yourself every day. We have not called on you, and we have not listened for your call to us. Without you, we have become tiny islands of self-concern. Our links with the rest of your children are stretched and broken. O God, we long for that loving community in which your reign is acknowledged and your purposes are served. Move us to that place, we pray. Amen.

Assurance of Forgiveness

God's grace has come to us in Jesus Christ. God restores us to a right relationship with the eternal, that we might rightfully value ourselves and all persons. Spiritual gifts are ours to claim. God is faithful and will strengthen us to face all circumstances. Praise God, the source of all things!

Collect

Child of humankind, born of God, reveal to us once more the power and glory which claims us all. Let your Word make its impact within and among us that we may accept your mission for us and enlist all our efforts in watchful service. Come to reign among us and rule in every heart. Amen.

Offertory Invitation

We have been enriched and strengthened in so many ways by the gifts of God. Now we have the privilege of sharing God's Word with the world. Our offerings enable our church's witness in this community and a caring outreach around the globe. Let us give as we have been blessed.

Offertory Prayer

Gracious God, we give our best to you, not out of guilt or fear, but with gratitude and faith. You have been our support in times of need. Every breath we take is a gift from you. We would be awake and watchful for opportunities to make a difference, to help others be alert for your presence, to value life in all its fullness, and to learn to care. We dedicate these symbols of thankfulness and all the days of our lives to those purposes. Amen.

Commission and Blessing

The time is coming when God will call us to account.
Be alert and watchful, serving faithfully day by day.
> *We will look around us for signs of God's presence.*
> *We will open our eyes to ways to be helpful.*
Use the gifts you have been given to the glory of God.
Let the testimony of Christ strengthen you in every way.
> *We will share our spiritual gifts in word and deed.*
> *We will seek to be shaped by the potter's hands.*
Grace to you and peace, from God and Jesus Christ.
Know that God is faithful and Christ walks with you.
> *With hearts full of gladness, we will do what is right.*
> *With great joy, our lives will show forth our faith.*
Amen. **Amen.**

(See hymns 1, 2.)

Isaiah 40:1–11   2 Peter 3:8–15a
Psalm 85:1–2, 8–13   Mark 1:1–8

CALL TO WORSHIP

The day of God is coming; lift up your voices.
Cry out with the strength God provides.
> *We await God's coming day with anticipation.*
> *We seek the peace and patience God provides.*

Comfort, comfort my people, says our God.
Speak tenderly to my suffering people.
> *We will prepare the way for One who is coming.*
> *We look forward to baptism in the Spirit.*

God will feed us like a shepherd.
God will gather us in gentle, caring arms.
> *God's hand is upon us in blessing;*
> *We are welcomed by God's steadfast love.*

INVOCATION

Righteous and holy God, your glory is revealed to us day by day as valleys of despair are lifted up and mountainous problems are leveled. In your presence, we see more than our immediate situation. We catch a glimpse of your eternal purposes. So come among us now and speak your word of peace. Feed us with your truth, and equip us to welcome Christ's coming. Amen.

CALL TO CONFESSION

God is patient with us, not wanting any to perish. Yet we have turned away from holiness and godliness. We have chosen to fit into society rather than give leadership for a new day. Let the church confess its failures.

PRAYER OF CONFESSION

God of glory, we confess that we have not recognized you in our midst nor listened for your voice. Our faith is fragile, and our iniquity goes unrecognized amid our massive self-concern. We have lived as if we have no need to account for the life we have been given. Our church is focused more on our own survival than on its mission in the world. We come to you today with sincere repentance for our neglect. We have failed to prepare the way for Christ's entry into our everyday environment. Pardon and change us, we pray. Amen.

ASSURANCE OF FORGIVENESS

God speaks tenderly to us and assures us that our debt has been paid, our sins forgiven, our paths made straight. God's glory is waiting to burst into the midst of all who accept the good news. Surely our salvation is at hand. Faithfulness will spring up from the ground, and righteousness will look down from the sky. Enjoy the baptism of the Holy Spirit!

COLLECT

God of good news, who sent John as a messenger to people of his day and who speaks to us in numerous words and deeds of the saints of all ages, open us now to receive what we most need today, that we may serve as a vital resource to others who are looking for meaning and hope in their lives. Amen.

OFFERTORY INVITATION

One way we prepare for Christ's appearance is to support the church's mission in our community and beyond. Our church's programs share good news, our outreach provides comfort and practical help, and our goals are nothing less than newness of life for all God's children. May our gifts reflect God's generosity.

OFFERTORY PRAYER

While we are waiting and preparing for Christ to appear, we are seeking, O God, to act as faithful followers. May our offerings extend the promise of salvation to people whose lives are broken by neglect, abuse, bad choices, and sinful ways. May these gifts offer hope to all whose suffering and loss seem too heavy to bear. May our church be a listening, caring presence for all its members, and through us for all those we meet in our work and leisure. Amen.

COMMISSION AND BLESSING

Announce the good news of Jesus Christ;
Prepare the way for Christ's witness to be heard.
> ***Christ brings hope for true peace to all people.***
> ***God is patiently waiting for us to claim this gift.***
Lead lives of holiness and godliness;
Enjoy treasures of heaven and earth that God offers.
> ***God's Word brings us both comfort and challenge.***
> ***We are accepted by God and commissioned for duty.***
You will be fed and blessed on life's way.
The baptism of the Holy Spirit will empower you.
> ***We turn our hearts and minds toward God.***
> ***We rejoice that we can be servants in Christ's name.***
Amen. **Amen.**

(See hymns 3, 4.)

Isaiah 61:1–4, 8–11   1 Thessalonians 5:16–24
Psalm 126 or Luke 1:47–55   John 1:6–8, 19–28

CALL TO WORSHIP

God is in our midst; do not fear.
God rejoices to renew our lives in steadfast love.
> *God gathers us for this time of worship.*
> *God claims us and promises us a home.*

Trust in God who is our strength and life.
Give thanks to God, the source of our salvation.
> *We will sing praises and exalt God's name.*
> *With joyous shouts, we will tell of God's glorious deeds.*

Rejoice in God, whatever your circumstances.
Remember the good fortune God has shared with you.
> *We will not worry as we seek God's peace.*
> *We open our hearts and minds to God's leading.*

INVOCATION

Loving God, we rejoice in this season of anticipation as we remember your promises and look forward to ways that you reveal yourself to us. May your presence be real to us in this hour. Strengthen us for victories over temptation, for renewal of our love for you and one another, for leadership and service in your church. We give thanks that you have called us into community and commissioned us to make a difference in the world. Equip us here for the tasks you set before us. Amen.

CALL TO CONFESSION

God's winnowing fork separates faithful ones from the unfaithful, honest ones from the dishonest, gentle ones from those who vent their anger against the innocent. God seeks to remove the chaff from our lives that we might recognize our own true worth as God's children. Let us seek God's healing.

PRAYER OF CONFESSION

All-knowing God, we confess our worry and anxiety over unimportant matters. We admit the fears that make us defensive instead of loving. We acknowledge our resentment over losses we have sustained and oppression we have suffered. We recognize that we have been far more concerned for our own welfare than for the building up of Christ's body, the church. In our congregation, we have focused on survival more than service. We look for what we can gain more than for what we can give. Re-establish your rule among us, we pray, and save us from ourselves. Amen.

ASSURANCE OF FORGIVENESS

God has good news of freedom for oppressed and captive people, of comfort for the brokenhearted and mourning ones, of hope for those who are devastated. God offers salvation and welcomes us into a covenant relationship. Surely our hearts will know joy, and our voices will ring with laughter. God is faithful and will grant us peace.

COLLECT

God of our baptism, whose messengers appear in strange places and unexpected times, keep us from missing the voices in the wilderness that speak your Word. Whether of warning or assurance or challenge, your message is one we would not ignore. May we, like John, help to prepare the way that our world may become a more wholesome and welcoming place for all people. Amen.

OFFERTORY INVITATION

Today God's voice is heard through the ministries we help to provide, here in our church, and in outreach to all the world's people. We bear witness to the light that is coming into the world through personal caring and corporate sharing. May all our giving be generous!

OFFERTORY PRAYER

In our unworthiness, O God, may we yet bring worthy gifts to honor the Messiah. May the brokenhearted be led to enriching new celebrations. May the lowly among us come to know their true worth as persons chosen by you to do great things. By your mercy, may the hungry be fed not only with bread but also with opportunities to feed others. We give ourselves as your servants, for no gift is complete without personal commitment. Thank you, God, for expecting great things of us. Our spirits rejoice in the coming of our Savior. Amen.

COMMISSION AND BLESSING

Rejoice always and pray without ceasing.
Give thanks to God, whatever your circumstances.
> **God has done great things for us.**
> **We rejoice that we are part of God's family.**

Listen for the word of the prophets.
Be open to the stirrings of the Holy Spirit.
> **The Spirit of God has come to us.**
> **We have a mission to accomplish for God.**

God is faithful and will stand by you.
You are valued in God's covenant community.
> **We are filled with joy as we go out to serve.**
> **We are thankful for the good news we carry.**

Amen. **Amen.**

(See hymns 5, 6.)

---

2 Samuel 7:1–11, 16   Romans 16:25–27
Luke 1:47–55 or Psalm 89:1–4, 19–26   Luke 1:26–38

CALL TO WORSHIP

Come apart to this place of rest and renewal;
Let your spirits rejoice in the presence of God.
> *We will sing of God's steadfast love for all people.*
> *We will proclaim God's faithfulness to all generations.*

God looks with favor on the humble and lowly.
God's covenant does not focus on rank or position.
> *God strengthens those who are weak.*
> *The proud are scattered in the thoughts of their hearts.*

Blessed are those who walk in God's light.
Blessed are all who say 'yes' to God's call.
> *Let the heavens proclaim the wonders of God.*
> *Let all the earth rejoice in Christ's coming.*

INVOCATION

We bring our spiritual hungers to this place, O God, hoping to be fed. We bring our weariness, expecting to find rest for our souls. We bring our dullness, asking that we might be alerted to those things that you consider important. We come because we want the scattered fragments of our lives to come together in a meaningful wholeness. You have promised to be with us. Reveal yourself to us here, we pray in the name of One who came to share our common lot. Amen.

CALL TO CONFESSION

The promises of God are meant for all to enjoy. Yet we have broken covenant and declared our independence from the Giver of Life. Then, when we are brought down from the thrones of our pretension, we wonder why. Let us confess the sin that separates us from God's promises.

PRAYER OF CONFESSION

Gracious God, in whom all things are possible, we confess that we have doubted what we cannot explain. We have sought strength and enjoyment apart from you. We have taken pride in ownership more than giving praise through stewardship. We have neglected to thank you, either in good times or when you have supported us during days of uncertainty. We have resisted the newness you offer. Forgive us, we pray, for installing ourselves as reigning deities. Lead us, rather, in paths of trust and obedience. Amen.

ASSURANCE OF FORGIVENESS

God does not turn away from steadfast love, even when we are unfaithful. The Rock of our salvation keeps covenant with us despite our iniquity. God's mercy is for all who humbly seek it. God fills the hungry with good things, but the rich are sent away empty. If we have chosen to receive forgiveness and to move away for self-absorption, we will understand God's pardon and live joyously within it.

COLLECT

God of unseen angels and unheard greetings, whose love for humankind continues even when we are inattentive, favor us now with a message we cannot ignore. Reign among us that we may respond to your call and serve with faithfulness in the ways you envision for us. Make us instruments of your peace. Amen.

OFFERTORY INVITATION

God gives us responsibilities in the church and the world to carry good news, to build and not destroy, to feed the hungry and house the homeless, to be faithful in all things. Our offerings are one sign of faithfulness and obedience.

OFFERTORY PRAYER

Our best we give to you, loving God, for you have given your best to us in the mystery of the incarnation. May our offerings proclaim Jesus in ways that will be received with joy. Send your Word to the world in this season through our caring service. May we share it with one another in ways that help us all to grow. We are your servants. The gifts we dedicate are already yours. Thank you for all the ways you have provided for us. Amen.

COMMISSION AND BLESSING

Inspired by God's presence, spread Advent good news.
Strengthened by the gospel, go out to serve.
> **Our spirits rejoice in the Savior's coming.**
> **Our lives are blessed by a merciful God.**
God has granted a beautiful earth for our home.
God appoints us as care-givers of the land and its people.
> **We are a covenant people, shaped by love.**
> **Wherever God sends us, we will go.**
God's steadfast love will go with you every day.
You will know the strength of God's mighty hand.
> **We will work with God to lift up the lowly.**
> **We will share good things with those who are hungry.**
Amen. **Amen.**

(See hymn 7.)

THE CHRISTMAS SEASON

CHRISTMAS
(PROPER 1)—A, B, C

Isaiah 9:2–7   Titus 2:11–14
Psalm 96   Luke 2:1–14 (15–20)

CALL TO WORSHIP

The splendor of God has been revealed among us.
A child has come to change all our ways.
> *We who have walked in the shadows have seen the light.*
> *We have given up the unnecessary burdens we carry.*

Authority has been assigned to the Wonderful Counselor.
Peace and justice will prevail through eternity.
> *We will leave judgment to God, whose equity we trust.*
> *We are free to rejoice in the beauty God reveals.*

Worship the One who breaks yokes and frees us.
Great is our God, and greatly to be praised.
> *Let the heavens be glad, and let earth rejoice.*
> *We are ready to declare God's marvelous works.*

INVOCATION

You keep surprising us, gracious God. Just when we get settled into our routines, you offer us a transforming birth. While we focus on greatness, you appear in humble circumstances among ordinary people, in out-of-the-way places. Amid the noise of our busyness, the angel song suddenly penetrates our dulled awareness, and we must listen again. O God, keep us from fear or cynicism, lest we miss this opportunity to hear good news that is meant for us, and for all this hostile unbelieving world in which we live. Amen.

CALL TO CONFESSION

The coming of Christmas challenges all our pretensions. We who have sought to organize and manage the world through our finite understandings are confronted with the wonder of Bethlehem. A baby carries God's revelation, and we are convicted of our neglect. Let us seek to reclaim God's mercy.

PRAYER OF CONFESSION

Awesome God, we confess our fear to let down our guard, to feel the wonder, to believe the good news. Why would love choose to live among us, who are so unloving in our words and deeds? Why would you choose to place Trusting Innocence in the hands of sinners like us? We are afraid to bow down, lest we be accused of sentimental weakness. We hesitate to embrace the joy, lest it turn to disappointment in the cruel realities of this world. Forgive us, God, and awaken the child within us, we pray, in Jesus' name. Amen.

ASSURANCE OF FORGIVENESS

The grace of God has appeared, bringing salvation to all, training us for lives that are self-controlled, upright, and godly. Jesus Christ has come to us as God's gift. In Christ, we are redeemed from iniquity and purified to live as God's own people. Glorify and praise God through your zeal for good deeds. Accept and live within the peace God provides.

COLLECT

Glorious God, greater than all our imagining, infinitely more vast than the universe you are creating, come to us once more in the simple complexity of a baby, the amazing wonder of new life, the stirring of hope within us and among us, that the world may be transformed in the image of Christ. May we respond with amazement and eagerness to share the wonder we experience here. Amen.

OFFERTORY INVITATION

We, who have known God's gracious hospitality, are invited to share together in ministry to the homeless, the forgotten, the weary, the lost of our world. Our offerings of gratitude remind us of God's claim on us and on all we possess. Let us make a generous response, in thanksgiving for all we have received.

OFFERTORY PRAYER

Thank you, God, for all the gifts you have given us. Most of all, we are grateful for the human child who became the embodiment of your Love. With our offerings, we worship the babe of Bethlehem and recommit ourselves as disciples of the man of Nazareth whom he grew up to be. May the ministry and mission of this church be true to our crucified and risen Savior, in whose name we pray. Amen.

COMMISSION AND BLESSING

Carry a song on your lips and joy in your hearts.
Let all the world observe the good news you convey.
Glory to God, glory to God in the highest!
May God's peace reign among all people!
As shepherds praised God for all they saw and heard,
We are commissioned to share Christmas joy.
A baby has become our Wonderful Counselor.
A child is pointing us to the way of peace.
The grace of God is your salvation, now and always.
Jesus Christ is the blessed hope who embraces us.
We join in glorifying and praising God.
We welcome the Christ into our hearts and homes.
Amen. **Amen.**

(See hymns 8, 9.)

Isaiah 62:6–12   Titus 3:4–7

Psalm 97   Luke 2:(1–7), 8–20

CALL TO WORSHIP

God reigns; let the earth rejoice.

God saves; may all humankind respond with joy.

> *We are the people of God, rescued and redeemed.*
> *God sends light to guide us on our way.*

Give thanks to God's holy name.

Praise God's goodness and loving kindness.

> *We are called to prepare the way for others;*
> *We have good news to share with the world.*

A child comes as God's sign of peace.

Glory to God in the highest.

> *We have come to see what God is doing.*
> *Let us glorify and praise God in our worship.*

INVOCATION

Come, righteous God, to the forsaken corners of our cities, to the ghettos of self-protection we erect around us, to troubled lives focused on things that do not satisfy. We cling to the story that you have acted in human history to bring light and hope and joy, even in the midst of fear, oppression, and suffering. You have offered to humankind the water of rebirth and renewal by the Holy Spirit. May this gathering awaken hope and open us to the gifts you are even now waiting to give us. Amen.

CALL TO CONFESSION

When the light of God's glory shines on us, we may be terrified as were the shepherds on a hillside near Bethlehem. Light reveals our secret sins, our unfaithfulness, our stubborn pursuit of our own agendas. Yet the light beckons us with the hope of a better way. Let us seek it as we make our confession.

PRAYER OF CONFESSION

Just and righteous God, the child in a manger leads us back to you. We have tried to ignore you, to deny your reality, to make it through life on our own. We have become accustomed to evil, to cynicism and exploitation, to dull routines and artificial excitements. O God, we long for something better. We want to rediscover integrity, faithfulness, and true joy. In the awesome simplicity of new-found life, amid the frightening complexity of all that distracts us from you, we repent and seek our freedom in Christ. Hear us, holy God. Amen.

ASSURANCE OF FORGIVENESS
God has heard our cries. God listens to our silent longing. God penetrates the doubts and fears that keep us from hearing good news of great joy. The Spirit is poured out on us richly through Jesus Christ our Savior, so that, having been justified by God's grace, we might become heirs according to the hope of eternal life. Praise God who rescues and makes whole.

COLLECT
God of all time and space, whose entry into human history on this tiny planet we celebrate in silent wonder, open our ears to the songs of angels, our hearts to the good news of great joy, our eyes to see you wherever you may appear. Then, in our amazement, grant us the will and courage to share our experiences in ways that will make a difference in our world, in Jesus' name. Amen.

OFFERTORY INVITATION
Who will clear away the stones of unbelief and false sophistication that keep people from bending their knees at the manger and opening their hearts to strangers? Who among us is committed to the inward spiritual quest and the outward journey of caring service? Let them, let us, demonstrate that commitment through a generous Christmas offering.

OFFERTORY PRAYER
Wonder-making God, your gifts are surprising and beyond our expectation. Thank you for gifting us once again with Christmas. We join ourselves and our offerings with the shepherds who returned to their work glorifying and praising you for all they had seen and heard. With Mary, we will ponder the words and music of this holy event. Transform us as messengers of good news that we may serve you with vision and high purposes in the days ahead.

COMMISSION AND BLESSING
Go out to spread the good news of great joy.
Salvation is offered to all of humankind.
> *Glory to God in the highest heaven;*
> *Peace on earth among all whom God favors.*
We have been justified by God's grace.
We are offered the rich hope of eternity.
> *Light and joy dawn for the righteous and upright.*
> *God guards the lives of all who are faithful.*
We are a holy people, chosen and redeemed.
By God's mercy we are granted new life.
> *We go out to tell the world what God is doing.*
> *Let us glorify and praise God in all we do.*
Amen. **Amen.**

(See hymn 10.)

CHRISTMAS
(PROPER III)—A, B, C

Isaiah 52:7–10   Hebrews 1:1–4 (5–12)

Psalm 98   John 1:1–14

CALL TO WORSHIP

Listen! Do you hear the sounds of joy?

Have you heard the messenger's good news?

> *The Word was with God from the beginning.*
> *In Jesus, the Word has come to dwell among us.*

Break forth into singing, people of God!

Your comfort and your salvation are at hand.

> *In Christ, we are empowered as God's children.*
> *We are gifted with grace and truth.*

Sing a new song and marvel at God's ways.

Make a joyful noise through all the earth.

> *We celebrate the true light that enlightens us.*
> *We rejoice in the gift of new life.*

INVOCATION

Speak to us again, God of glory, for we are slow to hear. Remind us of the good news, for we are prone to forget. Take us to see Jesus, for we have lost our way. We are weary and worn. We cry out for the truth that is eternal. O God, grant us the joy of your presence and the assurance of your steadfast love. Let the floods clap their hands; let the hills sing together in celebration of the Word made flesh. Amen.

CALL TO CONFESSION

The prophet tells of One who will come to judge the world with righteousness and the people with equity. Gazing at the manger, we are brought to our knees. In the simple trust of a child, we are judged. When the manger becomes a cross, we are convicted for our lack of love.

PRAYER OF CONFESSION

God of all worlds, we confess that we seek to create our own limited reality in which you have no part. We do not sense your glory or sing your praise. By our words and deeds, we deny Jesus as our brother, and reject Christ as Savior. We deal falsely with one another, caring more for our own reputation and comfort than for the common good. O God, we plead for forgiveness. By your holy arm, lead us to victory over our selfish impulses, and uphold us in your steadfast love.

Assurance of Forgiveness

We are assured that all the earth will see the salvation of our God. Forgiveness is available for all who seek to respond to God's love and do God's will. Our Creator claims us in the midst of time and for all eternity. God anoints us with the oil of gladness. We are empowered to be God's children, full of grace and truth.

Collect

Child of Bethlehem, lover of humanity, our crucified and risen Savior, grant that we may know the Word that gives light and life. Shine through us with joyous testimony to your truth so the way we live will make your love known to all we meet. Link us with one another as your beloved children who respond to your glory with gracious and truthful living. Amen.

Offertory Invitation

The ends of the earth will see the victory of our God when we give our best toward the realization of God's reign. Our offerings and our lives testify to what we really believe. As heirs of abundance, we have much to share.

Offertory Prayer

Thank you, God, for the Word that came to live among us, bringing life and a vision of glory. Thank you for your steadfast love and faithfulness even when we have not listened or responded to your will. May this offering represent our growing awareness of the larger vision to which you call us. We dedicate these tokens toward sharing the light of this season among the principalities and powers that seek to wrest the world from your hands. Draw our hearts to follow our treasure into the work you want us to do. Amen.

Commission and Blessing

How beautiful are the messengers who announce peace.
How welcome is the news of our salvation!
We have been given a new song to sing.
We will make a joyful noise to our God.
God, who spoke through the prophets, speaks to us.
God, who sent Jesus, also has a mission for us.
While the earth is our home, we are its stewards.
People of the earth are neighbors and kin.
As John witnessed to the light, so are we to do.
We are empowered to become children of God.
We will live our acceptance of God's gifts.
We will trust God and witness to the light.
Amen. **Amen.**

(See hymn 11.)

Christmas, Proper III   19

Isaiah 61:10–62:3   Galatians 4:4–7
Psalm 148   Luke 2:22–40

CALL TO WORSHIP

> Rejoice in God, who is our life and salvation.
> Christ has come to make us heirs of God's promises.
> > **God commanded, and we were created.**
> > **We are children of the Most High.**
> Praise God from the heights of heaven.
> Praise God, all people of the earth.
> > **God opens our eyes to see the light.**
> > **We will be called by a new name.**
> Men and women, youth and aged,
> Sing of God's glory; shout your praise.
> > **God has made us heirs of promise.**
> > **We will praise God's holy name.**

INVOCATION

Faithful God, by whose Spirit all people and places become holy, lead us by that Spirit today. We have come to celebrate a birth that offers us rebirth. We have gathered that you might claim us as heirs, with Christ, of eternal life. Unite our hearts and minds in a chorus of praise, that the life of this church might be quickened, renewed, and refocused. May your faithful people become a crown of beauty in your hands. Amen.

CALL TO CONFESSION

Come, all who are slaves of their own passions. Approach God, all who are bound by habits that destroy. In God's temple, there are many surprises. In God's presence, dreams are fulfilled. By God's power, lives are transformed.

PRAYER OF CONFESSION

We bring our prayers to you, gracious God, sensing that there is more to life than the ways we have known. We are drawn to the Messiah, yet we shrink from following where faith leads. We are afraid of what we might lose if we are guided by the Spirit. Thoughts of sacrifice and servanthood are not appealing to us. We are reluctant to enter into a close relationship with you. We think we know, better than you, what is best for us. Forgive our arrogance. Help us see the Christ. Amen.

ASSURANCE OF FORGIVENESS

Rejoice in God! Exalt God's name! You will be clothed with garments of salvation. They will fit you better than anything you have known. The robes of righteousness are not heavy burdens, but offer a freedom you have not felt before. You will become a crown of beauty, a new creation, in the hands of a loving God.

COLLECT

Surprising God, so often hidden from our view, yet appearing in unexpected times and places, open our eyes to your salvation. Shed your light on this worshiping community. Unite us in this time of prayer and praise that we may grow in your likeness, be filled with your wisdom, and become beacons of good news to the world. Amen.

OFFERTORY INVITATION

What seeds are we sowing for the sake of a more righteous and just world? Who will witness to God's intention that we live together as heirs to a rich, full life? It is our duty and our privilege to give our best that Christ may be revealed to all.

OFFERTORY PRAYER

With joyous praise, we return to you a portion of all you have given to us. May our giving exceed the demands of the law. You have invited us to sacrifices befitting our blessings. You have asked us to care for those less privileged. What we offer in these moments is a beginning. We will ponder again your amazing grace in granting us life, in offering the child Jesus to bring us back to you, and in giving us the name "Christian." Praise be to you, O God. Amen.

COMMISSION AND BLESSING

Go in peace, carrying God's word to the world.
Praise God, and tell the good news of a Savior.
> *Our eyes have seen an amazing gift.*
> *Our lives will witness to our salvation.*
Let praise fill all your waking hours.
Let your dreams reflect God's consolation.
> *We are not slaves to the excesses of our day.*
> *We are free to live by eternal values.*
God sends the Spirit to be our companion.
Welcome the Spirit's leading and guidance.
> *We are heirs of amazing blessings.*
> *We are gifted to become a blessing to others.*
Amen. **Amen.**

(See hymn 12.)

First Sunday after Christmas 21

Numbers 6:22–27   Galatians 4:4–7 or Philippians 2:5–13
Psalm 8   Luke 2:15–21

CALL TO WORSHIP

When the fullness of time had come, God acted.
Jesus came as a child among God's children.
> **In Christ, God reclaims us as heirs.**
> **We rejoice in God, who is parent to all humankind.**
From the mouths of infants, we hear God's truth.
Before a child, enemies are silenced.
> **How majestic is God's name in all the earth!**
> **How amazing is God's transforming power among us!**
God makes us stewards and gives us choices.
We are entrusted with good news for the world.
> **God's face shines on us in blessing**
> **God's favor rests on us and grants us peace.**

INVOCATION

Holy God, we greet you at the start of another year. As we mark time on our calendars, you see us within the timelessness of eternity. You esteem us more highly than we think of ourselves. You give us honor and glory we dare not expect. You entrust us with responsibility that often seems beyond our capacities. O God, how majestic is your name in all the earth! How amazing is the child lying in a manger! We call on the name of Jesus, for in that name we find our salvation, and in that name we gather now to worship. Amen.

CALL TO CONFESSION

We have visited the manger in this holy season. Our hearts have been touched by that tender scene. But as we return to the labors of every day, who will know where we have been? Let us confess our surrender to the secular.

PRAYER OF CONFESSION

Sovereign God, it is easy to forget whose we are. It is so hard to believe good news for long, and even harder to share it with a skeptical world. If we dare to praise and glorify you with our lips, we will need to do the same with our lives. Sometimes we are not ready to let your majesty shine through us. We are not ready to follow a grown-up Jesus in loving the unlovable and praying for enemies. Draw us to yourself, forgiving and empowering us as your children, we pray in Jesus' name. Amen.

ASSURANCE OF FORGIVENESS

God is mindful of you and has created you a little lower than God, crowning you with glory and honor. God puts all things under your feet, giving you dominion over the works of God's hands. To be entrusted with responsibility is good news. To be given a message to share shows God's ultimate trust. You are not a slave to this world but an heir of God who blesses and keeps you.

COLLECT

God of the shepherds, whose self-revelation is available to common folks like us, let your face shine on us in this time we are together. May we see you as we look into one another's eyes. May we feel your blessing as we struggle together to realize our potential. May we know your peace as the name of Jesus is lifted up among us. Help us carry that name and spirit to the world. Amen.

OFFERTORY INVITATION

The most important thing we have to offer is ourselves. We have more to give than we have dared to share. As we begin another year with the name of Jesus on our lips, let us rededicate our lives and our fortunes to the amazing story of God's love.

OFFERTORY PRAYER

May our offerings be large enough to honor you, God of majesty. We give thanks for the ways you have touched our lives with holiness. We are grateful for the witness of shepherds, for the faithfulness of truth-keepers, for the transformation of enemies into friends. All this you accomplish among us when we are open to your Spirit and generous in our response. Receive our lives as we dedicate these gifts to your service. Amen.

COMMISSION AND BLESSING

God bless you and keep you, today and forever.
Know the light of God's love, poured out for you.
> **God sends the spirit of Jesus into our hearts.**
> **We are heirs to God's love, through Christ.**
God will be gracious to you and lift you up.
God's peace will come to you along life's way.
> **When we look at the heavens God has made,**
> **What are we, that God cares about us?**
Even our doubts will be turned to joyous faith.
Our stumbling feet will carry us to new heights.
> **We will glorify and praise God for all we have seen.**
> **We will return to share good news we have heard.**
Amen. **Amen.**

(See hymn 13.)

Holy Name of Jesus   23

NEW YEAR'S DAY
(JANUARY 1)—A, B, C

Ecclesiastes 3:1–13   Revelation 21:1–6a
Psalm 8   Matthew 25:31–46

CALL TO WORSHIP

This is the time for worship and praise!
This is a day for song and celebration!
> *God calls us away from our toil.*
> *God invites us to examine our life and times.*

God wills our happiness and enjoyment of life.
God gives each of us important work to do.
> *God wants our work to give us pleasure.*
> *Our witness to God's glory brings fulfillment.*

Let us celebrate the past and anticipate the future.
Let us rejoice that God is present with us now.
> *There is a season for every matter under heaven.*
> *This is a time to heal and build up.*

INVOCATION

O God, our God, how majestic is your name in all the earth! You have gifted us with food and drink. You have been with us through times of laughter and days of weeping. You have comforted us in the midst of pain and confronted us in the needs of our neighbors. You have called us to responsibility for the well-being of this planet and the welfare of all your people. Come among us once more to equip us for the tasks you set before us in this new year. Amen.

CALL TO CONFESSION

How often we fail to discern the times! How easily we tear down when the moment calls instead for building up! How often we speak when silence is called for! How tempting it is to look for a harvest when we have not yet planted! Let us pray for God's pardon.

PRAYER OF CONFESSION

Amazing God, as we ponder your vast creation, we are awed by what we see and all we cannot see. We have been so busy that we have forgotten how small and insignificant we are amid the far reaches of time and space. Yet you honor and value us as if each of us were your crowning achievement. You care for us as if we were of highest worth. O God, reorder our priorities so we can begin to live up to your high expectations. Forgive our faltering ways. Embrace us in your tender mercy. We long to be made new. Amen.

ASSURANCE OF FORGIVENESS
What has been is now wiped away. Today begins a new year in which God offers new life. God intends for you to inherit the holy realm prepared for those who embrace all God's children in their concern. God crowns you with glory and honor and entrusts all you touch to your care. In communion with God, you will find pleasure in the tasks you are given to do.

COLLECT
Sovereign God, who sent Jesus to be our shepherd, teach us to be a faithful flock, feeding the hungry, offering pure water to those who thirst, welcoming the stranger, clothing the naked, caring for the sick, and visiting those in prison. Grant us compassion for all who mourn, for all who suffer, for all who confuse their own desires with your will. May we listen and hear and heed your call to faithful discipleship so your new heaven and earth may be realized among us. Amen.

OFFERTORY INVITATION
There are hungry people who have no food. There are hurting people with no one to bring comfort. There are people suffering injustice who have no one to take up their cause. There are many without faith or hope who have never known the love of God. We can give time and money to answer their need.

OFFERTORY PRAYER
For all we have gathered through our toil, we give you thanks, O God. For all that we have claimed at the expense of others, we beg your forgiveness. May the programs we support through our offerings fulfill your expectations of us, here in this community and wherever you direct us to act. We seek to treat all people as a little less than God, made in your image and valued by you, crowned with glory and honor. Use us and our gifts to establish your realm. Amen.

COMMISSION AND BLESSING
Go forth renewed and equipped for this new year.
God gives us all a business to be busy with.
God is mindful of us and cares about us.
Whatever our circumstances, there is a witness we can make.
Measure the time and the conditions of each occasion.
Seek the will of God for yourself and all you meet.
For everything there is a season.
In all times and places we will seek to serve Christ.
Reach out to the least of your sisters and brothers.
As you help them, you honor the Christ.
God crowns our lives with glory and honor.
We will enjoy the gifts God entrusts to us.
Amen. **Amen.**

(See hymn 14.)

SECOND SUNDAY AFTER CHRISTMAS— A, B, C

Jeremiah 31:7–14
Psalm 147:12–20

Ephesians 1:3–14
John 1:(1–9), 10–18

CALL TO WORSHIP

God gathers us from the farthest parts of the earth.
God brings together a great variety of people.
> *Surely God will meet us here.*
> *Surely God will save the people.*
Some come weeping, in need of consolation.
Some are confused, needing to find a straight path.
> *We are a great company of seekers.*
> *All have stumbled and need a blessing.*
Come with radiant delight before our God.
Come with joyous dancing and singing.
> *God offers us life in a watered garden.*
> *God brings us joy and gladness and abundance.*

INVOCATION

We praise you, O God, for the comfort you offer and the bounty you bestow. Where you reign, there is peace. In your word, there is power. We seek your presence so we might receive a spiritual blessing. Grant wisdom and insight to your gathered people, that we might know the mystery of your will. We have welcomed a baby in Bethlehem. Now we seek to learn more fully our inheritance in Christ. Share with us again the gospel of salvation, we pray in Jesus' name. Amen.

CALL TO CONFESSION

We have heard the word. Why have we not believed? We have encountered truth. Why have we failed to live by it? Answering the "whys" is not as important as making the changes necessary for life in all its fullness. Let us ask God to help us redirect our lives.

PRAYER OF CONFESSION

We confess to you, God of our ancestors, that we have heard your word but ignored its witness. We have nodded agreement with your truth, but we follow our own ways. Your commands are frozen on paper, for we do not warm to their possibilities for our lives. As the word became flesh in Christ, we pray it may come alive in us. Melt our rigid perceptions and prejudices. Break down our resistance to change. Link us together in a community of faith, boldly receptive to the gospel. We want to be a communion of forgiven and forgiving sinners.

Assurance of Forgiveness

To all who receive Christ, who believe in that name and trust in that love, God gives power to become children of God. When we are born of the Spirit, we receive grace upon grace. Light shines into our lives to bring understanding and empowerment. The goodness of our God makes us radiant witnesses to God's truth. Let it be so among us!

Collect

O Word of life, made flesh in Jesus, speak to us now. May we see your glory, experience your grace, and live your truth. Remind us of the love we knew at our birth, the love even now being reborn within us. We seek this, not so much for our own enjoyment as for those whom you call us to meet and greet in your name. Grant us to live as your under-shepherds to all in need of your love. Amen.

Offertory Invitation

How will the nations hear God's word if the church is unfaithful? Who will seek the lost if we do not care? Who will teach the young if we have no time for them? Who will uphold true values against the compromises that demean human life? What we return to God can make a difference.

Offertory Prayer

Use our gifts, holy God, to sound a word of hope in our world. Let them reach beyond this place to care for lonely, frightened, hurting people. Extend them among the children and youth who need to know someone cares. Lift up among us those lasting values that enrich lives and make them whole. To these ends, we dedicate our offering and ourselves. Amen.

Commission and Blessing

Scatter with radiance in your hearts.
Go out to proclaim God's word by your deeds.
> *We seek to walk in the light God gives us.*
> *We will act on the truth God reveals.*
Carry God's commands as a beacon to guide you.
Share them that others may find new life.
> *We will testify to the light we have received.*
> *We will listen for truths we have not yet heard.*
The gospel of salvation is good news for the world.
It is meant for you to embrace and enjoy.
> *God transforms our mourning into gladness.*
> *God lifts our spirits to songs of joy.*
Amen. **Amen.**

(See hymn 15.)

Epiphany and the Season Following

Isaiah 60:1–6
Psalm 72:1–7, 10–14

Ephesians 3:1–12
Matthew 2:1–12

CALL TO WORSHIP

Come, join the search for all God will reveal.
We are the church, committed to an encounter with mystery.
> *God has sent light to dispel our fears.*
> *The glory of God has risen upon us.*
The gospel of Christ reveals God's grace.
We share in the promise of Jesus Christ.
> *We gather together and lift up our eyes.*
> *Our hearts thrill to the sight and our lips rejoice.*
Through us, the wisdom of God will be made known.
There is rich variety to meet each one where we are.
> *The radiance of truth surrounds us.*
> *Boldly and confidently, we approach our God.*

INVOCATION

God beyond our knowing, grant us today new glimpses of who you are and what you intend for us to be. The powers of this earth bow before you in humble adoration. Mighty nations are tiny blips on the screens of your eternity. Our lives are insignificant except as you enlist us to be a part of your eternal purposes. You draw us irresistibly toward the light. We are attracted to your revelation. We need the sense of purpose you engender among us. Come, Holy Mystery, to reveal as much of your truth as we can stretch to understand and receive into our lives. Amen.

CALL TO CONFESSION

The God of justice and righteousness calls us to account for the ways we invest our hours and our resources. Amid the oppression and violence that many endure, God listens for our voices and watches for our works. What have we done with the commission entrusted to us by God's grace?

PRAYER OF CONFESSION

God of sovereigns and commoners, we confess that we are often more impressed with famous people than we are with your amazing glory. The rulers of this earth are more real to us than the One who reigns over time and eternity. Your priorities are not foremost in our lives. We reach for power and popularity more than for justice for the poor. We are more focused on prosperity than on relief for the oppressed. Our pursuits do not satisfy; save us from their fragmenting grip in our lives. Cause a new epiphany among us, we pray. Amen.

ASSURANCE OF FORGIVENESS

God will judge us with righteousness and deliver us from the oppressive greed to which we have succumbed. The showers of God's blessings will fall on us like rain on new-mown grass. Peace will abound in the hearts of those who give help to the poor and needy. God commissions us, as fellow heirs with Christ, to fulfill the mission given to the saints.

COLLECT

Honored God, before whom the treasures of the wise men are pale tokens of devotion, we are strangely moved by their ambitious journey and unhesitating response. Help us to value whatever we have to give you and rise to the challenge of giving our best to honor Christ. Speak to us that we might be led along the road you want us to travel. Remove from us both pretense and timidity, that we may draw others to follow the star.

OFFERTORY INVITATION

No gift is too small, except to the giver, for we cannot receive what we are unwilling to share. The riches God entrusts to us cannot satisfy those who hoard them for their own purposes. They are a delight only when they are invested on our knees before the manger.

OFFERTORY PRAYER

We reach for the boundless riches of Christ, even as we give the tithes and offerings we have pledged. An abundance of things does not satisfy, and the wealth of nations cannot buy peace. Therefore, we join our efforts in the church to make a difference in the world, not through instruments of oppression but through the power of love. Employ our gifts in the service of Jesus Christ, we pray. Amen.

COMMISSION AND BLESSING

Arise, shine, for your light has come.
Take that light into the world and spread it around.
> *We see more now than when we came together.*
> *We are ready to hear the world's cries and feel its pain.*
Your hearts will thrill and rejoice in your Savior.
Give yourselves as servants of the Gospel.
> *Christ has numbered us among the saints.*
> *We are part of God's eternal purpose.*
You are commissioned and empowered to serve.
Look for the star that will lead you day by day.
> *In boldness and confidence, we make our witness.*
> *In the strength God supplies, we become helpers of the needy.*
Amen. **Amen.**

(See hymn 16.)

FIRST SUNDAY AFTER EPIPHANY
(BAPTISM OF JESUS)

Genesis 1:1–5   Acts 19:1–7
Psalm 29   Mark 1:4–11

CALL TO WORSHIP

The powerful voice of God created all worlds.
That same voice calls us to worship.
> *Ascribe to our God glory and strength.*
> *Come before God's glorious majesty.*

God's strength shakes the wilderness.
That same strength is offered to people of faith.
> *The flames of God penetrate our cold hearts.*
> *May God bless all people with true peace.*

Come together to remember your baptism.
Gather to celebrate the Spirit's gifts.
> *The heavens open to us at the Word of God.*
> *Surely God forgives and makes whole.*

INVOCATION

In the beginning, O God, you fashioned a universe. Each star and planet had its beginning in you. Out of the void, you brought light and life. Through eons of creativity, you have acted, and today we are here, inheritors of an amazing process, tiny specks in the limitless reaches of time and space. And you are here, waiting to greet us. As you acted in our baptism, you are acting still to make all things new within us and among us. Let your light awaken us and your Spirit empower us for faithful living. Amen.

CALL TO CONFESSION

John the Baptizer appeared in the wilderness, proclaiming a baptism of repentance for the forgiveness of sins. We, who have received the gift of baptism, recognize the need to confess our sins to remind ourselves of our finitude and of God's amazing grace.

PRAYER OF CONFESSION

Creator God, you have created us, but we have chosen to go our own way. You have reclaimed us, but we have, by our arrogant attitudes and actions, rejected the claim. You have sent your Holy Spirit to break into our controlled and unimaginative routines, and we have not appreciated that burst of creative energy. We are ready now, ready to admit that our ways are full of dangerous byways. Our mistakes and failures have often come because, in our false pride, we have not listened to you. Save us again by your forgiving love. Amen.

ASSURANCE OF FORGIVENESS

A voice from heaven said to Jesus: "You are my own Child, the Beloved; with you I am well-pleased." Jesus Christ passed on that gift to those who dared to follow. We, too, are beloved children of God, loved, forgiven, and sent on a mission. All who are truly sorry for their sin are relieved of its burden and are recreated in God's image. Celebrate God's strength and glory!

COLLECT

Powerful God, whose voice penetrates the wilderness of our deceits, and whose transforming reality is symbolized in the act of baptism, take us now to the River Jordan, that we might share Jesus' moment of emptying self to receive your Spirit in all its power. Move us to remembrance that we have been baptized, that your grace was poured out on us, not because we earned it, but because of your amazing generosity. Amid the wonder of it all, we would accept once more Christ's call to discipleship. Amen.

OFFERTORY INVITATION

In thanksgiving for all we have received, we enlist in the ministry Christ demonstrated and inspired. We have nothing apart from God's gifts. We have everything when we allow God's Spirit to work through us. This offering demonstrates the depth of our awareness.

OFFERTORY PRAYER

Mighty God, you have given us everything we have. You have granted us life. You have poured out abiding love on our behalf. You have made us rich. We share out of this awareness, and because we care about people who do not know you, people who have not shared your abundance, people who have defied your commandments, people who need your love. Bless our gifts to do the work you intend. Amen.

COMMISSION AND BLESSING

God gives strength to those who will receive it.
God will bless the people with peace.
> *We need the strength God will provide.*
> *We accept peace as God's generous gift.*
Listen to the majesty of God's voice, calling you!
Glorify God's name in your work and worship.
> *We have been baptized in the name of Jesus.*
> *The triune God has blessed and empowered us.*
Then go out as a new creation in Christ.
Let others see how God is changing you.
> *We are unworthy servants of the Most High.*
> *Yet we are ready to do what God expects.*
Amen. **Amen.**

(See hymns 17, 18.)

I Samuel 3:1–10 (11–20)   I Corinthians 6:12–20
Psalm 139:1–6, 13–18   John 1:43–51

CALL TO WORSHIP

God is calling. Do you not hear?
You are being called by name, for a purpose.
> **God, you have searched us and know us.**
> **You discern our thoughts from far away.**

Do not confuse the siren calls of the world for God's call.
Do not confuse the values of this world for God's values.
> **You know, O God, when we sit and when we stand.**
> **You know when we lie down and where we go.**

Your words and your deeds are known to God.
You were known to God before you were born.
> **Your knowledge of us is more than we can understand.**
> **Your thoughts embrace us amid all you have created.**

INVOCATION

We have come together, listening God, because you have spoken your word of summons and welcome. We are drawn irresistibly to the promise of your presence and by the persistence of your call. Speak to your servants here in ways we can understand. We want to hear the message you intend for us. We want to listen, not because someone else needs to have it told to them, but because we ourselves are needy sinners. Your expectations of us are high and holy. We tremble before you, eager for the heavens to be opened in our midst for our transformation. Amen.

CALL TO CONFESSION

We can hide nothing from God, who knows our every thought. God is aware of sins we have not recognized. Whenever we have broken a solemn trust, whenever we have acted on selfish impulse, whenever we have trampled the feelings of others or ignored their need, God has noticed. We cannot be right with God unless we examine ourselves and repent.

PRAYER OF CONFESSION

O God, our lives are an open book to you. Help us to recognize in ourselves what you have seen there. Remove the distortions that keep us from acknowledging our sin. Awaken in us a sorrow over the wrong we have done and the good we have neglected. Create in us an earnest desire to change. O God, we are in touch with the pain we have caused and the pain within us. Because of your love and care, we can face and overcome the sins we here confess. Amen.

ASSURANCE OF FORGIVENESS

God has heard your cries and felt your pain. Your struggles to know yourself are prompted by God's love. God leads the community of faith beyond what is lawful to what is holy. We are not our own; we are members of Christ. We are one in the Spirit. By God's grace, we are turning from self-serving ways to selfless ministries. Above all else, we who were bought with a price seek to honor and glorify God.

COLLECT

Law-giver and God of the prophets, whose all-seeing eye has sought us out and whose voice has called us into the community of saints, confront us here with eternal verities and relevant truth. Guide our discernment of our mission and our choice of words to the world. Speak to us, for we are ready to listen. Commission us, for we are willing to serve. Amen.

OFFERTORY INVITATION

We have been bought with a price. God has made a costly investment in humanity. For love's sake, God sent Christ among us. For love's sake, we make the offering of ourselves and our resources the high point of our worship.

OFFERTORY PRAYER

We have heard you calling us, loving God, in the cries of your children—cries for bread, for justice, for relief. We have seen you beckoning to us amid the corporate greed and social distortions of our day. We have felt the pain of sisters and brothers caught up in damaging relationships that violate your holy temple within them. We want to help, and we believe your church can be Christ's healing presence for them. Show us the way to be messengers of your gentle judgment and powerful good news. May our offerings be used for the transformation of church and society, individuals and groups. Amen.

COMMISSION AND BLESSING

Jesus said, "Follow me," so Philip followed.
Jesus says to us, "Follow me!" Will we follow?
 We do not always know where Jesus will lead.
 But we hear the call, and we intend to follow.
Philip found Nathaniel and led him to Jesus.
There are many we know whom Jesus is seeking.
 It is often difficult to share our faith with friends.
 But we hear the call, and we intend to invite them.
Jesus promised, " You will see greater things than I have shown you."
We are Christ's messengers of revelation today.
 Wonderful are the works of our God.
 Christ is our mentor, our Savior and friend.
Amen. **Amen.**

(See hymn 19.)

Second Sunday after Epiphany　　35

Jonah 3:1–5, 10

Psalm 62:5–12

1 Corinthians 7:29–31

Mark 1:14–20

CALL TO WORSHIP

For God alone our souls wait in silence.
Our hope is from God, our fortress.
God is our rock and our salvation.
God is our refuge and our deliverance.
Trust in God at all times, in all places.
Pour out your hearts to the One who hears.
All people are valuable in God's sight.
No one is more important than another.
Worship God, who is ready to speak to us.
Open your lives to God's steadfast love.
All power in the universe belongs to God.
Yet God depends on our faithful service.

INVOCATION

We await your message, God of all places and times. Sometimes we do not like what we hear, but we know we need to listen. Your message is inclusive and fair, while we like to make distinctions that favor us and our friends. You call us out of our comfort zones to do new things and try better ways. You direct us to reach out to people with whom we seem to have little in common. Speak your truth to us in this service so we can carry it to the places where you want us to go, to the people you are eager to reach. Amen.

CALL TO CONFESSION

God's word sometimes comes as a warning. How often we have pushed aside the word we find unpleasant. Even if we grudgingly acknowledge its truth, we like to postpone any action to change. God comes to us today, saying that our days are fewer than we think. The time for us to repent is now.

PRAYER OF CONFESSION

Sovereign God, we reluctantly confess that we have installed our own gods in our lives. They take our time. They use our resources. They exact from us care and devotion. We do not like to hear that our way of life is endangered. Yet we sometimes realize that innocent steps into self-indulgence are really deliberate strides away from you. We hear distant echoes of warning and judgment. O God, we want to return to you before it is too late. We repent of everything in our lives that cuts us off from you. Hear our prayer. Amen.

ASSURANCE OF FORGIVENESS

The people of wicked Nineveh proclaimed a fast and put on the garments of repentance. They begged God to turn around what seemed so inevitable—their own destruction. God listened, and they were saved. The present form of our world is passing away. God has better things in store for us than we have yet known. Our lives, enlisted in God's realm, can count for something good. Forgiven and forgiving people make a difference.

COLLECT

God, whose reign is nearer than we have realized, and whose realm is available to us even here and now, speak your invitation to us today in ways we have never fully heard before. Confront us again with the good news you want us to share. Enlist us in reaching out to the world with love and joy, so all may be saved from calamity and know the fulfillment you intend for every person. Amen.

OFFERTORY INVITATION

When our riches increase, we are tempted to put our trust and confidence in them. But riches are not meant to satisfy us. They are placed in our hands that we might accomplish some good purpose. Giving through the church grants us that opportunity.

OFFERTORY PRAYER

God of steadfast love, we pray that you will love the world through the moneys we dedicate today. We pray that your work of transformation will be carried forward by our gifts. As a church, we seek to follow where Jesus leads. As individuals, we heed the call to discipleship. Bless our efforts to fish for people—for their sakes, not our own. Amen.

COMMISSION AND BLESSING

God sends us out into the world with good news.
God directs us to warn and to give assurance.
> *We are disciples of Jesus Christ.*
> *We have been commissioned and blessed.*
We go out as people who know our own weakness.
We rise above our shortcoming in the strength Christ gives.
> *We will trust in God at all times.*
> *We will speak God's truth in love.*
The reign of God is drawing near to us.
It can be realized in our lives here and now.
> *We accept God's rule among us.*
> *We are citizens of God's realm.*
Amen. **Amen.**

(See hymn 20. "Follow Where Jesus Leads," *Whispers of God*,
pp. 171–72, is based on the texts for this Sunday.)

Deuteronomy 18:15–20   1 Corinthians 8:1–13
Psalm 111   Mark 1:21–28

CALL TO WORSHIP

Great are the works of God, and greatly to be praised.
God's righteousness endures forever.
>   *We come together as a congregation of believers.*
>   *We give thanks to God with whole hearts.*

God is gracious and merciful and trustworthy.
At all times, God is mindful of the covenant.
>   *The works of God's hands are established among us.*
>   *We can count on God's righteousness and faithfulness.*

Awe before God is the beginning of wisdom.
All who approach God in fear have good understanding.
>   *Holy and awesome is God's name.*
>   *We call on God to empower our worship.*

INVOCATION

God of the prophets, help us to recognize your voice among the competing claims of our day. Raise up in our midst authentic witnesses to your truth. Be present with us now to guide our prayers and praise. Let us not presume to know your message without careful listening or to speak your word without discerning the Spirit. Light your fires within us so we may heed your summons and give our best in your service. Amen.

CALL TO CONFESSION

We are called to confession if we have distorted God's word, knowingly or unknowingly. We are invited to repent if our freedom in Christ has led others astray. We join in prayer together because the church is not yet the perfect body of Christ. Let us seek God's forgiveness.

PRAYER OF CONFESSION

Faithful God, we have claimed to have more knowledge than we really possess. We have presumed to judge others on the basis of our limited understanding. We have grasped for freedom without taking full responsibility for our actions. Our witness is weak, and is directed primarily toward those with whom we prefer to associate. By our actions, some of our sisters and brothers are excluded, some are misled, and some are unjustly accused. If we have violated another's conscience, if we have caused someone to fall, we are deeply sorry. For failing to do all Christ expects of the church, we repent and seek your forgiveness. Amen.

ASSURANCE OF FORGIVENESS

All who love God are known by God, whose intention is that we live by eternal values, in loving relationship with one another. God applauds our efforts to rid our lives of pseudo-gods we create, habits that destroy, and prejudices that divide. We count on God to understand us, to free us from our bondage to sin, and to dwell among us, transforming our lives. Praise God forever and ever!

COLLECT

All-powerful God, whose revelation in Jesus Christ communicated authority and wisdom and strength among people who lived long ago, let your word today address the unclean spirits in our midst, that your church may more fully represent Christ in today's world, reaching out in love to all who need food, inspiration, direction, care, and healing. Amen.

OFFERTORY INVITATION

An important way to give thanks to God is through sharing the bounty we have been honored to receive. We can never do enough to earn God's generous blessings. We can only express our gratitude by passing on our gifts. It is a privilege to be able to give.

OFFERTORY PRAYER

By giving away some of the wealth we cherish so much, we keep ourselves focused on who you are, gracious God, and on what you expect of us. As the body of Christ, we seek to be a healing force in our world. May the offerings we present be used in ways that encourage healthful behaviors among us in the church, within our community, and as far as our influence can reach. Receive us and our gifts, we pray in Jesus' name. Amen.

COMMISSION AND BLESSING

Go out to witness to the good news you have heard.
God is even now raising up prophets among us.
We thank God for this time of being together.
We are grateful for freedom to worship and grow.
God is establishing truth among us, inviting us to learn.
Dare to question and explore, as disciples of Jesus.
We praise God for insight and guidance we have received.
We delight in ways we are able to help others.
God will supply us with words for our witness.
We will be led to offer others appropriate help.
All honor and majesty and glory be to God!
May we never stop praising God with our lives!
Amen. **Amen.**

(See hymn 21. See also "We Give You Thanks," *Whispers of God*,
pp. 172–73, based on the same scriptures.)

Fourth Sunday after Epiphany   39

Isaiah 40:21–31   1 Corinthians 9:16–23

Psalm 147:1–11, 20c   Mark 1:29–39

CALL TO WORSHIP

Worship God, who is from everlasting to everlasting!
The God of creation does not faint or grow weary.
> *How good it is to sing praises to our God!*
> *How expansive is God's understanding of us!*

The whole universe is subject to God's power.
Creation continues as the universe expands.
> *God rules all time and space, yet cares about us.*
> *God is pleased with all who reflect steadfast love.*

Sing to God with great thanksgiving.
Praise God with the best you have to offer.
> *We lift up our eyes to see God's wonders.*
> *We open our ears to receive God's message.*

INVOCATION

Powerful God, before whom we are as nothing, we dare to approach you because you assure us that we are not like mere grasshoppers to you. Our individual potential is not hidden from you, and the faithfulness of your church is important to you. We have gathered with great expectation, seeking to have our strength renewed and our hope restored. Make yourself known among us as we unite in your praise. Amen.

CALL TO CONFESSION

Come away from your pretensions to examine your relationship with God. Break away from your illusions of independence to realize your responsibility in the church. Claim your unity in Christ with all God's children. Then realize how much you need to confess brokenness and seek healing.

PRAYER OF CONFESSION

Who are we to claim equality with you, Ruler of all worlds? Yet we try to order you around when it is we who should be taking orders. At times, we act as if we can get along without you. In our church, we often pretend that we don't need other congregations. We hoard the gospel as if it were our possession, and thus we do not follow its mandates. We bend your law to our own whims and then excuse our disobedience. Forgive us, God. We are not worthy to carry the name of Christ. Restore us to yourself, we pray. Amen.

ASSURANCE OF FORGIVENESS

God calls each of us by name. Every community of faith is known to God, whose understanding is unlimited. The One who knows our hearts is eager to forgive the truly penitent and to empower those who have grown weary. Your strength is being renewed in these moments. You will mount up with wings like eagles. You will run and not be weary. You will walk and not faint. Praise God!

COLLECT

Compassionate Savior, at whose touch people are healed and by whose word lives are transformed, show yourself to us now; touch our lives; speak to us. We do not seek these gifts for ourselves alone, but for the sake of the gospel. May your message be proclaimed among all people, drawing us all into the community you intend, where God reigns and love prevails. Amen.

OFFERTORY INVITATION

We have an obligation to proclaim the gospel. We are entrusted with a commission. So we give freely of our time and abilities where we are, and we send and support the witness of others where we cannot go. Let us continue to give generously.

OFFERTORY PRAYER

Thank you, God, for showing us a better way to live than we are able to devise for ourselves. Thank you for reaching out to win our hearts. Thank you for Jesus Christ, for the ministry that extended your love to the least and the lost, for the powerful presence that offered wholeness to those who were sick or brokenhearted, for the prayers that demonstrated how we, too, can be in communion with you. In gratitude, we dedicate this offering. Amen.

COMMISSION AND BLESSING

Go out to serve. Someone needs you today.
What you have to give will be helpful to someone.
We pray God will open our eyes to needs around us.
We will look for ways to be helpful.
Go in the name of Jesus Christ, who sends us.
Speak a healing word. Do a caring deed.
God binds up wounds of the brokenhearted.
Surely God will empower our ministry.
God strengthens the powerless and helps the weak.
God's power will be in you when you pray.
We shall run and not be weary.
We will serve in the strength God supplies.
Amen. *Amen.*

(See hymn 22.)

2 Kings 5:1–14   I Corinthians 9:24–27
Psalm 30   Mark 1:40–45

CALL TO WORSHIP

Come to rejoice together; God is present with us.
Sing praises to God, all you faithful ones.
> *We are restored to life morning after morning.*
> *We will extol our God, who lifts us up.*

Come to be washed and cleansed, forgiven and freed.
Renew your commitment to the One who calls us.
> *We have come to listen for God's word to us.*
> *We will give thanks to God's holy name.*

Come to enter the race for an imperishable goal.
Proclaim the joy of serving in God's name.
> *We are here to find where God will send us.*
> *We are ready to serve in Christ's name.*

INVOCATION

We come to you, gracious God, as a community of people who realize all is not well with us. We come longing for a wholeness that eludes us. At times, we flee from you. We are afraid to let you get too close. But today we dare to enter your presence with the intention of letting you heal us and draw us close. Hear us, O God, and be gracious to us. O God, be our helper. Turn our mourning into dancing, so our souls may praise you and not be silent. Touch us with your love. Amen.

CALL TO CONFESSION

The recognition of our sins is not difficult, but we are reluctant to acknowledge them. Coming to God in prayer is not an onerous task, but we build walls that make an approach to God more difficult. Now is the time to let down barriers so communication can flow freely.

PRAYER OF CONFESSION

Where are you, God? We confess that we have ignored you for so long that we feel out of touch. When we have a sudden need, it feels as if you are hiding from us. On those days when it seems we are down in a pit, and there is no way out, we do not dare to trust that you are there. Instead, we look for help in the wrong places and pursue our own ideas of what is best for us. Forgive us, O God, and teach us healthy self-control and responsiveness to your will. Amen.

Assurance of Forgiveness

As Jesus chose to heal the leper, God chooses to forgive and reconcile us to our best selves. We can take off our sack-cloth to put on garments of joy, for God turns our mourning to dancing. God's favor rests on us and strengthens us. We are cleansed and made whole. Give thanks to God, whose welcome is for each one of us and for all of us together.

Collect

Gracious God, whose pity is on all who cry out to you, and whose cleansing power is offered to all who are mired in sin, keep us from running aimlessly or hurting others. Help us to listen to your promises, respond to your word, and learn to proclaim your good news for the healing of all humanity. Amen.

Offertory Invitation

When our physical health is threatened, most of us would invest our resources where there is hope for healing. When our spiritual health is shattered, when brothers and sisters have wandered far from the wholeness God intends, can we do any less? We bring our treasure for God's blessing, praying that our hearts and many others' may follow and know God's grace.

Offertory Prayer

Thank you, God, for the opportunity to invest in the healing ministry of the church. As we reach out to offer hope of wholeness to our fragmented world, we find new meaning for our lives. We are grateful for your faithfulness even when we do not respond. We rejoice that your love is constant through our long nights of weeping and days of suffering. Even in these moments, we celebrate the joy of giving. Amen.

Commission and Blessing

In life and in death, we praise God.
With every breath, we give thanks to God's holy name.
We will praise God in our daily activities.
We will share good news of God's faithfulness.
God's healing presence is ever available to us.
God's quiet faithfulness transforms our spirits.
We are glad for evidence of the Creator's hand.
We rejoice in experiences of God's watchful care.
Be alert for God's invitations and commands.
Listen for God's call to you where you live.
God gives us abilities to match these expectations.
We are receiving strength for the race of life.
Amen. **Amen.**

(See hymn 23.)

Sixth Sunday after Epiphany　　　43

Isaiah 43:18–25   2 Corinthians 1:18–22
Psalm 41   Mark 2:1–12

CALL TO WORSHIP

Do not cling to old ways of doing things.
God is creating a new day among us.
We have wearied of calling on God.
Yet our Creator offers us water in the wilderness.
Happy are those who look beyond their own troubles.
All who seek to help others will find new life.
The call of God is gentle but persistent.
God waits for our offer to serve in Christ's name.
Surely God is faithful and will be with us.
Blessed be our God from everlasting to everlasting!
All praise to Christ Jesus, who forgives and heals.
All praise to the Spirit, who makes all things new.

INVOCATION

Faithful God, we recognize your abiding "Yes" to us when we are in deep need. We come to you now, aware of some of the continuing issues in our lives that paralyze us and separate us from you. We have lived for so long at less than our best that we seldom recognize our need for your healing touch. We are attracted by your promises and drawn by your love. Bring healing and peace to us that we might become instruments of healing in our world. Amen.

CALL TO CONFESSION

We have burdened our Creator with our iniquities and wearied our God with our transgressions. Yet God awaits our return and is eager to listen to our prayers. Let us confess our need to the One who is ready to listen.

PRAYER OF CONFESSION

God of the future, we have made a habit of looking backward to what has been instead of forward to what may yet be. We are so focused on the past that we miss your vital presence with us day by day. We deny you by our neglect, for we have not honored you with our sacrifices, listened for your word or watched for your appearing. We have sinned against you. How can we ask for a word of forgiveness or seek your gracious healing? Yet we must, for we cannot continue the way we are. Amen.

Assurance of Forgiveness

Be assured that God is ready to forgive. Our transgressions are blotted out. God delivers us and remembers our sins no more. Give thanks that our infirmities are healed and our lives enriched. Let us walk in God's ways as people who claim our baptism and respond to God's revelation. Amen.

Collect

Amazing God, whose visit among us in Jesus Christ draws us together in worship, look upon us here, for we are paralyzed in so many ways and are in need of healing. May your Word minister to us in such a way that we can stand up for all that is right and good, and walk courageously where you would have us go, offering healing to a hurting world. Amen.

Offertory Invitation

For the healing of nations and individuals, for the re-formation of the church, to the honor and glory of God, we bring our offerings of time, talent, and treasure. God is not pleased with tokens but calls for wholehearted commitment. May this time of giving reflect our integrity as Christians.

Offertory Prayer

With joyous thanksgiving, we offer ourselves and our substance to honor you, our Creator. In consideration of the poor, both those who lack basic necessities and all who are spiritually destitute, we dedicate this offering. We want to be responsible stewards of all the resources gathered by our church and of all the bounty you have entrusted to us individually. Show us the way, gracious God. Amen.

Commission and Blessing

Rise up from all that weighs you down.
Walk confidently into God's future.
God is doing new things among us.
We seek to live as God's chosen people.
Trust in God and in one another.
Know that God is ever with you to sustain and heal.
We feel God's welcome and hear God's call.
All around, we see evidence of God's activity.
Receive the Spirit in your hearts.
Say "Amen" to the glory of God through Christ.
Come, Holy Spirit, to enliven us.
Go with us, O Christ, to make us whole.
Amen. **Amen.**

(See hymn 24. Another hymn using the scriptures for this Sunday is "Blessed Are God's People," *Whispers of God*, pp. 174–75.)

Hosea 2:14–20   2 Corinthians 3:1–6

Psalm 103:1–13, 22   Mark 2:13–22

CALL TO WORSHIP

Rise up in heart and mind to bless God's holy name.

Open your arms and your souls to receive the covenant.

> **We are here to praise God and to receive mercy.**
> **We have come in response to God's steadfast love.**

God welcomes you and offers renewal.

Compassion and competence are God's gifts to you.

> **God is merciful, gracious, and slow to anger.**
> **God protects us and allows us to lie down in safety.**

God calls you to use your gifts for the sake of justice.

God seeks to equip you here to make a difference.

> **God raises us up as followers of Jesus.**
> **God equips us as ministers of the new covenant.**

INVOCATION

Living God, we read your Word in the lives of people who embody your Spirit. Some of them surround us today and link us to you. All of us have the potential to become your letters to the world. That is what we want to be. That is why we gather, to find that integration of faith and deed, trust and discipleship, that will make us authentic witnesses to your steadfast love. Make yourself known among us so we will experience your presence inside us and in all the gaps between us. Amen.

CALL TO CONFESSION

God calls us from our idols and seeks our complete devotion. God summons us from half-hearted beliefs to whole-hearted trust. God invites us to identify the enemies within us so they may be overcome.

PRAYER OF CONFESSION

O God, so many things are important to us that we cannot keep track of all of them. So many activities fill our calendars that we often have no time to meditate and pray. You become to us a compartment of life rather than the whole of it. We do not sense your embrace because we have not allowed you to be the center of our lives. We hear Christ's call to discipleship, but we do not want to associate with the friends Jesus chose. We hesitate to receive the newness you offer. O God, forgive us, heal us, recreate us, we pray. Amen.

ASSURANCE OF FORGIVENESS
God does not deal with us according to our sins, nor repay us according to our iniquities. As far as the heavens are high above the earth, so great is God's steadfast love toward all who trust and obey. As far as the east is from the west, so far does God remove our transgressions from us. God's compassion is greater than that of a parent, and God's forgiveness is sure. Bless God, every soul!

COLLECT
Inclusive God, whose welcome for tax collectors and sinners includes us all, and whose dominion is over the earth and over all worlds, teach us now to prepare new wineskins to hold the new insights from your Word which we are about to receive. Fill us with confidence to take an active role in the mission to which you call us. Amen.

OFFERTORY INVITATION
Justice for the oppressed, good news for sinners, strength for life's journey—these gifts God offers us and bids us to pass on. Our mission begins in reaching out to one another and extends to encompass the whole world in love and care. What is returned to God in these moments represents our commitment to that mission.

OFFERTORY PRAYER
As ministers of your new covenant, O God, we bring these offerings. May they impart new life to the sisters and brothers we know and to many we will never meet. Help us to soar with the eagles as we give of ourselves. Bless the work of our hands as we reach out in your name. May all your people feast at the banquet table of your love. We want to help make that possible. Amen.

COMMISSION AND BLESSING
You are ministers of a new covenant in the Spirit.
Go forth into the world, equipped for your ministry.
Empowered by the Spirit, we go out to serve.
Granted new life, we are eager to make our witness.
You are competent representatives of Jesus Christ.
Follow where the Savior leads you.
We are letters from Christ to the world.
We seek to follow the Great Physician.
Go to the sick who need a physician.
Call on the unrighteous who need a Savior.
Bless God in all the places where God reigns.
Bless God, O my soul! Bless God, O my soul!
Amen. **Amen.**

(See hymn 25.)

Deuteronomy 5:12–15   2 Corinthians 4:5–12
Psalm 81:1–10   Mark 2:23–3:6

CALL TO WORSHIP

This is a holy day set aside for worshiping God.
Draw near to meditate and pray, as God commands.
> *We are freed from our labors for this time of praise.*
> *Let us bring our songs of joy and thankfulness.*

Blow trumpets on this festal day.
Sound tambourines and lyre and harp.
> *We sing aloud to God, our strength and salvation.*
> *Our hearts and voices join in a chorus of praise.*

Listen, and hear the voice of God.
Give up your burdens to the One who cares about you.
> *We are not slaves to any earthly power.*
> *We are willing servants of the Most High.*

INVOCATION

Light of lights, shine into our gloom, granting knowledge of your glory in the face of Christ Jesus. In many ways, we are afflicted but not crushed; perplexed but not driven to despair, struck down but not destroyed—for we are confident of your presence wherever we go. Reassure us now that you are with us. Feed our hungers, heal our brokenness, melt away our conflicts, that we may be knit together in the body of Christ to continue the work of Jesus in our world today. Amen.

CALL TO CONFESSION

We hold the treasures of heaven in clay jars. The gifts of God are defaced by our poor choices, by our self-serving desires, by our willful disobedience. We become enslaved to habits that destroy. We become addicted to activities that waste our time and energies. We need to seek forgiveness and a better way.

PRAYER OF CONFESSION

Holy God, help us know ourselves as we are, and set before us a vision of what life could be if we followed your law. We admit our short-sighted views. We act in ways that seem to meet our immediate interests without considering the long-term results. We let our appetites rule us. We squander the gift of time in frivolous pursuits. We ignore your Word as if it were unimportant. We flee from your presence in doubt and rebellion. O God, we cannot escape you here. We want the life you offer in Jesus Christ. Forgive and help us, we pray. Amen.

ASSURANCE OF FORGIVENESS

God restores us to wholeness and grants us new opportunities for life. No matter how far we have strayed into the ways of death, we can begin again as free and forgiven children of God. Our burdens are lifted, our spirits are renewed, as God's love is rekindled within us and in all our relationships. Praise God.

COLLECT

God of our sabbath times, from whose presence we can never hide and whose purposes are always beyond our understanding, teach us to use our sabbath times in ways that are pleasing to you and helpful to others. May we be instruments of healing, not instigators of division. Make us bearers of life-giving good news, not purveyors of death. Fill us with hope that we may share with the world, in Jesus' name. Amen.

OFFERTORY INVITATION

Stretch out your hands. They are gifts from God. With them, you have been able to do your work. Open your minds. With them, you have been able to solve problems. Rejoice that God has so richly blessed you and now offers you the opportunity to extend blessings to others. Let us give generously.

OFFERTORY PRAYER

Thank you, God, for the privilege of giving. We have received so much! Now it is a joy to share. All we have belongs to you. You empower our earning and our use of the treasures we possess. We want to do good with everything we have received. Bless today's offering and tomorrow's spending with insight, compassion, and responsible stewardship. May our giving for others reflect your generosity toward us. Amen.

COMMISSION AND BLESSING

Let the life of Jesus be visible in you this week.
Pass on to others the love you have received.
>   *We will live each day as a gift from God.*
>   *We will seek to live as God has commanded.*
Lift someone's burdens; carry another's load.
Bring them to Christ, who bears all things for us.
>   *We will listen for cries for help from people around us.*
>   *We will seek to offer what they need from us.*
The glory of God will be seen in your actions.
You will be a light to the people you meet.
>   *We will do good, as God empowers us.*
>   *We will seek to let God's light shine through us.*
Amen. **Amen.**

(See hymn 26.)

LAST SUNDAY AFTER EPIPHANY (TRANSFIGURATION)

2 Kings 2:1–12

2 Corinthians 4:3–6

Psalm 50:1–6

Mark 9:2–9

CALL TO WORSHIP

God summons us from the sun's rising to its setting.
Listen, for the mighty One speaks to us.
   Our God comes and does not keep silence.
   Through fire and tempest, God is with us.
God gathers those faithful to the covenant.
Be quick to respond to God's invitation.
   We seek a double share of the prophet's spirit.
   We look for a vision to claim our souls.
Open your ears to the good news of the gospel.
Open your eyes to the glory of God.
   We have come to share knowledge of Jesus Christ.
   We gather, seeking transformation and empowerment.

INVOCATION

Speak to us, Mighty One, for we are eager to listen. Bless us, as we cry out to you for strength and vision. You have acted in times past to save your people. Save us now. You have sent prophets to change the world. Change us now. You have granted light in Jesus Christ. Shine on us now. Let us see your glory. Lift us to the mountaintop in this time of prayer. Stay close to us to melt away our doubts, and do not leave us, we pray, through Christ. Amen.

CALL TO CONFESSION

The whirlwind pace of our lives becomes so all-consuming that we may forget our origins. Our busyness separates us from knowledge of God's glory in the face of Christ. Now in these quiet moments apart from our everyday distractions, we seek to renew our relationship with God and be restored to wholeness.

PRAYER OF CONFESSION

When the gospel is veiled from us, mighty God, we feel alone. How easy it is to lose our direction and go the wrong way! At times, we feel as if we are perishing under the demands of our day, unable to see clearly what is most important. We become enslaved to our routines and enticed by shallow distractions. We fill all our hours with doing so there is no time for reflection and prayer. Forgive us, O God, and restore balance to our lives. Amen.

Assurance of Forgiveness

God promises light for our nighttime and guidance on our way. In Christ, God lifts the veil so we can catch a glimpse of glory. There is peace to be found in the midst of turmoil. There is freedom and quiet even amid our busyness. We are released from our slavery to things, and lifted up beyond the limitations of our habits. God forgives us and offers new meaning to our lives.

Collect

Transforming God, in whose love we become new people able to see others in a new light, help us to view Christ beyond the blinders of our culture as one whose way is relevant and exciting in our time and place. In the name of Jesus Christ, make us servants who participate in the transformation you envision for our world. Amen.

Offertory Invitation

Through our offerings, we support prophetic leadership, provide possibilities for mountaintop experiences, and enable the teaching ministry of our church. Our generosity can make a difference in the lives of people we will never know and in our own lives as well. Let us give from our hearts in deep thanksgiving.

Offertory Prayer

Use our gifts, mighty God, to bring light where there is gloom, hope where there is despair, peace where there is turmoil. May Jesus Christ be proclaimed among us and around your world. May righteousness and justice prevail in spite of differences. May we inherit a double portion of the prophets' spirit to discern clearly the ways you would have us go. We dedicate ourselves and our offering to these ends. Amen.

Commission and Blessing

It has been good for us to be together.
Now we scatter to share good news.
> **God has visited earth in human form.**
> **In Jesus Christ, the beloved of God, humanity is blessed.**
Light from the gospel has been revealed to us.
We are becoming lights to the world.
> **It is an awesome responsibility to reflect God's glory.**
> **Ours is a wonderful opportunity to show God's love.**
God will not leave us or forsake us.
God's presence is constant and dependable.
> **We depart with confidence and joy.**
> **We will carry the knowledge of Christ in our hearts.**
Amen. **Amen.**

(See hymn 27. "Speak, Mighty One," *Whispers of God*, p. 176, is based on the same scriptures.)

THE LENTEN SEASON

Joel 2:1–2, 12–17 or Isaiah 58:1–12　　　　　　2 Corinthians 5:20b–6:10
Psalm 51:1–17　　　　　　　　　　　　　　　　　Matthew 6:1–6, 16–21

CALL TO WORSHIP

Blow the trumpets; summon all God's servants!
Call a solemn assembly for people of all ages.
> *We respond to God's mercy and steadfast love.*
> *We are drawn by God's saving grace.*

Sound an alarm among all who have forgotten God.
Turn back with fasting and repentance.
> *We want to worship God with our whole being.*
> *We intend to be genuine in our praise and service.*

God's blessings penetrate our gloom and despair.
God gathers us into the holy presence.
> *Surely we will be washed and cleansed.*
> *God will teach us, and we will learn.*

INVOCATION

Gracious and merciful God, we return to you with hearts that long for healing and minds that seek meaning for our days. Examine us and all our ways. Keep us from the self-delusions that overlook our sin and ignore our alienation. We tremble as we sense your presence. We are afraid to face your judgment. Yet we are eager to be reconciled to you. We want to know you more fully and serve you more faithfully. Come among us in convincing ways on this holy day and in this season. Amen.

CALL TO CONFESSION

God knows our false piety and religious pretense. All that we say and do is known to God. We can hide nothing from our Creator. Now is the time to bare our souls before God.

PRAYER OF CONFESSION

God of steadfast love, we tremble before you. We know our transgressions. We have rebelled since our earliest days, shutting you out of our lives. We have doubted your presence, ignored your blessings, and resented your inclusiveness. It is hard to be truthful with others and within ourselves. Our worship has slipped into dull routine. Our sacrifices have been superficial. Blot out our iniquities, we pray, and wash us clean. Renew our spirits in the joy of your salvation. Amen.

ASSURANCE OF FORGIVENESS

The grace of God is abundantly present to change our lives. God lifts us above our transgressions and cleanses us from our sin. In Christ we are restored to the wholeness God intends for us. Our contrite hearts and receptive spirits welcome the deliverance we are offered. Open your mouths to declare God's praise. Open your lives to accept the transformation that comes with forgiveness.

COLLECT

All-seeing God, you know our motives as well as our deeds; nothing we think or do is a secret from you. May our piety grow out of love for you, our generosity out of genuine care for others, our prayers out of deep thankfulness for the treasures you entrust to our stewardship. Guide our time of fasting and self-examination toward the deepening of our faith and the effectiveness of our service, in Christ's name. Amen.

OFFERTORY INVITATION

When you give, do not let your left hand know what your right hand is doing. Give, not to be praised or thanked, but to praise God and proclaim the good news of salvation.

OFFERTORY PRAYER

In our relationship with you, loving God, we have everything we need. We are rich, and have much to share. With joy and gladness, we dedicate our offerings to the work you call us to do. Lead us, by this investment of our money, to greater investment of our time and skills in the ways of heaven. May our love be genuine, our speech truthful, and our leadership patient and kind as we labor to bring others to your holy mountain. Amen.

COMMISSION AND BLESSING

Go forth in the steadfast love of God.
Spread the good news of salvation from sin.
> **Our spirits have been fed in this time of worship.**
> **Our lives have been cleansed by a merciful God.**
Share with others the joy of living in God's grace.
Let your fasting and sacrifices be a blessing to others.
> **Our lips will declare God's praise.**
> **Our secret alms will extend God's love.**
We are assured of God's continuing presence.
The One who knows our hearts accepts us as we are.
> **We will seek to grow in truth and purity.**
> **We will use well the time and resources God gives.**
Amen. **Amen.**

(See hymn 28. Previous volumes of worship resources contain a number of Ash Wednesday hymns based on these same texts.)

Genesis 9:8–17   1 Peter 3:18–22
Psalm 25:1–10   Mark 1:9–15

CALL TO WORSHIP

Welcome to the time of covenant renewal.
The God of our salvation greets us here.
> *We are reminded of God's promises to us;*
> *We remember the promises we have made.*

Sense the Spirit descending on us now.
Hear God's welcoming voice.
> *Surely God is with us.*
> *We can hear God calling our names.*

See the rainbow in the sky.
Wonder at God's steadfast love.
> *All creation proclaims the wonders of God.*
> *We come together to learn what God wants to teach us.*

INVOCATION

Lead us in your truth this day, gracious God. We long to know your ways and to
be guided by your Spirit. Direct us into that realm where your purposes govern
the hearts and minds of all your children. We want to grow in the likeness of Jesus, to learn to live in ways that are pleasing to you. We wait for you now, eager to
respond to your instruction. Let nothing cut us off from you or separate us from
one another, not only in this time of worship but as we face the challenges of another week. Amen.

CALL TO CONFESSION

In our day, we cannot escape temptation, for it comes in so many forms, from so
many sources. As Jesus was tempted, so are we. But we have yielded to temptation,
and Jesus did not. Sometimes we do not even recognize the sins into which we
have slipped. We seek to recall them now. Repent, and believe in the good news.

PRAYER OF CONFESSION

Have mercy on your church, O God, for we forget the covenant into which you
call us. We muddle along in our self-serving schemes rather than waiting on your
word. We follow the path of least resistance without seeking your higher way. We
forget our baptism into a faith community built on trust and forgiveness. We turn
from the vision of heaven to the treacherous hell of competing egos. O God, we
turn to you to lead us to a new day. According to your steadfast love, forgive us,
we pray. Amen.

ASSURANCE OF FORGIVENESS

God is faithful to the covenant, even when we forget. In mercy and steadfast love, God lifts us above the sins of our youth and the transgressions of today. Christ brings us to God that we might receive a new spirit and a good conscience. We are God's beloved children who are welcomed into God's realm right here, right now, in the midst of life.

COLLECT

Loving God, whose realm was revealed to humankind in Jesus of Nazareth, open your heavens to us that the Sprit may come among us, reclaiming us, helping us to know our infinite worth in your sight, strengthening us to cope with temptation, equipping us to minister in Christ's name. May our faithfulness draw others into your covenant community, where mutual trust and joyous service unite us in Christ. Amen.

OFFERTORY INVITATION

We dare to believe that the Power holding together the infinite reaches of time and space has entered into a covenant relationship with people on this tiny planet, that God gives us responsibility to be co-creators in the covenant community which is intended for all humanity. Our giving is dedicated to that end.

OFFERTORY PRAYER

Thank you, God, for the signs and wonders that reveal your presence. Thank you for the covenant fulfilled in Jesus Christ. We want to do our part to share your love with the world. Use our offerings and our lives to bring a realization of your reign among us. Extend your realm by re-creating the church as a true representation of Jesus Christ. May we be humble, teachable, and faithful as we seek to lead others into covenant community. Amen.

COMMISSION AND BLESSING

The time is fulfilled; God's reign is now.
Hear and believe the good news Christ offers.
We are children of God, beloved and blessed.
We are a covenant community with a mission.
Be open to all God wants to teach you this week.
Seek God's leading every day through Lent.
This is a season for renewal and recommitment.
We will turn to God in prayer every day.
God will teach you and lead you in truth.
God's mercy and steadfast love will surround you.
We will live as people of the promise.
We go out rejoicing in our baptism, in Christ.
Amen. **Amen.**

(See hymn 29.)

SECOND SUNDAY IN LENT

Genesis 17:1–7, 15–16   Romans 4:13–25
Psalm 22:23–31   Mark 8:31–38 or Mark 9:2–9

CALL TO WORSHIP

We are invited to walk with God.
We are welcomed by God as people of the covenant.
How awesome to stand in the presence of our Creator!
We bring our praise to glorify God.
God calls us by name and gives us new names.
We are summoned to faithfulness and fruitfulness.
God not only speaks to us but also listens.
God hears our cries and meets our need.
Let the ends of the earth remember and turn to God.
Let the families of all nations worship the Creator.
We will pay our vows to the One who calls us.
We praise the God of all nations and all peoples.

INVOCATION

In trust and confidence, we call on your name, almighty God, eager to know you more fully and serve you more faithfully. We have heard your amazing promises given to our ancestors in the faith. We seek your word for us in our day, for we want to grow strong in our faith as our ancestors did in theirs. As they gave you glory and praise, we gather to do the same. As they passed on their faith to new generations, we seek to teach and live in such a way that our children and their children will be drawn to minister in your name. Amen.

CALL TO CONFESSION

In this season, when we reexamine our lives and find our faith tested, we often discover a barrenness within. Our relationship with God is weak, not because God has turned away, but because we have failed to trust the Almighty or spend time in prayer. We have not sought God's answers to our daily problems. Let us be honest with our Creator in this time of prayer.

PRAYER OF CONFESSION

God of our ancestors, we come to you, confessing that we have set our minds on human things. We have sought to gain the world—so many things to buy, so many things to do. Yet we are not satisfied. Life's meaning eludes us. Your ways seem out of date; your promises appear as the hopes and dreams of a past generation. But in our hearts we sense an eternal design which is for all generations, a way of life more satisfying than we have allowed ourselves to explore. O God, we confess our need for you.

ASSURANCE OF FORGIVENESS

God's face is not hidden from those who truly seek. God does not withhold love from us when we go our own way. When we open our eyes to see God's works, when we open our ears to hear God's word, when all our senses are alert to God's leading, we will realize how we have been blessed by an unseen hand, forgiven and restored to wholeness. God offers us the opportunity to live as ones in tune with the universe, filled with hope, upheld in love, dwelling in covenant.

COLLECT

God of all generations, whose revelation in Jesus Christ calls us to self-denial and risk-taking service, we dare to listen for your call, knowing that it may draw us out of step with the expectations of our culture, realizing that you may lead us away from our dependence on things we have accumulated. We take that risk, longing for the day when all the families of the nations shall worship before you. Amen.

OFFERTORY INVITATION

Those who want to save their life will lose it, and those who lose themselves for Christ's sake and for the gospel will be saved. We are invited to give all we have and all we are to the realization of God's will among us. A portion of that we bring today as our offering.

OFFERTORY PRAYER

Glorious God, we dedicate these gifts as an expression of our faith. You alone know how much we share and how much we withhold. You know the extent of our trust and the depth of our commitment. May this act of giving draw us closer to you and extend a blessing to all who are helped through our sharing. Amen.

COMMISSION AND BLESSING

Dare this week to follow where Jesus leads.
Dare to love the unlovable and care about others.
>   *We want to follow in the footsteps of Christ.*
>   *We want the poor to eat and be satisfied.*
Do not be ashamed to challenge values of our culture.
Dare to question all that denies God's reign.
>   *We want to live with faith, hope, and love.*
>   *We want to extend God's rule to all people.*
The promises of God are for you and for all.
God will make you exceedingly fruitful.
>   *We will trust the promises of God.*
>   *We go out to live as covenant people.*
Amen. **Amen.**

(See hymn 30.)

Second Sunday in Lent   59

THIRD SUNDAY IN LENT

Exodus 20:1–17

1 Corinthians 1:18–25

Psalm 19

John 2:13–22

CALL TO WORSHIP

The heavens are telling the glory of God.
The firmament proclaims God's handiwork.
We celebrate the steadfast love of God, our Creator.
Surely God is faithful to all who live in covenant.
From the sun's rising to its setting, the creation speaks.
Day and night, earth's creatures announce God's works.
The commandments of God are clear, enlightening the eyes.
God's law is perfect, calling forth our best.
God's foolishness is wiser than human wisdom.
God's weakness is stronger than human strength.
The ordinances of God are true and righteous.
In following them, we gain wisdom and strength.

INVOCATION

All-wise and all-loving God, we are drawn together in this place because all our knowledge and discernment is not enough to give meaning to our lives. All the pieces of our busy days need a center, and we have come to see that center in the "foolishness" of the cross. There, Love went the distance for us. There, the paths of service were lifted up above our passion for personal gain. We are frightened by what you might ask of us, but we long for the wholeness only you can offer. Let the words of our mouths and the meditations of our hearts be acceptable to you, O Lord, our rock and our redeemer. Amen.

CALL TO CONFESSION

The psalmist declared that our souls are revived by God's perfect law. We are confronted by that law today. At its center is the love of God revealed in Jesus Christ. It is more desirable than all the gold in the world. Let us confess those things in our lives that keep us from realizing that love.

PRAYER OF CONFESSION

We have come to your temple, loving God, because this is your place, not ours. We confess that we sometimes forget whose house this is. We forget that all the world belongs to you as we scramble for all we can claim for ourselves. Our actions deny your love, which is at the heart of your perfect law. Our minds have justified the bending and breaking of your law to suit current trends and feelings. We cry out for forgiveness and the opportunity for a fresh start. Clear us of hidden faults and redeem us from those we recognize and confess. Amen.

ASSURANCE OF FORGIVENESS

When our prayers become more than pious words; when, in awe before God, we truly seek forgiveness; the Almighty becomes for us a guiding presence. We are healed, strengthened, and set free from our slavery to sin. In steadfast love, God claims us, saying: You are my people. Dare to walk in the footsteps of Jesus.

COLLECT

Everlasting God, whose law is perfect and whose judgments are just, speak and act among us today to challenge all we do in your church and in our lives that is out of step with your law so we may be raised to new life and become authentic witnesses to your love in all we do, wherever we go, that the world might come to know and serve you. Amen.

OFFERTORY INVITATION

The commandments invite us to a sabbath time in which we give ourselves completely to the worship of God. The gifts we bring are important, but even more, we are invited to commit ourselves to God's foolishness, to the way of love. May it be our passion to extend love to all of earth's people.

OFFERTORY PRAYER

We bring our offerings, O God, not to buy your favor, but to express our gratitude, not to support an institution, but to further your mission. We support the church in its efforts to challenge the false wisdom that pervades our culture. We seek to make this community of faith a center of values that are consistent with your will. May we be zealous in your service, willing to sacrifice for love's sake, and eager to embrace your word in our everyday living. Amen.

COMMISSION AND BLESSING

You have been embraced by God's power and love.
Dare to face the world, bearing God's wisdom.
> *We proclaim the crucified one, Jesus Christ.*
> *The power of love is not destroyed by death.*
Be careful in your use of God's name.
Live in awe that God chooses you as a witness.
> *The law of God is perfect, reviving the soul.*
> *The precepts of God are right, rejoicing the heart.*
The scriptures will guide us toward God's truth.
God's steadfast love will sustain us.
> *We will seek to keep the spirit of the commandments.*
> *Self-giving love toward God and humanity will guide us.*
Amen. **Amen.**

(See hymns 31, 32. "Let All Our Words," Whispers of God, p. 180, centers especially on the Ten Commandments.)

Fourth Sunday in Lent

Numbers 21:4–9   Ephesians 2:1–10
Psalm 107:1–3, 17–22   John 3:14–21

Call to Worship

Light has entered our world; rejoice!
Light is God's gift to each, and to all together.
> *Give thanks to God for days of watchful care.*
> *The steadfast love of God endures forever.*

Let those whom God has redeemed rejoice!
Let them tell the world of God's good news!
> *We will thank God for wonderful works.*
> *We will rejoice in God's love for all humankind.*

By God's word, we are delivered from destruction.
By God's mercy, we are healed and made whole.
> *Our voices will join in songs of joy.*
> *Our lives will offer sacrifices of thanksgiving.*

Amen.   *Amen.*

Invocation

God of infinite patience, we call on you once more, knowing that you have every reason to question our coming together. We have worshiped without expectation. We have gathered without diligent preparation, as if meeting you laid no requirements on us. Amid the complexities of our lives, we have forgotten to set aside times to be still before you. Sometimes we feel as if we are bitten by snakes all week long, so we assemble here for some relief and healing. O God, will you meet us as we are? Amen.

Call to Confession

Our time of penitence before God gives us the opportunity to rid ourselves of the weights we carry, the lingering sense that we have not lived up to our full potential, that we have cheated others, that we are disoriented and mired down in troubles of our own making. Let our individual confessions be gathered up in the confessions of the church.

Prayer of Confession

Healing God, we are sick through our sinful ways. We are impatient, complaining, and troubled. We love the night because it hides the evil we have done and the doubt that shows on our faces. By our self-indulgent habits, we are destroying ourselves and depriving others. As a church, we seem content to be dead in our trespasses, for we are afraid to embrace the changes that come with the new life you offer. We cry out to you in our trouble. Save us from our distress. Amen.

ASSURANCE OF FORGIVENESS

God loved the world so much that Jesus Christ was sent to show us the way to eternal life. We are not condemned, but offered saving grace. Come to the light. Let its warmth melt away our resistance to God's truth. We are re-created in Jesus Christ that we may do the good that God intends and make that goodness our way of life. Praise God!

COLLECT

Loving God, who sent Jesus to earth to share our common lot and bring eternal life into our midst, help us to believe and to trust. Show us the light of your revelation and help us to welcome its presence in the life of this congregation as we gather and when we scatter to our daily activities. May we consciously represent you in all our deeds so that the world may come to a saving knowledge of your grace. Amen.

OFFERTORY INVITATION

In joyous thanksgiving, we offer sacrifices of time and resources to announce God's healing grace to the world. It is our privilege to participate in God's wonderful works to humankind, to share the steadfast love that is saving us, and to offer life to those who are perishing.

OFFERTORY PRAYER

For life-sustaining gifts that we so often take for granted—for shelter, food, and meaningful tasks to do; for your steadfast love that awakens us and raises us from our sinful ways; for your word that guides and heals us—we give you thanks, gracious God. As we invest a part of all you entrust to us to further the ministries of the church, may we show to others the immeasurable riches of your grace in Jesus Christ. Make this church a beacon of hope for the world. Amen.

COMMISSION AND BLESSING

God sent Jesus that the world may believe.
God sends us into the world to share that good news.
In Christ, we are not condemned to perish.
Christ came to offer us abundant life.
Let everyone see the light you have received.
Live openly as people enjoying the love of God.
Let those whom God has redeemed say so.
Let us give thanks for God's steadfast love.
We are alive together in Christ Jesus.
God offers to all the gift of eternal life, beginning now.
By grace, we have been saved through faith.
We will live in the light and thus share good news.
Amen. **Amen.**

(See hymn 33.)

Fourth Sunday in Lent   63

Jeremiah 31:31–34   Hebrews 5:5–10
Psalm 51:1–12 or Psalm 119:9–16   John 12:20–33

CALL TO WORSHIP

The days are surely coming, says our God;
The day is here to affirm a new covenant.
>   *We call on God's steadfast love and mercy.*
>   *We seek a strong and vital relationship with our God.*

God's law will be written on our hearts.
Our Creator claims us and forgives our faithlessness.
>   *We are eager to know the God who loves us.*
>   *We are ready to learn God's intention for us.*

God offers us the joy of salvation.
Our brokenness can be healed and wholeness restored.
>   *We are open to the new and right spirit God offers.*
>   *We seek guidance for our daily living.*

Amen.   *Amen.*

INVOCATION

As Jesus offered up prayers and supplications to you, O God, we cry out to you to-day. You know our losses and our fears. You understand our suffering and pain. We wish to see Jesus, to know the healing touch felt by so many. We want to hear a reassuring voice. We long to see a new day when evil is overcome and wrong cannot prevail. Lift us up and draw us to yourself as we worship in this hour. Equip us for our daily living as we seek to be true to your covenant with us. Amen.

CALL TO CONFESSION

The doubts and inattention that mark our response to God summon us now to confess our sin. The promises of God which we have ignored draw us back to consider the covenant God offers. The obedience of Jesus can inspire in us a reverent submission to God's will. Let us seek forgiveness and reconciliation.

PRAYER OF CONFESSION

Have mercy on us, O God, according to your steadfast love. Wash us thoroughly from our iniquity and cleanse us from our sin. We know more of our own transgression than we have been willing to admit, even to ourselves. We cannot escape from the sin that clings so closely. By our actions and our neglect, we have done what is evil in your sight. May your judgment help us to face the truth about ourselves. Then wash away the stain of our iniquity. Create in us clean hearts, and renew our spirits. We are ready for a new life. Amen.

ASSURANCE OF FORGIVENESS

We are welcomed into God's redeeming presence. We are children of our Creator who loves us. We are brothers and sisters of Jesus, who was obedient to God and faithful to the law of love, even in the face of the cross. Through suffering, Christ became the source of eternal salvation for us, realized when we embrace the covenant in truth and faithfulness. The burden of our sin is lifted from us. New life is ours to enjoy.

COLLECT

Loving God, in whose service there is both risk and honor, we want to see Jesus, not to prove a theory, but to experience a presence; not to observe from a distance, but to become involved; not just to listen, but to follow and to serve. Lead us beyond a quest for personal security to a passion for the lifting up of all human life to the promises of eternity. Amen.

OFFERTORY INVITATION

What are we ready to die for? How much of ourselves and our resources will we risk for the sake of the gospel? Jesus invites us to follow as disciples and servants, risking everything for the sake of God's love.

OFFERTORY PRAYER

We dedicate these offerings to the proclamation of your word, the teaching of your ways, and the living of your will for all humankind. We reach out with joy and gladness to offer your love to the world. May these gifts enable the sharing of your presence with many who have not experienced a sense of their own value as your children. As we keep covenant with you, we would also share its joys and obligations with our neighbors. Amen.

COMMISSION AND BLESSING

God has written the law of love within us.
We are empowered to live according to that law.
> **We have experienced God's presence together.**
> **That presence will sustain us as we scatter.**

God's wisdom has been planted in our hearts.
It is different from the wisdom of this world.
> **We dare to live as forgiven and forgiving sinners.**
> **We risk showing love to those who seem unlovable.**

We are people of God, accepted and loved.
We are followers of Christ, commissioned for service.
> **Where Christ leads, we will follow.**
> **Where our service is needed, we will go.**

Amen. **Amen.**

(See hymns 34, 35. "Within Your Temple," *Whispers of God*, p. 181,
is based on all the scripture texts for this day.)

SIXTH SUNDAY IN LENT
(PASSION SUNDAY)

Isaiah 50:4–9a   Philippians 2:5–11
Psalm 31:9–16   Mark 14:1–15:47 or Mark 15:1–39

CALL TO WORSHIP

Come to prepare yourselves for this trying week.
Watch and pray with One who was betrayed.
> *Our times are in God's hands.*
> *Surely God will deliver us from this terror.*

Awake from your sleep; God is asking for your best.
Remain alert; much will be required of you.
> *We want to be faithful in our work and witness.*
> *We seek to honor Christ in worship and service.*

God offers you the tongue of a teacher.
God sustains you with the strength of Christ.
> *We will listen for God's word.*
> *We will speak on behalf of justice and truth.*

INVOCATION

We come before you with good intentions, gracious God, but our lives are full of sorrow and distress. In our suffering, we cry out to you. From the misery of rejection and failure and brokenness, we turn to you. In humility, we empty ourselves of the problems that so often overwhelm, that we might see the Christ. Draw us near the cross to experience the confident witness of our Savior, find the strength to live as forgiving people, and catch a vision that looks beyond our own situation to the greater needs of our sisters and brothers. Amen.

CALL TO CONFESSION

Do not hesitate to face your brokenness. Be bold to confess your fears. The cross is not a pleasant gathering place but a place where we can find strength. Christ's loving witness cannot be matched, but it will empower all who are open to its transforming power. Come to experience the grace of God.

PRAYER OF CONFESSION

O God, we are not worthy to bend our knees before you. Too often, our actions have shouted, "Crucify!" Our fears have led to denial. Our self-interest has prompted false witness. We have compromised our integrity to avoid criticism. We have bowed down to false gods whose fleeting promises seem momentarily attractive. We are so confused! We want to do what is right, but we do not want to suffer. We would like to get rid of the burden of our mistakes, but we find it difficult to change. O God, deliver us from ourselves. Amen.

ASSURANCE OF FORGIVENESS

Christ has witnessed your tears of remorse. Your sins are forgiven. Your past is wiped clean. With courage and confidence, take up the cross of Christ. Help to carry the burden of the world's sin. What you do for others is not done alone. Christ is with you to strengthen your shoulders and your voices, to deliver you from enemies and persecutors, to raise you up to new life. Trust God, whose help is ever available.

COLLECT

Loving God, whose presence becomes real to us when we sink to the depths of despair, whose care dawns on our awareness when we have felt your absence, minister to us through the Word who became flesh to dwell among us, that we may take the risks of faithfulness as Christ did. Teach us the love that will go all the way to the cross so we will not be discouraged but will serve with caring persistence until the world believes. Amen.

OFFERTORY INVITATION

We empty ourselves that we might serve. We divest ourselves of excess wealth so we will be free of encumbrances. All that we have and all that we are, we invest in the cause of Christ. Some of it we offer now to further the ministries of the church.

OFFERTORY PRAYER

God of extravagant generosity, we bring costly sacrifices to honor you. Our gifts are a measure of our devotion. May they communicate good news to the world, not as a faint whimper, but as a rousing proclamation. May they sustain the weary and witness to unbelievers. May the act of giving increase our own devotion even as it opens new possibilities for neighbors we have not yet met. Amen.

COMMISSION AND BLESSING

We have remembered the story of Holy Week.
Denial and betrayal we, too, have known.
> *We are aware of the violence around us.*
> *We have recognized the violence within us.*
The sorrow of this week could weigh us down.
Yet working through grief can bring new life.
> *By facing up to evil, we lose our fears.*
> *By pointing to a better way, we help our neighbors.*
We are appointed as teachers and listeners.
We are equipped for trusting servanthood.
> *The cost of love is worth any price.*
> *To live by love is to find fulfillment.*
Amen. **Amen.**

(See hymn 36. When celebrating the passion of Jesus on this Sunday, consider "We Bring Our Sorrows," *Whispers of God*, pp. 182–83.)

Sixth Sunday in Lent (Passion Sunday)   67

SIXTH SUNDAY IN LENT
(PALM SUNDAY)

Isaiah 50:4–9a
Psalm 118:1–2, 19–29

Philippians 2:5–11
Mark 11:1–11 or John 12:12–16

CALL TO WORSHIP

Blessed are those who delight in worship.
Blessed are the ones who come in God's name.
> *Give thanks to God, all who assemble here.*
> *God's steadfast love endures forever.*

Let all who follow Christ sing God's praise.
Because of God's help, we are not disgraced.
> *Open the gates of righteousness that we might enter.*
> *The works of God are marvelous in our eyes.*

This is the day that our God has made;
Let us rejoice and be glad in it.
> *Hosanna! Let every knee bend before Jesus!*
> *Let every tongue welcome Christ's reign! Hosanna!*

INVOCATION

This is your day, holy God. Every day belongs to you. We would empty ourselves before you so there will be room for your entrance into our minds and hearts. Our times are in your hands. This precious gift of life is ours, in trust, from you. We give thanks, for your steadfast love endures forever. That love, expressed in the life of Jesus, dared to challenge those centers of power that lived by other standards. We come to declare that love today. Reign among us, we pray. Amen.

CALL TO CONFESSION

Will we wave our leafy branches today and hide them tomorrow? Will our hosannas melt into another chorus of death? Will we, like the builders of old, reject the stone that is meant to hold all things together? Is Jesus Christ truly the cornerstone of our lives? Let us admit the truth about ourselves.

PRAYER OF CONFESSION

Sovereign God, we confess that we are as fickle as the crowds in Jerusalem. When everything seems to be going well, we join the hosanna chorus, but in times of weariness or rebellion, praise can turn to insult. We hide our faith when it is under attack and link ourselves with the scoffers. When there is opportunity to speak a good word for Jesus Christ, we are silent. Our church lifts an uncertain word before the world, for we, its members, have not been faithful. We need your forgiving love today, O God, more than ever. Hear our prayer! Amen.

ASSURANCE OF FORGIVENESS

God answers us and offers salvation. In the mystery of God, One came among us, fully human yet fully divine, to lead us to the throne of grace. Though in the form of God, Jesus emptied himself, taking a slave's role in humble service to humanity. This was for our sakes, that we might bend our knees before God in humility and trust. We are saved in God's steadfast love!

COLLECT

Loving God, whose gift of salvation in Jesus Christ is so often ridiculed and rejected, we are ready to offer our coats and gathered branches to prepare the way today. We will join in singing the songs of praise and will even dare to shout hosanna if others do. Free us, we pray, to enter fully into the joy and gladness of welcoming the One who comes in your name, for we know you have called us to carry good news to a waiting world, that every tongue might confess Christ's reign, to your glory. Amen.

OFFERTORY INVITATION

What shall we give in the name of One who gave everything for us? What do we offer in thanksgiving for the steadfast love proclaimed in Jesus Christ? How will good news be carried to the centers of power in our world today? What we give will make a difference.

OFFERTORY PRAYER

What you have done for us is marvelous in our eyes, gracious God. Our gifts can never match your goodness toward us. Your saving grace, your healing light, your personal sacrifice are so far beyond our imagining! We can only offer ourselves, all we have and all we are, in response to the coming of Christ Jesus. Hosanna in the highest! Receive, O God, our humble service. Amen.

COMMISSION AND BLESSING

God has given us light.
We are sent into the world to share that light.
> *This is God's doing; marvelous in our eyes.*
> *We will carry the light of Christ to the world.*
God has offered us the keystone of life.
We are called to build lives where God can dwell.
> *We offer ourselves as homes for God's spirit.*
> *We will make room for God's rule within us.*
Give thanks for God's reign among us.
Praise God, whose steadfast love endures forever.
> *Hosanna in the highest heaven!*
> *We trust in God and seek to serve in Christ's name.*
Amen. **Amen.**

(See hymn 37. See also "Come, O Christ of God," *Whispers of God*, p. 182.)

Isaiah 42:1–9   Hebrews 9:11–15
Psalm 36:5–11   John 12:1–11

CALL TO WORSHIP

You are called to an eternal inheritance.
It is waiting for you to claim it today.
We are people of a new covenant in Christ.
By the life and death of Jesus, we are redeemed.
Through the resurrection, we are raised to new life.
Rescued from dead works, we serve the living God.
How precious is God's steadfast love!
We take refuge in the shadow of God's wings.
Come to feast on the abundance of God's house.
Gather to drink from the river of God's delights.
In God, we find the fountain of life.
In the light of God's love, we see light.

INVOCATION

Just and righteous God, we present ourselves before you, eager to receive your spirit and walk in your ways. Rescue us, we pray, from the crushing burdens we carry— the losses, failures, brokenness, and guilt that weigh us down. As you created the heavens and gave life to the earth, come to us now with new breath for your people. Remind us of the covenant which you offered us in our baptism. Let your light shine through us to dispel the fearfulness that keeps us from discerning your truth. Amen.

CALL TO CONFESSION

In this holy week, we are called away from our praise of idols. We are summoned from our comfortable ruts to forge new pathways. We are called from our arrogance to a life of humble faithfulness. Let us confess our rejection of God's challenge.

PRAYER OF CONFESSION

God over all worlds, we confess our tendency to see you with our own limitations. Sometimes we cannot see you at all. We hear no voice. We feel no presence. So we assume there is no God we can trust, and we turn our attention to things we can see and touch and measure. They become our idols. Rather than discipline ourselves through quiet times of openness to your word, we shut our ears and set our minds on other things. We reject you and turn away from your call. Save and purify us, we pray. Amen.

Assurance of Forgiveness

God restores our dimly burning wicks to full brightness. With justice and mercy, God lifts our faint spirits and recalls us to fullness of life. God renews the covenant of our ancestors in Jesus Christ, promising us an eternal inheritance that we can begin to realize immediately. To the upright of heart, God offers salvation. Receive and believe God's promises!

Collect

Giver of Life, whose love raises the dead and gives breath to all people, send your spirit among us to sharpen our awareness, deepen our appreciation, and heighten our devotion to the Christ at whose feet we seek to learn. Through the days of Holy Week, as Jesus faces rejection and death, help us to be as caring as Mary and as intent on service as Martha, that our participation in the new covenant may bring light to the world. Amen.

Offertory Invitation

Come with your costly gifts in the name of One whose sacrifice pointed the way for your salvation. Give, because you have been raised to new life and you long for others to have that experience. Bring your best, bring yourself, as an offering to God, for the sake of all God's people.

Offertory Prayer

How precious is your steadfast love, O God! How amazing was the ministry of Jesus Christ! Equip us so to love, that others may believe because of our message. Use the resources we dedicate here to extend that witness in our community, to go where we cannot go, to reach many we may never know. Bless each gift and giver, in Jesus' name. Amen.

Commission and Blessing

The high priest of good things commissions us.
Go out as a light to the nations.
>   **The breath and spirit of Christ is within us.**
>   **Our deeds can shine with God's love.**
Arise from dead works to serve the living God.
Let every thought and deed be an act of worship.
>   **We will not grow faint or be crushed.**
>   **We seek justice for the earth and its people.**
The poor need our help; the blind need to see.
Millions in bondage long to be free.
>   **A new day is dawning, and God gives us light.**
>   **We will declare the wonderful works of God.**
Amen. **Amen.**

(See hymn 38.)

Isaiah 49:1–7   1 Corinthians 1:18–31
Psalm 71:1–14   John 12:20–36

CALL TO WORSHIP

God chooses what is weak to shame the strong.
God calls us to the way of love, not power.
> *We are here to learn God's foolishness;*
> *We have come to consider our call.*

God's foolishness is wiser than human wisdom.
God's weakness is stronger than human strength.
> *God is our rock and our fortress.*
> *Injustice and cruelty will not prevail.*

Let your mouths be filled with praise to God.
Rejoice that God invites your service.
> *We rejoice to sing of God's saving grace.*
> *We are happy to enlist as servants of Christ.*

INVOCATION

God of all wisdom and truth, you are our hope and our trust. We have leaned on you from our birth, and we need you as much today as ever. Perhaps our need today is greater than ever before. We have seen so much of the world's cruelty. We have felt its pain. The news we hear around us day after day is not good. As we walk through the shadows of Holy Week, we are troubled, confused, and afraid. How can right prevail against so much that is wrong? Meet us here to reassure and strengthen us for all we must face. Amen.

CALL TO CONFESSION

We live in a society that has little regard for weakness and scoffs at self-abasement. Look out for number one, we say, and don't give anything away. Into that world during this holy week rides one who looks on our grasping world with pity and love, inviting us to examine our lives before a loving God.

PRAYER OF CONFESSION

O God, we have spent our strength for nothing and vanity. We have accepted false values as our guides, while turning away from the wisdom you seek to teach us. The way of love seems dangerous and foolish. The cross becomes a stumbling block for us when we are asked to accept its risks as a way of life. We do not want to die in order to bear fruit. We like our advantages. We like to think we deserve them. O God, deliver us; make haste to help us discover true meaning and purpose for our days. Amen.

Assurance of Forgiveness

Jesus said to those who followed: Whoever serves me, God will honor. As God restores the penitent to wholeness, we are lifted up, given courage, and strengthened to do for Christ those things that only we can do. Walk in the light, and carry that light to chase away the shadows in which so many dwell. Believe in the light, and become children of light, disciples of Jesus. Christ.

Collect

Parent of us all, we wish to see Jesus. We want to follow. We have promised to serve. But the way is not clear. We find it hard to hear your voice amid the clamor of competing claims. There is no clear vision for our church today. Draw us to your Word. Plant it inside us so we may bear fruit, scattering the seeds of your love far and wide. Amen.

Offertory Invitation

The cross is foolishness to those who are perishing, but to us who are being saved, it is the power of God. We are called to extend the witness of the cross among all who are perishing, in person and through our offerings. Our gifts are a measure of our love and evidence of our thankfulness.

Offertory Prayer

As we hope in you, O God, we bring ourselves and our gifts to praise you. May the coastlands listen and the heartland give heed to your promises and your judgment, O Creator of all. May all our resources be put to uses that are pleasing to you. Bless and multiply our efforts to do good and follow where Jesus leads. Amen.

Commission and Blessing

Believe in the light; become children of light.
Let your light shine, that the world might believe.
> **God sends us out as a light to the nations.**
> **We will shine for Jesus Christ, the wisdom of God.**
Those who hoard life will lose it.
All who give it away for others will find eternity.
> **We proclaim Christ crucified,**
> **A stumbling block to some and foolishness to many.**
God's foolishness is wiser than human wisdom.
God's weakness is stronger than human strength.
> **We will hope continually and praise more and more.**
> **Our trust is in God, who is ever faithful.**
Amen. **Amen.**

(See hymn 39. "O God, Our Refuge," *Whispers of God*, p. 184, and "Come, O Christ," *Refreshing Rains of the Living Word*, pp. 194–95, are additional hymns for this day.)

WEDNESDAY OF HOLY WEEK— A, B, C

Isaiah 50:4–9a

Hebrews 12:1–3

Psalm 70

John 13:21–32

CALL TO WORSHIP

Through the gathering of clouds, we come to worship.
As the shadows deepen, we gather in mutual support.
> *We are remembering the lonely walk to Calvary.*
> *We recall the pioneering faith of Jesus.*

Other clouds surround us in this hour.
We are uplifted by memories of saints we have known.
> *We are surrounded by so great a cloud of witnesses!*
> *Let us lay aside the weight of clinging sins.*

This is the hour to leave our sins at the cross.
We are here to equip ourselves for life's race.
> *Let us take up the race of life with joy!*
> *With Christ, we will not grow weary or lose heart!*

INVOCATION

Eternal God, we speak with more courage than we feel. Make haste to help us amid the confusion and fears that mark our days. We know there are hostile adversaries to your truth all around us. Sometimes we join them, in spite of our best intentions. We need to know your freeing presence among us here. Lift us from our weariness that we might stand up together against wrong. Awaken our ears and teach us, so we may become faithful witnesses to the glory of Jesus Christ. Amen.

CALL TO CONFESSION

God confronts us in our rebellion, seeking to draw us back to active growth as disciples and committed service as apostles of good news. Let us confess our separation from God and our grievances against our neighbors.

PRAYER OF CONFESSION

O God, we confess that we have used our tongues to complain rather than to teach. We have used our interests and skills to create idols rather than to serve you. When others have opposed us, we have retaliated. When you confront us, we make excuses. We flee from the cross, lest our comforts be jeopardized. We avoid those who seem hostile to us rather than seeking reconciliation. We ignore the plight of others who are struggling, for we do not want to pay the price of involvement. You are our only hope and help, gracious God. Deliver us without delay from these sinful barriers to communion. Amen.

ASSURANCE OF FORGIVENESS

God awakens the love within us as we are being healed of our anger and weariness. God is ever available to help us build the self-discipline we need to relate constructively to each life situation. God rescues us from shame and disgrace, vindicating us in the face of false accusations. Rejoice and be glad in the salvation you are receiving!

COLLECT

Holy God, whose presence in Jesus Christ has drawn us closer to you, we give thanks that our humanity is affirmed and our potential for good celebrated as we gather for instruction. Teach us to value the opportunity to serve with Christ that we might grow daily in understanding and commitment, not so much for our own fulfillment as to glorify our Savior and introduce others to discipleship. Amen.

OFFERTORY INVITATION

The bread we have received is meant to be shared. The lessons we have learned are meant to be passed on. The witness we have heard must not be silenced by our neglect or inactivity. So we come again to a time of offering ourselves and our substance.

OFFERTORY PRAYER

In the name of Jesus, the pioneer and perfector of our faith, we offer our money and our lives in sacrifice and service. May what we do ourselves, along with the ministries we support, glorify Christ and enlist others as disciples and apostles. We rejoice in this opportunity to give and to stand with Jesus through the turmoil of this difficult week. Amen.

COMMISSION AND BLESSING

Disciples, we are called to renewed faithfulness.
The way before us will not be easy.
> *We are prepared to follow where Jesus leads.*
> *We, too, will be pioneers of love.*

Resolutions made in the sanctuary will be challenged.
We will need to stand together against the world's values.
> *We will not grow weary in well-doing.*
> *We will not let the work of Christ be put to shame.*

God is our help and our deliverer.
God's saving grace goes with us today and always.
> *Great is our God and greatly to be praised.*
> *We go out, assured of God's love and salvation.*

Amen. **Amen.**

(See hymn 40. "O Sovereign God," *Refreshing Rains of the Living Word,*
pp. 195–96, and "Be Pleased, O God," *Whispers of God,* pp. 184–85,
reflect the same scriptures.)

Exodus 12:1–4 (5–10), 11–14
Psalm 116:1–2, 12–19

I Corinthians 11:23–26
John 13:1–17, 31b–35

CALL TO WORSHIP

This shall be a day of remembrance for you.
You shall celebrate it as a festival to God.
> *We will pay our vows to God before all the people.*
> *We will offer our sacrifices of thanksgiving.*

This is a time for remembering the Last Supper.
You are called to the table to celebrate with Jesus.
> *We have gathered to break bread together.*
> *We will lift up the cup of salvation.*

This is the hour when we are recalled to the command:
You shall love one another, as I have loved you.
> *We remember that Jesus washed the disciples' feet.*
> *In covenant with Christ, we seek to serve.*

INVOCATION

On this day, O God, you link us with sisters and brothers who celebrate the Passover, even as we remember an upper-room gathering that began a new observance. We thank you that on the night of his betrayal, Jesus took a loaf of bread, and when he had given thanks, broke it and said, "This is my body that is for you. Do this in remembrance of me." Similarly, he declared a new covenant in his blood and directed us to drink, remembering his death. Take us back to that room that we may know Christ's presence and be transformed in this hour. Amen.

CALL TO CONFESSION

Come, all who have resisted help from another out of pride or desire for independence. We cannot be Christian alone. We are dependent on God. We are in debt to Christ, who humbly washed the disciples' feet, then broke bread with them to announce his impending death.

PRAYER OF CONFESSION

We cannot deserve the sacrifice of Jesus Christ, made on our behalf. We have resisted the servant role as beneath our dignity. We do not care to wash feet. Why should we stoop down before people who may deny and betray us? O God, we confess under the shadow of the cross that our faith wavers before threat, and our love is limited by self-interest. We want to serve without sacrifice or inconvenience. We need forgiveness and the courage to love by those higher values that Jesus represents. Amen.

ASSURANCE OF FORGIVENESS

God hears our voices and listens to our supplications. Our spiritual ancestors found relief from the plagues in Egypt and freedom from bondage when they cried out to the living God. So, too, those who seek to know and serve God today are offered the cup of salvation. It overflows with love that enables us to love one another.

COLLECT

God of all worlds, whose intent for humanity on this tiny planet was lived out in Jesus of Nazareth, teach us to love one another as you have loved us. Help us to learn from Jesus as disciples devoted to ministries of caring. Fill us with compassion for all who suffer, that our responses to them may become ever more Christlike. Amen.

OFFERTORY INVITATION

What can we offer to our Savior, who welcomes us as honored guests at table and serves us with love and compassion? How will we respond to the God who thus affirms our worth and calls us to discipleship? Everything we possess is ours by God's grace. How we use it is the measure of our faith. Let us present our expressions of thankfulness.

OFFERTORY PRAYER

We celebrate the love we only dimly comprehend—your love for us, O God, in Jesus Christ. We have vowed to serve you, to minister to one another in Christ's name, and to pass on the love we have received. Remembering the upper room, we consecrate this offering and rededicate ourselves to the ministries you set before your servant people. Amen.

COMMISSION AND BLESSING

Jesus went out from the table to a time of prayer.
We who have communed with Jesus are invited to pray.
> *We need to reflect on what Jesus has done for us.*
> *We need to enter into conversation with God.*
God is ready to hear what is on your minds.
God is available to answer the longing of your hearts.
> *Our lives have been touched by the ministry of Jesus.*
> *We have met Christ at the table, and we are changed.*
Love one another as you have been loved.
Live as disciples of Jesus Christ.
> *We intend to care for others as Jesus did.*
> *We seek the courage to love as Jesus loved.*
Amen. **Amen.**

(See hymn 41. Other Holy Thursday hymns may be found in previous books by the author.)

Holy Thursday   77

Isaiah 52:13–53:12   Hebrews 10:16–25 or Hebrews 4:14–16; 5:7–9
Psalm 22   John 18:1–19:42

CALL TO WORSHIP

Let the ends of the earth remember and turn to God.
May all families of the nations worship together.
> *Dominion belongs to God who rules over all.*
> *We will bow down to the dust and rise up to live.*

Future generations will hear of God's love.
We will proclaim deliverance to people yet unborn.
> *The law of God is written on our hearts.*
> *Our minds hold in memory all that God requires.*

My friends, have confidence to enter the sanctuary.
Come with true hearts in full assurance of faith.
> *We seek to provoke one another to love and good deeds.*
> *We will encourage one another to hope in God.*

INVOCATION

It is hard to believe what we have heard, O God. How could a ministry of love be so blatantly rejected? Who would despise the teacher and healer who reached out to common people with acceptance and affirmation? Support and sustain us now as we recall the horror of Jesus' final hours. May the anguish we observe point us beyond death to catch glimpses of the light you seek to reveal to us. Lead us through the crushing pain and agony to challenge the violence that is ever more prevalent among us. We believe it is your will that we live in unity and peace. Amen.

CALL TO CONFESSION

We have a high priest who sympathizes with our weaknesses. Jesus, who was tested as we are, bids us come to the throne of grace with boldness that we may receive mercy and find grace to help in time of need.

PRAYER OF CONFESSION

We turn away, righteous God, rather than look at the marred features of our Savior. We join in the mockery and denial lest we, too, become objects of scorn. Our sins separate us from your love, not by your choice but because of the barriers we erect. We draw swords in anger. We lash out with cutting words. We complain about our lot. We neglect worship and shrink from service. We are influenced far more by the crowd than by our Creator. Save us from the powerful clutches of our poor choices. Amen.

ASSURANCE OF FORGIVENESS

You have heard the cock crow, and you have confessed your guilt. Jesus' eyes meet yours, and they are filled with compassion and forgiveness. Today you are empowered to take up the cross, not as a burden but as a privilege. You can feed the hungry and quench people's thirst. You can say the healing word and offer the reassuring touch. You can stand for justice when others choose what is expedient. You can work for peace amid the prejudice and hatred that divides. You will live triumphantly in the face of death.

COLLECT

Loving God, whose investment in humanity was challenged at Golgotha, and whose faithfulness sustained Jesus through suffering and death, lead us through the story of Good Friday to face our own pain and alienation. Draw us to the foot of the cross, there to sense the power of love to change lives, beginning with our own. Amen.

OFFERTORY INVITATION

What will we sacrifice in the name of one who risked everything for love? For what cause were we born, and how deeply are our lives invested in the truth of the gospel? We give, not to prove our love, but to express our thanks.

OFFERTORY PRAYER

Thank you, God, for living among us in the role you intend for all rulers. We long for the reign of love among us when all will act for the common good and none will be hungry or afraid. We are not content to dream of such a day, but intend to work for its realization. Thus we bring our offerings and ourselves to rededicate what is already yours to the realization of your will. We are at your mercy, and we serve at your behest. Amen.

COMMISSION AND BLESSING

Good Friday is here, and Easter is not yet.
Still, the promise is before us to seek its power.
God's arm has been revealed to us.
God's revelation in Jesus turns our lives around.
Surely Christ has borne our infirmities and diseases.
Unconditional Love was wounded for our transgressions.
Jesus suffered and died for our healing.
The faithfulness of Christ offers us wholeness.
Let us hold fast to our hopes, without wavering.
Let us provoke one another to love and good deeds.
We will gather together for mutual encouragement.
We seek fullness of life in the midst of death.
Amen. **Amen.**

(See hymn 42. See previous books by the author for other
Good Friday hymns.)

Job 14:1–14 or Lamentations 3:1–9, 19–24   I Peter 4:1–8
Psalm 31:1–4, 15–16   Matthew 27:57–66 or John 19:38–42

CALL TO WORSHIP

Through the gloom of this day, our souls are bowed down.
Yet God's mercies are new every morning.
> **Though prayers seem unanswered, we cry out to God.**
> **Great is God's faithfulness day to day.**

Though our bones are broken, we hope in God.
Through bitter affliction, we continue to trust.
> **We seek refuge in God who is righteous.**
> **God is our strong fortress, to save us.**

Our times are in God's hands.
We look to God to deliver us from our enemies.
> **We will discipline ourselves to pray.**
> **We will hold one another in constant love.**

INVOCATION

Incline your ear to us, O God, for we are caught up in the experience of death. Our days are full of trouble. We feel like flowers withering away. When we die, our mortal remains are laid away, and we cannot be roused. Loving God, do you remember us when we die? Will we live again? On this foreboding day, we need your reassurance. It is so hard to look beyond endings when we are grieving. We seek the peace you alone can give. Amen.

CALL TO CONFESSION

Face to face with death, confronted here by the One who judges the living and the dead, we join in confessing the sins that have led to our brokenness and despair. Our individual deeds and our corporate neglect have killed much that is good within and among us. We come as one body, seeking healing.

PRAYER OF CONFESSION

Meet us, Holy One, in our misery. We have used our freedom as license to pursue our own selfish pleasures without regard to others. As individuals and as a church, we are centered on ourselves. We have fashioned idols that substitute for a vital relationship with you. We flee from suffering, seeking to drown our sorrows in excesses that destroy. We are afraid of being called to account. Yet, in this time of endings, we truly want to change, to learn to discipline ourselves, to grow in love. Save us and help us, O God! Amen.

ASSURANCE OF FORGIVENESS

God's face shines on all who are truly penitent. When we sincerely desire to change, we can feel God's love that has been waiting for us, surrounding us, inviting us into relationship. This is the day of preparation for joys that are yet to come. Let God's forgiving love become real to you, and to all of us together. Already we are hearing rumors of good news!

COLLECT

God of the saints and of undercover Christians, whose faithfulness is constant and whose mercies are renewed every morning, we hope in your steadfast love. With the secret disciples, we reverently carry the body of Jesus, seeking to be joined together with one another in the body of Christ, your holy church. Prepare us now for resurrection, that all your children may be brought to life. Amen.

OFFERTORY INVITATION

We are called to endure suffering and to offer sacrifices for the sake of the gospel and for a dying world. As we live for the realization of God's will among us, we offer ourselves, not just the tokens we have brought to share, as an offering to God, who is recalling us to the vision of Jesus Christ.

OFFERTORY PRAYER

God of endings and new beginnings, we bring our offerings, anticipating that you have much more for us to do than we have yet undertaken. There are contributions we can make that we have not yet imagined. Surrounded by your assurances, and living in hope, we ask you to bless us and all our gifts that we may join in the mission to which you call us with joy and zeal. Amen.

COMMISSION AND BLESSING

We cannot stay at the tomb; we have work to do.
In the midst of our sorrow, we are called to listen.
There are many who want to tell their stories.
There are many who need to be lifted from death.
Let your grief open you to the suffering of others.
Let awareness of your own sin put you in touch with theirs.
We will not judge others but welcome them.
As we listen, we will also care in the spirit of Jesus.
Work and wait with openness to good news.
See the promises of new life that are emerging.
Our times are in God's hands.
We are drawn by God's love to new acts of service.
Amen. **Amen.**

(See hymn 43.)

THE EASTER SEASON

Acts 10:34–43 or Isaiah 25:6–9　　　　　　I Corinthians 15:1–11 or Acts 10:34–43
Psalm 118:1–2, 14–24　　　　　　　　　　　　　John 20:1–18 or Mark 16:1–8

CALL TO WORSHIP

This is a great and joyous festival day.
Come to celebrate amazing good news.
> *We gather for worship in awe and wonder.*
> *The tomb is empty; death is not the last word.*

Sing songs of praise, for God is good.
God's steadfast love endures forever.
> *God has answered our prayers with salvation.*
> *Jesus Christ is alive and we, too, shall live.*

Open your hearts and minds to the risen Christ.
You are greeted by name and welcomed here.
> *This is the day that our God has made.*
> *Let us rejoice and be glad in it.*

INVOCATION

We greet the dawning brightness of this special day with hopes renewed. We have known grief and sorrow, loss and tears, fear and failure. Meet us here, living Christ, for we need this time of resurrection. We need your healing presence. We need your word of greeting that welcomes us into the community of faith in spite of our doubts and faithlessness. You are the Great Teacher. We have come to learn from you. We want to be your disciples. Amen.

CALL TO CONFESSION

The apostle Paul wrote to the church at Corinth: "I handed on to you as of first importance what I in turn had received: that Christ died for our sins. . . ." In the mystery of that atoning sacrifice, we come to this time of prayer, bringing our sins to the door of the empty tomb.

PRAYER OF CONFESSION

We cannot truly worship you, loving God, until we recognize how unloving we have been. We cannot truly live until we admit the many ways we have been dwelling in death. We cannot know forgiveness until we honestly face the wrong we have done and the good we have neglected. We admit before you now the anger and spite we have carried in our hearts, the doubts and fears we have allowed to paralyze us, the misplaced priorities that have led us away from your will and way. Help us break down the barriers we have erected so we can experience new life today. In Jesus' name. Amen.

ASSURANCE OF FORGIVENESS

God shows no partiality, but in every nation anyone who fears God and does what is right finds forgiveness and acceptance. The One who came to embody love among people is ordained by God as judge of the living and the dead. In Jesus' name, our sins are forgiven, and we are being saved. The grace of God is extended to each of us on this day of resurrection. Praise God!

COLLECT

God of empty tombs and abundant surprises, who announces new life in the face of death, dry our tears of grief and calm the anguish of our losses as we listen for amazing good news. Help us to find our identity in the person of Jesus Christ. Be to us a living presence, that the story of Easter may become our story, and we can embody its hope for the whole world. Amen.

OFFERTORY INVITATION

When we have seen the Christ, that makes all the difference in our view of life. When we have encountered life, we can no longer pursue the ways of death. When we realize how much we have received from a loving God, our gratitude pours forth in eagerness to share good news with the world.

OFFERTORY PRAYER

We consecrate all we have brought to share, that the message of today may spread through the streets and across the lands, beginning within these walls and bursting out for all the world to hear and observe. May the glad songs motivate practical ministries. As forgiven and forgiving people, we take new life into the marketplace, into our jobs and schools, into our social life and leisure hours. May all we offer express true thankfulness. Amen.

COMMISSION AND BLESSING

In Christ, we have been rescued from death.
At the cross, we have learned the cost of true love.
In Jesus, we have observed courage and faithfulness.
At the empty tomb, we have met the power of Love.
Continue to sing the glad songs of victory.
Dare to live the welcoming message of God's grace.
Christ has appeared to us in the joy of this day.
We have been empowered to reach out to others.
The One who was rejected holds the key to life.
The key of unconditional love is passed on to us.
We have seen the risen Christ, and we are changed.
We have been chosen as witnesses to resurrection.
Amen. **Amen.**

(See hymns 44, 45. *Whispers of God*, pp. 187–88, includes three hymns based on the readings for Easter Sunday.)

Isaiah 25:6–9   I Corinthians 5:6b–8
Psalm 114   Luke 24:13–49

CALL TO WORSHIP

Tremble, O earth, in the presence of your God.
It is an awesome thing to be surprised by God.
When we sit at table, there is a presence with us.
When we break bread, the love of Christ is revealed.
We are invited to the mountains for a feast.
We are lifted up to see the bounty of the earth.
God wipes the tears from our faces.
The disgrace we have known is taken away.
Let us be glad together, rejoicing in salvation.
Let us meet one another with sincerity and truth.
Let us not be strangers to one another.
God calls us into the family of faith.

INVOCATION

Come to stay with us, O risen Christ. We will try not to be startled or terrified
when you make yourself known. Grant your transforming peace to this assembly
of your people, that we may listen to learn and understand, not to take issue and
find fault. We want to celebrate with you, to hear your teaching with sharper clar-
ity, to be strengthened for service in ways that challenge and stretch us. This is the
hour for which we have waited. Keep us from worship that is merely routine.
Amen.

CALL TO CONFESSION

The risen Christ invites us to get rid of all the crumbs of malice and evil that linger
within us, for they multiply like yeast in times of difficulty. It is not easy to identify the potential malignancy within us when everything is going well. We open
ourselves to self-examination and humble confession to our God.

PRAYER OF CONFESSION

Your church is less than faithful, righteous God. We want to represent our risen
Savior, but we forget that Jesus loved the unlovable, forgave the unforgivable, and
welcomed sinners. We set limits on inclusiveness and break bread only with those
who qualify to sit at table with us. We do not recognize your presence in people
who seem different from us. Seldom is there passion for discipleship among us.
Forgive us and renew your church, O God. Amen.

Assurance of Forgiveness

Death and disgrace are not God's intention for the church. Rather, God lifts the shroud from us, reaching out to heal our brokenness and save us from our prejudices. Day after day, God comes to us in the persons and situations before us, inviting us to become as Christ to our neighbors and to see in them the One who is known to us in the breaking of bread. Because we are forgiven, let us also forgive.

Collect

God of amazing surprises, dwelling unrecognized in the stranger among us, open our eyes, sharpen our hearing, increase our sensitivity to the presence of Jesus Christ, lest we miss the opportunities you place before us. Keep us alive to the issues of our day so we will be ready to speak the word or take the action that will bring your will to realization. Amen.

Offertory Invitation

When those who are hungry beg for food, the church is there. When shelter is needed, Christians respond. When the scriptures need interpretation, we struggle together to hear the truth. To support our ministries to one another and to the world, we make generous offerings, as God has blessed us.

Offertory Prayer

To share the peace of Christ, to confront the doubts that we face on every hand, to feed our bodies and our spirits, we offer these tokens of thanksgiving. May our church make a powerful witness in this place, wherever we scatter during the week, and in situations where others must go for us. Strengthen our witness here and everywhere, we pray. Amen.

Commission and Blessing

We have been fed in our time together.
Go out now to enjoy the feast of life that God offers.
> *We will be glad and rejoice in God's saving grace.*
> *We celebrate all the signs of God's love around us.*

Be alert to the wondrous surprises of our Creator.
Be receptive to the possibilities for new insights.
> *We look forward to our walk with Jesus.*
> *Surely the risen Christ accompanies us day by day.*

Continue in openness to the scriptures.
Let the words of Christ find a home in you.
> *This day, we have been clothed with power.*
> *We have witnessed the celebration of love's triumph.*

Amen. **Amen.**

(See hymn 46. See also "Come, Share the Joy," *Whispers of God,*
pp. 189–90.)

Acts 4:32–35
Psalm 133

I John 1:1–2:2
John 20:19–31

CALL TO WORSHIP

Life has been revealed to us in this Easter season.
Gather once more to testify to life.
We declare to each other what we have experienced.
In community we find the life God intends.
Early believers were of one heart and soul.
We, too, are called to find common ground in Christ.
How very good and pleasant it is
When kindred live together in unity.
Peace be with you as we celebrate resurrection.
Christ is with us to renew our faith.
We are here to testify to God's grace.
We will share our story and ourselves.

INVOCATION

You pour out upon us the oil of gladness, gracious God, as we gather in the name
of our risen Savior. You have given us the Word of Life; we have heard and seen
your greatest of all gifts and testify to that experience by our presence here. Let Jesus Christ be known among us, in our conversation and in our prayers. May our
thoughts center on the message that light has come to chase away the shadows,
community has been born to remove our isolation, joy has been heaped upon us
that we might share it with the world. Amen.

CALL TO CONFESSION

Life with eternity in it is God's present gift to us. We have heard it, but we are slow
to believe. We have received it, but we are slow to trust. It is ours to enjoy, but we
have not lived it. Let us discuss the matter with our Creator.

PRAYER OF CONFESSION

We have taken the name Christian, but few of us are known primarily by that
name. We have experienced Easter radiance, but we seldom reflect the light of our
risen Savior. We have heard the message of salvation, but it grows cold on our lips
and is of little influence on our lives. Sometimes we delude ourselves that, because
we are basically good people, there is no sin in us. We deceive ourselves, and the
truth is not in us. Sin is separation from you, and we have allowed great chasms
and built high walls to keep you out of our lives. Forgive us, we pray. Amen.

ASSURANCE OF FORGIVENESS

John wrote to the early church: If we walk in the light as Christ is in the light, we have fellowship with one another, and the blood of Jesus Christ cleanses us from all sin. If we confess our sins, God, who is faithful and just, will forgive us. Christ is the atoning sacrifice for our sin. When we are of one with God through Christ, we extend forgiveness to our sisters and brothers, that all may come to faith and have life in Jesus' name. Amen.

COLLECT

Ever-present God, who by the power of the Holy Spirit transforms us individually and as a church to be your dwelling place, confront us here in the midst of our doubts, grant us your peace while we face our fears, and increase our trust that we may embrace life in all its fullness. Speak to us now the word that we need, empowering us to be a unifying presence in our broken world. Amen.

OFFERTORY INVITATION

Among the first Christians, there were no needy people because those who were rich brought their resources to be shared. They gave up their advantages so the needs of all could be met. Out of the rich legacy they have passed on to us, we bring our tithes and offerings in thanksgiving for all God's gifts.

OFFERTORY PRAYER

We offer to you our common stewardship, loving God. We want to be faithful in meeting one another's needs and in serving the world in Christ's name. The gifts we bring today will not mark an end to our giving. We sense that you are sending us, as Jesus was sent, to share light with the world. Thus, we dedicate our time and effort as a further offering. May life and faith be extended to many through us. Amen.

COMMISSION AND BLESSING

You are sent into the world as a sign of God's love.
Go forth, carrying God's peace to all you meet.
> *We will live in unity with our kindred;*
> *We will listen and speak as God guides us.*

You are commissioned as a bearer of God's forgiveness.
Announce good news, sharing your testimony.
> *It will be our joy to reconcile others to God.*
> *We will extend to them the fellowship of light.*

The grace of Jesus Christ has been poured out on you.
God ordains a blessing for you: life forevermore.
> *Our fears are unlocked; our faith is renewed.*
> *We will invite our neighbors to share the joy.*

Amen. **Amen.**

(See hymn 47. The short hymn "We Seek to Walk in Light," *Whispers of God*, p. 190, reflects the same scriptures.)

Acts 3:12–19   1 John 3:1–17
Psalm 4   Luke 24:36b–48

CALL TO WORSHIP

God has set apart those who are faithful.
Our Creator will hear us when we call.

> *God puts gladness in our hearts and minds.*
> *We will lie down in safety and sleep in peace.*

Beloved, we are God's children now.
What we will be has not yet been revealed.

> *We are here to remember Jesus Christ.*
> *We want to be like the One who lived by love.*

Our faith strengthens us for each day's living.
God empowers our ministries of caring.

> *We trust God whose children we are.*
> *We look forward to what God will reveal to us.*

INVOCATION

God of our ancestors, author of life, source of Easter good news, we are drawn together again by the mystery of life and death. We call on you, so far beyond our knowing, with a mixture of faith and doubt. Let your face shine on us as we put our trust in you. Draw together the fragments of our busy lives around the central core of love which you provide, that we might relate to one another as whole people. Grant us a fuller sense of what is right and good, and help us to live at our best. Amen.

CALL TO CONFESSION

In his preaching, the disciple Peter reminded his listeners that no one can escape the collective guilt that allows innocent people to suffer. The mob action that sent Jesus to the cross was fed by fears and anger we are reluctant to claim. Yet we, too, reject the Holy One, by our neglect if not by deliberate intent. Peter invites us to repent and turn to God that our sins may be wiped away.

PRAYER OF CONFESSION

We are disturbed and distressed, O God, by the evil that surrounds us. It is hard to view many people we see as your children: murderers, abusers, those who cheat others and profit at their expense. We feel like victims. Why should we confess our sins when there is so much evil beyond our influence? Yet we know we do not abide in your love. We sin by turning away from sisters and brothers who are also beloved by you, however they may differ from us. We seek the forgiveness you promise and the health you offer. Amen.

Assurance of Forgiveness

Forgiveness of sins is proclaimed to all who repent and seek new life in Christ. The peace of God dwells in us when we honestly examine ourselves, exposing our wounds to Love's healing and our self-deceit to Love's correction. Beloved, we are accepted by God whose will for us is a joyous freedom in Christ Jesus.

Collect

God of amazing surprises, whose proclamation of peace through the risen Christ startles us yet washes over us with refreshing joy, we are eager to see Jesus and to trust that the purity of life we know through him is worth emulating. Put us in touch with truth that cleanses and makes whole so we can relate to others in ways that reconcile and redeem. Amen.

Offertory Invitation

With gladness in our hearts, we offer our best to God in this act of commitment and sacrifice. We give because repentance and forgiveness of sins is to be proclaimed in the name of Jesus Christ to all nations, beginning where we are. Let us give according to our faith.

Offertory Prayer

We give with joy, gracious God, for you have been with us even when we were unfaithful. You have kept us in safety through times of grave distress. We can call on you in all times and places, in life and in death, knowing that your strength is available to sustain us. We give now that your church may be empowered in the proclamation of good news and the transformation of human life. Amen.

Commission and Blessing

Put your trust in God as you face another week.
Good affirms you and claims your faithfulness.
We will open our eyes to the goodness of God.
We seek to follow faithfully where Christ leads.
Turn away from vain words and seeking after lies.
Seek the purity of life we find in Christ Jesus.
We pray for honest insight as we seek truth.
O that we might see the good in ourselves!
We have been touched by mystery and wonder.
Let us live as God's beloved children.
What we will become has not yet been revealed.
We are confident in God's will for us.
Amen. **Amen.**

(See hymn 48. "Faith in the Name of Jesus," *Whispers of God,* p. 191, is based on these texts.)

FOURTH SUNDAY OF EASTER

Acts 4:5–12   I John 3:16–24
Psalm 23   John 10:11–18

CALL TO WORSHIP
> The Good Shepherd invites us to green pastures.
> We are refreshed beside still waters.
> > *We have been given everything we have.*
> > *God offers us everything we need.*
> When we walk through shadowed valleys, God is with us.
> We are comforted and reassured.
> > *God leads us in the right paths.*
> > *Our cups are filled to overflowing.*
> God welcomes us to the table where love is expressed.
> We are invited to partake of the truth God offers.
> > *We have received plenty that we might share.*
> > *We are called to be God's helpers.*

INVOCATION
Good Shepherd, we meet in your name, confident that we are known and loved
by you. Here we draw close to one another and to you, expecting to be empowered by fresh insights to live as your people. We want to care for one another in
life-giving ways. We seek to reach out to those who deny you or suspect us. Help
us grow in love that is genuine in its caring and self-sacrifice. We embrace the
wholeness you offer and dare to risk acceptance of a healing role for ourselves and
this faith community. Equip us for service beyond this hour of meeting. Amen.

CALL TO CONFESSION
All of us have taken vows of loyalty to Jesus Christ. We have made promises in
words that have not been lived out in truth. We have too easily pushed aside God's
commands in favor of our own desires. We are more interested in pleasing ourselves than in pleasing God. Let us return to the one who is our Origin to re-
attune ourselves to God's intent for us.

PRAYER OF CONFESSION
Good Shepherd, we have wandered down the strange pathways of our world. We
have ventured into dead-end streets that looked more inviting than the narrow ways
marked out by the signposts of your love. We have trusted other voices and turned
away from your truth. We have accepted your gifts without acknowledgment. We
have failed to use our overflowing cups to fill the cups of sisters and brothers who
need what we could offer. Forgive us, we pray, and restore us to your fold. Amen.

ASSURANCE OF FORGIVENESS

Hear the good news. By the name of Jesus Christ, our sins are forgiven, and we are restored to wholeness. God's love will abide with us as long as we share it with others. Our souls will be fed when we focus on feeding others. We will be empowered by prayer and generosity.

COLLECT

God of love, whom Jesus knew as a caring parent, remind us of your commandments that it may become our heart's most earnest desire to pass on your love in truth and action. Grant us the courage to risk life itself that others may see Christ abiding in us and thus come to know your goodness and mercy. Amen.

OFFERTORY INVITATION

Bring your good deeds as an offering to God. Present to the Good Shepherd your firm commitment to care for others in the spirit of Christ. We cannot simply dedicate our money, hiring others to carry out the mission of the church on our behalf. We, ourselves, are called to give leadership and comfort. The giving that God expects includes our time and talents as well as treasure.

OFFERTORY PRAYER

How can we express our thanks, O God, for the one who laid down life itself in witness to your love for all people? We are aware that many have not experienced that love. We see their need, and we want to respond. Use what we offer to you to bring healing and peace to others not of this fold. Draw us together as one flock in the care of one shepherd, Jesus Christ, in whose name we pray. Amen.

COMMISSION AND BLESSING

We are invited to make God's house our home.
We are sent out into God's world to serve.
> **God has been with us through life's most foreboding valleys.**
> **We have been equipped to help others on their journeys.**
When we ask God for what we need, God provides.
When we are obedient, we know God abides in us.
> **God leads us by still waters and restores our souls.**
> **God knows us better than we know ourselves.**
God's love in Jesus Christ has blessed us.
We have received the gift of God's own Spirit.
> **Surely goodness and mercy will pursue us through life.**
> **We will dwell in the house of our Good Shepherd.**
Amen. **Amen.**

(See hymn 49. Another hymn on the texts for this Sunday is "Jesus Christ Is Our Good Shepherd," Whispers of God, pp. 191–92.)

Acts 8:26–40   I John 4:7–21
Psalm 22:25–31   John 15:1–8

CALL TO WORSHIP

Come to worship God whose love was revealed in Jesus.
Let all the ends of the earth turn to our God.
> *We will worship the Almighty and sing praises.*
> *We will proclaim good news to others.*

Beloved, we are called to love as God loves us.
We are to love one another as sisters and brothers.
> *Everyone who loves is born of God and knows God.*
> *We seek to let God's love be perfected in us.*

Remember that you have been baptized.
God claims you and has high expectations of you.
> *Christ is the vine; we are the branches.*
> *We will bear fruit when we abide in the vine.*

INVOCATION

Open our senses to your direction, amazing God, so we may be alert to opportunities you give us. Fill us with good news to share with those who seek meaning for their lives. We are here because we need the good news ourselves. There is much in life that we do not understand. We seek to know your Word and to be led by it. Recall us to the vows of our baptism, reconfirming in us the covenant promises that link us to you and to one another. As we meet you here, our hearts are lifted up in praise. May our worship glorify your name and be pleasing to you. Amen.

CALL TO CONFESSION

Sense the love of God that seeks to live in us. Remember the times you have felt connected to the true vine, Jesus Christ. Listen again to the promise and challenge: If you abide in me and my words abide in you, ask for whatever you wish and it will be done for you. . . . bear much fruit and become my disciples.

PRAYER OF CONFESSION

O God, we have ignored our origin in you and denied your rule over the nations. We have pursued illusions of self-interest rather than abiding in your love. We have turned away from brothers and sisters as if they were enemies to be hated. We are afraid to love those who differ from us or who have the power to harm us. We hesitate to take the risks of caring for fear that we may be hurt. Discipleship seems too demanding. O God, release us from our fears and failures to trust your love and live with bold generosity. Amen.

ASSURANCE OF FORGIVENESS

There is good news for all who sincerely repent and seek a living, growing relationship with God. Those who are open to the gift of God's love are blessed with the capacity to extend love to others and thus experience the depth and riches of life that God intends for us. When we love one another, God's love is perfected in us.

COLLECT

Loving God, whom we praise and glorify as disciples of Jesus Christ, cleanse us today by your word so we may rejoice once more in our baptism and aspire to the perfection of love among us and throughout your world. Prune away the dead debris of our fears and failures so we may become productive branches in the church, reaching out to feed a world starving for genuine love and yearning for community. Amen.

OFFERTORY INVITATION

God loves us so much that Jesus was sent to be the atoning sacrifice for our sin. The balm of love was offered for our healing so we might be reconciled to God and one another. What will we offer in thanksgiving for so great a gift?

OFFERTORY PRAYER

We give, gracious God, because we are grateful. Your love has sustained us through many trials and temptations. We are thankful for those who have guided our attempts to understand the scriptures. Your loving judgment has provided the pruning our lives require in order to bear fruit. We give in order to extend to others the blessings we have received and to continue the ministry we need as we seek to abide together in your love. Amen.

COMMISSION AND BLESSING

Live for God every moment of every day.
Take time to bow down in gratitude for God's love.
   We seek to live as people who know God.
   Because we are loved, we dare to love others.
Do not be afraid to witness to your growing faith.
Do not hesitate to show the fruits of abiding in Christ.
   We will turn to the perfect love that casts out fear.
   We will tell of that love to future generations.
You have been equipped and empowered by love.
God is filling your life with purpose and energy.
   We love because God first loved us.
   We go out to serve as apostles of Jesus Christ.
Amen. **Amen.**

(See hymn 50. "Praise, All Congregations," *Whispers of God*, pp. 192–93,
grew out of the readings for this week.)

Acts 10:44–48   1 John 5:1–6
Psalm 98   John 15:–17

Call to Worship

Come all who are born of God;
Abide in the love revealed in Jesus Christ.
> *We come in response to the one who calls us friends.*
> *We are here in obedience to Christ's command.*
Remember God's steadfast love and faithfulness.
Let hands and voices echo God's praise.
> *Let our lips pour out a joyful noise.*
> *Let our hands reflect a serving Savior.*
Sing a new song to God who does marvelous things.
Obey God's commandments which are not burdensome.
> *We clap our hands and sing for joy.*
> *We live by faith that conquers the world.*

Invocation

Come, Holy Spirit, to lift us from empty routines to the surprising joy of your love. Loosen our tongues to praise you with sincere delight. Open our hearts to trust your leading through times of difficulty and days of despair. Calm our doubts and guide us through the mires of fear. You have called us together for mutual support in a time of worship that unites our spirits. We remember that we have been baptized in the name of Jesus Christ. Teach us to follow where Christ leads. Amen.

Call to Confession

God judges the world with righteousness, and the peoples with equity. God knows all that we have done and all that we avoid. God is aware of our obedience to the way of love and our rebellion against it. We are invited to confess all that God already knows so healing and freedom can be ours in Christ Jesus.

Prayer of Confession

Ever-present God, we confess to you our unloving thoughts and deeds. We live by standards that we bend and break in our own favor, while ignoring the commandments you have given. We find it hard to love everyone, for so many act in unloving ways. It is easier to treat people as things than to listen for their needs. We withhold ourselves rather than offer our lives, even for our friends. We hoard the gifts you entrust to us instead of letting them bear fruit for you. Cleanse us from these destructive ways, freeing us to love as you have loved us, we pray in Jesus' name. Amen.

ASSURANCE OF FORGIVENESS

Even now, God is giving us victory over the limitations we impose on ourselves. When we trust God's love, we can emerge from the shell of self-protection to celebrate the joy of friendship in Christ. We can dare to show love that is not dependent on others' responses. We can serve without the need for recognition. Praise God!

COLLECT

Creator of friendships, whose love lifts us from mindless servitude to caring community, we thank you for the guidance of your commandments and the promise of joy in Jesus Christ. We seek to love as we have been loved, to risk life itself for the sake of our sisters and brothers, and to bear fruit that will last. Grant us the strength and courage we need. Amen.

OFFERTORY INVITATION

We are people whom God has blessed with many gifts. God has done marvelous things for us. How will we, who have been baptized by water and the Spirit, respond to God's generosity?

OFFERTORY PRAYER

Generous and loving God, we dedicate to your service the work of our hands, the earnings of our time and efforts, and our vision for the future. May faith sustain us as we offer our best to you in praise and thanksgiving and joyous dedication. We seek to work for the reign of your truth and extension of the friendship granted to us in Jesus Christ. Let our offering bear fruit in the lives of all who are helped by it. Amen.

COMMISSION AND BLESSING

Friends of Christ, carry God's love into the world.
You have been chosen and appointed to bear fruit.
May the Holy Spirit inspire our words.
May God's love in Christ empower our deeds.
Sing of the victory of self-giving friendship.
Witness to the saving power of love.
In Christ, we are no longer servants but friends.
We are learning to love as we have been loved.
God judges the world with righteousness.
Our efforts are accepted with steadfast faithfulness.
We clap our hands with appreciation and joy.
The law of love is reigning in our hearts.
Amen. **Amen.**

(See hymn 51. "Make a Joyful Noise," *Whispers of God*, pp. 193–94, is
another hymn centered on these texts.)

Sixth Sunday of Easter   97

ASCENSION (OR SEVENTH SUNDAY OF EASTER)—A, B, C

Acts 1:1–11

Psalm 47 or Psalm 93

Ephesians 1:15–23

Luke 24:44–53

CALL TO WORSHIP

Come together expecting great things.
Wait for the promises of God.
Is this the time when God will come to reign?
Will we receive power and authority?
In God's time, the Holy Spirit will come to you.
You will be empowered as faithful witnesses.
We are here to learn about all that Jesus did.
We are ready to listen to all that Jesus taught.
Clap your hands, all you peoples;
Sing praises to God, sing praises.
God is ruler over all the earth.
We seek to experience God's rule in our lives.

INVOCATION

Appear to us again, risen Savior, for we have lost sight of you. We have come to find you here so we may recognize you among all who suffer. We seek wisdom and revelation to cope with the confusion we face every day amid competing claims. We are here to remember the authority with which you spoke so we may walk amid the rulers of our day, speaking in Christ's name. We who seek to be your body, the church, need the eyes of our hearts enlightened so we may once more embrace hope and know your joy. Amen.

CALL TO CONFESSION

If the people of Galilee spent too much time looking up toward heaven, perhaps our problem is that we spend too little. In our busyness, we do not examine our busyness. Are we about God's business? Are we on a spiritual quest in the midst of all our doing? Let us confess the way things are between ourselves and God.

PRAYER OF CONFESSION

O God, it is hard for us to wait for anything. We want instant answers and immediate gratification of our desires. We are more acquisitive than grateful. We forget the amazing riches of your gifts to us and only want more. We do not take time simply to enjoy being in your presence, singing your praises, delighting in your love. Forgive us for our arrogant, selfish pride and our neglect of values and relationships that would supply all we really need. Amen.

ASSURANCE OF FORGIVENESS
Forgiveness is yours to receive and to proclaim to all nations. The power of God at work in Christ, is offered to us: the power of love to make a difference among us. Let us give thanks that we are restored as sons and daughters of the Living God who promises to us the baptism of the Holy Spirit.

COLLECT
Holy God, whose word has come to us through the law of Moses, in the poetry of the psalms, and in the passion of the prophets, speak to us again through the Word made flesh in Jesus Christ, who calls us as witnesses in our own times and places. May we know your blessing and empowerment, not for our own satisfaction but that we might share good news and practical help with confidence and joy. Amen.

OFFERTORY INVITATION
We are called as witnesses to God's love for us in Jesus Christ, to the ends of the earth. Our glorious inheritance is meant to be shared with brothers and sisters in our community and throughout the world. May our generous gifts praise God and give radiant testimony to the faith we share.

OFFERTORY PRAYER
May our offerings leave no doubt that you are head of our church and the inspiration for our lives. Empower our ministries with the fullness of Christ that we may be inclusive in our outreach and effective as teachers and healers. Help us to find joy in our praying and in our serving. For these purposes and to the glory of your name, we dedicate our money and our lives. Amen.

COMMISSION AND BLESSING
Return to your homes with great joy.
Look around you to see how God is blessing you.
> **God has opened our minds to understand the scriptures.**
> **We are surrounded with evidence of God's care.**

Delight in God's revelation and wisdom.
Embrace the hope to which you have been called.
> **We have been baptized by the Holy Spirit.**
> **We are empowered to be Christ's disciples.**

Clap your hands and sing your praises.
Let your spirits be lifted up with rejoicing.
> **We are witnesses to God's presence with us.**
> **God is with us when we are together and when we part.**

Amen. **Amen.**

(See hymn 52. Other hymns by the author on the Ascension texts include *Whispers of God*, p. 194; *Refreshing Rains of the Living Word*, pp. 207–8; *Fresh Winds of the Spirit*, book 2, pp. 215 and 216.)

Acts 1:15–17, 21–26   I John 5:9–13

Psalm 1   John 17:6–19

CALL TO WORSHIP

We are together today because Christ has claimed us.
We are called to be the body of Christ in today's world.
> *Who are we to make such a claim?*
> *Who would see Jesus Christ when they look at us?*

It is not our claim that brings us together.
The church is not our private club.
> *We are not here just for ourselves, for our own needs.*
> *We are drawn together by a larger purpose.*

We have been called by Christ for a mission.
The gathered community is sent out into the world.
> *We are here to be equipped for ministry.*
> *We have been chosen as apostles of good news.*

INVOCATION

Watch over us, holy God, as we take time to pray and to meditate on the continuing impact of Easter on our lives. Jesus Christ has become for us the measure of life. He represents to us your gift of love and eternal life. We are a resurrection people no longer bound by fear of death but freed to become witnesses to the light. Nourish us to become like trees, planted beside streams of water, that flourish and bear much fruit because of your constant attention and abundant provision for our needs. Be known to us here in this hour. Amen.

CALL TO CONFESSION

Each of us is allotted a ministry only we can carry out. When we betray this trust and turn aside to pursue our own limited agendas, who will share the story only we can tell? Who will testify to the God who gives us life through Jesus Christ?

PRAYER OF CONFESSION

In the name of Jesus Christ, we pour out our Prayer of Confession. We have been called together into the church to live the resurrection faith, to embody Easter and touch lives as Jesus did. We have not done this well. Our vision has been narrow and limited. Our testimony has been timid and self-protective. We listen to the wrong advisors and complain when things do not go our way. Forgive our limited commitment and low expectations that deny the Body of Christ as the strong force for good that we are meant to be. Help us rediscover the delight and joy of full commitment. Amen.

Assurance of Forgiveness

God hears our prayers and forgives. No longer are we like chaff that the wind drives away. We are not numbered among the wicked who have no place in the congregation of the righteous. As forgiven and forgiving sinners, let us embrace our chosenness and live up to our calling.

Collect

Eternal God, revealed to us in ways we can begin to understand through Jesus Christ, show us now what you expect of us as we seek the unity for which Jesus prayed. May we find joy in your word as we share it with others. May we discover your truth that unites us with all your children everywhere in acts of self-giving love that bring us closer to your realm. Amen.

Offertory Invitation

All that we possess is a part of God's gift to the world. God's gift in Jesus Christ reminds us that what is entrusted to us is meant to be shared. May the joy we discover in God's word be passed on through our generous giving.

Offertory Prayer

Here, O God, is some of the abundance you have allowed us to manage for you while we are on this earth. May it be enough to draw us closer to you and to all whom we seek to help. May our hearts follow our treasure into growing devotion to your truth and expanded commitment to the unity in love that Jesus sought for all your children. Bless this offering, and increase our joy in giving. Amen.

Commission and Blessing

You have been chosen as disciples and apostles.
Your task is to learn and proclaim God's Word.
> *We are learning from the life of Jesus.*
> *We are seeking to live in ways Jesus taught.*
You do not belong to the world but to God.
You are in the world as bearers of God's truth.
> *We find delight in the discovery of God's law.*
> *May it be a part of us, day and night.*
God's love is our guardian and protection.
God gives us eternal life in Christ Jesus.
> *God, who knows our hearts, accepts us.*
> *The love of God follows us wherever we go.*
Amen. **Amen.**

(See hymns 53, 54. "Grant Us Your Joy," *Whispers of God*, p. 195, is derived from the same scriptures.)

Pentecost and the Season Following

Acts 2:1–21 or Ezekiel 37:1–14   Romans 8:22–27 or Acts 2:1–21
Psalm 104:24–34, 35b   John 15:26–27; 16:4b–15

CALL TO WORSHIP

The day of Pentecost has come, and we are together.
Will the works of God be known among us today?
> *We live in the valley of dry bones.*
> *Around and within us is emptiness.*

God comes to us as a gentle breath or violent wind.
Catch your breath, God's breath, and live.
> *There are stirrings deep within that give us hope.*
> *There is a Spirit linking us to one another.*

The fires of love dispel life's shadows.
God's Spirit comes to give us new life.
> *Surely God is in this place!*
> *May the glory of God be known among us today!*

INVOCATION

Amazing God, how manifold are your works! The earth is full of life you have created, in forms too numerous to count. You have linked us, your people, to the earth and to all living things. We are interdependent. We can survive only if we have reverence for life. Come among us now to make your ways known. Help us to dream dreams and see visions of your intentions for this world and for your church. Amen.

CALL TO CONFESSION

Like the first disciples, we have much to learn about sin and righteousness and judgment. Almost without conscious awareness, we slip into the valley of dry bones, devoid of meaning and hope, unable even to pray. But together we can join our voices, asking that our spirits will awaken to new possibilities.

PRAYER OF CONFESSION

When your face is hidden from us, mighty God, we forget that there is more to life than the daily pursuits that occupy our attention. We are weak because we have not tapped the resources you place within us. We are engaged only by what we can see and touch and hear. Our frantic self-centeredness dries up our bones and we lose hope. Call us out of the graves in which we have chosen to live, the deep ruts that keep us from knowing the fullness of life you reveal when we welcome your Spirit. Amen.

ASSURANCE OF FORGIVENESS

In hope we are saved. The Spirit helps us in our weakness, intercedes for us, and guides us into all truth. God seeks to restore us to the fullness of life, to offer us hope, to assure us of our worth and value. Feel the flames of God's love resting on us, empowering us to love and serve in Christ's name.

COLLECT

Spirit of truth, come among us to guide us in the footsteps of Jesus. Amaze and astonish us with the gifts already present among us. Awaken us to the wind and tongues of fire waiting to fill us with new life and vigorous hope. May our meditations be pleasing to you and our service to others be truly helpful, that your great and glorious day may be realized in our midst. Amen.

OFFERTORY INVITATION

God has given us food in due season, opening a kind and loving hand to fill us with good things. The face of the ground is continually renewed each year so we can reap its bounty. Likewise, our spirits are renewed. Our offerings are but a small expression of thanks.

OFFERTORY PRAYER

How manifold are your works, amazing God! When there are dry-bones times in our lives, we can look to you for new breath and hope and renewal of life. Your Spirit comes, and we are lifted up and linked to one another. We bring our offerings as an expression of thanksgiving for all your gifts. May your glory be proclaimed in all we give and all we do, when we are together and when we scatter to do your will in other places. Amen.

COMMISSION AND BLESSING

God's Spirit is being poured out on this church.
We carry it with us into our everyday world.
> *With joy and amazement we scatter to serve.*
> *God's love is changing us and granting new life.*
Our children will share new insights.
People of all ages will dream and see visions.
> *God is inspiring us in fresh ways.*
> *We are filled with hope for each new day.*
The Spirit will help us in our weakness.
We will be guided in all truth.
> *Each day we will practice what we are learning.*
> *Throughout our days we will continue in prayer.*
Amen. **Amen.**

(See hymn 55. See also "On This Day of Expectation,"
Whispers of God, p. 196.)

TRINITY SUNDAY
(FIRST SUNDAY AFTER PENTECOST)

Isaiah 6:1–8   Romans 8:12–17
Psalm 29   John 3:1–17

CALL TO WORSHIP

Ascribe to God glory and strength;
Worship God in holy splendor.
> *The splendor of our Creator meets us here.*
> *We are filled with awe before our God.*

The voice of God is powerful and full of majesty.
God offers strength and peace to all people.
> *God's voice thunders over the waters.*
> *God's strength empowers our response.*

Holy, holy, holy is the God of hosts.
The whole earth is full of God's glory.
> *The universe is God's dwelling place.*
> *There is no place from which God is absent.*

INVOCATION

O God, you are beyond our wildest imagining. When we speak of you, there are no words to describe your majesty and power. We know you best in Jesus of Nazareth who shared your love with all he met. He called for our rebirth as your children, cleansed by water and the spirit. We come together seeking renewal of the vows made at our baptism. We want to be faithful as Christ was faithful. We want to be fruitful in the work you give us to do. Bless our worship that we may be a blessing to others. Amen.

CALL TO CONFESSION

In the midst of a time of grieving, the prophet Isaiah went to the temple to pray. There he had a vision of God's majesty, that moved him to recognize his unworthiness and sin. Sometimes we think we have nothing to confess, until we are confronted by the awesome presence of the Creator of all things. In awe before God, we come to seek forgiveness and reconciliation.

PRAYER OF CONFESSION

God of all worlds, we confess that we are too much people of the flesh, living in slavery to our possessions and our fears. We are so attached to our little corner of the world that we find it difficult to identify with people whose experience is far different from our own. We do not want to suffer with the homeless, the hungry, the refugees, the oppressed. We turn away from the suffering of Jesus to pursue temporary advantages. We act like just another human organization, not the body of Christ making a difference in the world. O God, forgive us and reclaim us as your children. Amen.

ASSURANCE OF FORGIVENESS

God always claims us and loves us. When we confess our lostness and seek new birth in the Spirit, putting to death our selfish pursuits, we can receive what God always offers, participation in God's realm. We are born anew to life which already partakes of eternity. The cleansing coals of forgiveness touch our lips, taking away our guilt and blotting out our sin. Receive this gift from God.

COLLECT

Wind of God, blowing among the crowds at Pentecost, sweeping across the generations to claim us, may we be born of the Spirit. Speak to us of heavenly things in the midst of our earthly pilgrimage so we may live, not for ourselves, but for the well-being of the whole human family. Send us as messengers of good news and bearers of your peace. Amen.

OFFERTORY INVITATION

As a sign of our rebirth in the Spirit, we offer back to God all that we have received in this life. This time of giving is a sacred symbol of our intent to live as God intends. We lift up our tiny tokens of thanksgiving, entrusting to the ministry of this church, here and around the world, not only these gifts but ourselves as well.

OFFERTORY PRAYER

Receive our offering, God of glory, that our church may come alive in the Spirit. May these gifts, and the way we live our lives each day, proclaim the good news of Jesus Christ. Strengthen us in our giving. Help us to be generous enough to experience the joy you find in showering us with more than we can ever give away. Thank you for the gift of Jesus Christ. Amen.

COMMISSION AND BLESSING

Together, we catch a glimpse of God's glory.
Scattered, we carry that vision into the world.
> *We need courage to live what we have seen.*
> *We need confidence to pass on the joy.*
God offers strength for our journey.
God blesses us with peace amid the world's tensions.
> *We are people of the Spirit, released from slavery.*
> *We are children of God, bearing witness every day.*
God asks: "Whom shall I send? Who will go for us?
Who will tell of my love for all the world?"
> **God has touched our lips and our hearts.**
> **We dare to say: "Here am I; send me!"**
Amen.

(See hymn 56. Another hymn of similar title, "Holy, Holy, Holy God," *Whispers of God*, p. 197, is based on the same scriptures.)

PROPER 4

Sunday between May 29 and June 4
(if after Trinity Sunday)

I Samuel 3:1–10, (11–20)	(or Deuteronomy 5:12–15	2 Corinthians 4:5–12
Psalm 139:1–6, 13–18	Psalm 81:1–10)	Mark 2:23–3:6

CALL TO WORSHIP

Listen, for your name is being called.
Beyond the range of human voices, God is calling.
> **We have come to observe a sabbath time.**
> **We have gathered to worship at God's command.**

Listen for the unfamiliar voice you have ignored.
Listen for the solemn charge God gives.
> **We are called away from things we have pursued as gods.**
> **Our iniquity has separated us from the one true God.**

Wonderful are the thoughts and works of God!
God's light is ready to shine in our hearts.
> **Even clay jars can be open to the light.**
> **May the power of light cleanse and heal us!**

INVOCATION

Speak to us, O God, for your servants are trying to listen. Amid the noisy claimants for our attention, our ears tingle at the prospect that you have a message for us. Here we are, gathered that you might search us and know us. We are wonderfully made in your image. Inspire us to live up to that image. Show us how to proclaim Jesus Christ in our daily decisions so we can witness to your love through deeds of kindness and words that empower. Amen.

CALL TO CONFESSION

By a strong hand, we are summoned from our unfaithfulness to face our sins before God. The One who listens and rescues gives us a solemn charge: Do not try to hide from me the iniquity I already know. Face up to your sin and let go of it.

PRAYER OF CONFESSION

Before a word is on our tongues, O God, you know it completely. Before we confess our broken vows, you are aware of them. Our unfaithfulness to you and to people around us is evident to you. You observe our sinful secrets and our blatant rebellion. Nothing we say or do escapes your notice. Test our sincerity now as we confess to you our individual and shared wrongdoing and neglect. Melt our hardness of heart that we may be forgiven and cleansed from our iniquity. Amen.

ASSURANCE OF FORGIVENESS

The God who punishes blasphemy also forgives those sincerely repentant. The God who is acquainted with all our ways welcomes us into the light of knowledge of God's glory in the face of Jesus Christ. Let the life of Jesus be visible to others through you. Stretch out your hand to help those who need a caring touch, a kind word, some practical assistance. What you give away will return to you as joy.

COLLECT

Loving God, whose law of love is greater than all our human ordinances, and whose care for humankind exceeds all our deserving, lead us to look for the good in our neighbors, and to celebrate the goodness we observe, that together we might grow toward your perfect intent for us in Christ Jesus, in whose name we pray. Amen.

OFFERTORY INVITATION

We bring our offerings, not to win God's favor, but to express our thanks. We give because we cannot truly live if we only receive. It is our privilege to respond to God's mercy by doing good with the resources entrusted to us. Let us give with generosity and joy.

OFFERTORY PRAYER

In answer to your call, gracious God, we have opened our ears for your instruction and our eyes to the needs of our sisters and brothers. Alone, our helpfulness is limited, though often greater than we have imagined, for you are with us. Together, our effectiveness is multiplied, and your work is made visible. Bless our sharing and our sacrifices that your rule of love may grow among us and extend to all we meet. Amen.

COMMISSION AND BLESSING

Our sabbath times are for our own growth.
They are also for the renewal of our compassion.
> *Our lives are saved to be a benefit to others.*
> *Our days are enriched when our blessings are shared.*
Praise God for creating and caring for us.
Give thanks for God's continuing knowledge of us.
> *God speaks encouragement and challenge to us.*
> *God honors us with tasks to do.*
Go forth to let your light shine in the gloom.
Let the life of Jesus be known through you.
> *We are affected but not crushed, perplexed but not despairing.*
> *In all times, God is with us; praise God!*
Amen. **Amen.**

(See hymn 57. The Gospel and Epistle lessons for the day are reflected in part in the hymn "Great God, We Bring," *Whispers of God*, p. 198.)

PROPER 5

Sunday between June 5 and June 11
(if after Trinity Sunday)

I Samuel 8:4–11, (12–15), 16–20, (11:14–15) Psalm 138	(or Genesis 3:8–152 Psalm 130)	2 Corinthians 4:13–5:1 Mark 3:20–35

CALL TO WORSHIP

> Gather to give thanks with your whole heart.
> Rejoice in God's love and faithfulness.
> > *We bow down, for this is God's holy temple.*
> > *We pour out our thanks in songs of praise.*
> God answers us when we call.
> Our Creator increases our strength of soul.
> > *Great is the glory of our God!*
> > *We rejoice in God's steadfast love.*
> Wait for God, and hope in God's Word.
> Open your hearts to the holy presence in our midst.
> > *Our ears are attentive to the voice of God.*
> > *We open our lives to God's direction.*

INVOCATION

Our souls wait for you, O God. Our ears are attentive to your word. We hope for a clear understanding of your will for us. Let this time of meeting draw us together in unity, with a sense of direction and purpose for our church and our individual lives. Renew us within so that nothing we face around us can undermine our faith or cause us to despair. Claim us all as sisters and brothers of Jesus Christ, and help us to reflect this kinship in all we do or say. Amen.

CALL TO CONFESSION

God does not forsake us, but we often choose other rulers. We abdicate responsibility for our own lives, in relation to our Creator, turning instead to entertainers, politicians, and financial wizards as our hope. In worship, we are recalled to our primary accountability to God.

PRAYER OF CONFESSION

We confess, O God, that we often act as if we know better than you what is right for us. We make decisions without considering your larger purposes. Our own convenience and desires are more important to us than your commands. We go our own way and then blame others for our mistakes. Our inner confusion creates division and brokenness. We hide from you rather than admitting our needs. O God, we want to face our sin and find forgiveness. Help us! Amen.

Assurance of Forgiveness

The One who raised Jesus from the dead offers us new life today. Our sins are forgiven. Our lives are cleansed. Our inner nature is being renewed. God does not forsake us. We are the work of God's hands, the object of steadfast love. Meet the world with the assurance that you are loved, valued, and empowered as an ambassador of God's eternal realm.

Collect

Gracious and loving God, who in Jesus Christ has called each one of us to recognize that we are all sisters and brothers and members of your family, unite us today as a community of faith, listening to your word and finding in it our greatest hope and highest joy. May we hear the words of your mouth and give thanks for your steadfast love and faithfulness. Amen.

Offertory Invitation

Many of our resources are committed to time payments, taxes, rent, or mortgages. Our need for food, shelter, and clothing take precedence in our lives. We also confuse wants with needs, the more and more affluent we become. Where is our thanksgiving to God in all this? And our commitment to love God and neighbor as ourselves? We give in proportion to our faith.

Offertory Prayer

Thank you, God, for your faithfulness. We bring ourselves and some of what we have accumulated to praise you and do the work you call us to do. Fulfill your purpose for this church as you enlist our offerings and our lives. In amazement at the work of your hands, we reach out our hands to help others and invite them to join us. In our labors for you, we will not lose heart. Help us to do your will. Amen.

Commission and Blessing

God's grace has been poured out on us.
We are invited to share it with more and more people.
We seek to live so God's grace is evident.
We will consult with God in our decision-making.
Go into the world to serve, to the glory of God.
May your thanksgiving increase day by day.
Our praise will not cease when we leave this place.
All the world is God's temple, a place to give thanks.
We are brothers and sisters of Jesus Christ.
The Holy Spirit has come among us and abides with us.
We have good news to share, so we will do it!
May our thanksgiving proclaim God's glory!
Amen. **Amen.**

(See hymns 58, 59. The Gospel and Epistle lessons for the day are reflected in "Grace Extends to All," *Whispers of God,* pp. 198–99.)

PROPER 6

Sunday between June 12 and June 18
(if after Trinity Sunday)

I Samuel 15:34–16:13	(or Ezekiel 17:22–24	2 Corinthians 5:6–10,
Psalm 20	Psalm 92:1–4, 12–15)	(11–13), 14–17
		Mark 4:26–34

CALL TO WORSHIP

It is good to give thanks to God!
Come to make music to our Creator.
> **God knows our troubles and remembers our need.**
> **Our petitions are answered and our hearts' desires fulfilled.**
Declare God's steadfast love and faithfulness.
Seek God's help in the sanctuary.
> **We know that God will help the anointed ones.**
> **Our pride is in God alone.**
Listen for the voice of God, speaking to us again.
How great is our God, our rock and defender!
> **God will respond when we call.**
> **We will bear fruit for God as long as life endures.**

INVOCATION

We turn to you, God of all worlds, knowing we can depend on you when earthly rulers stumble and fall, when other relationships are strained and broken, when we are faced with difficult challenges. It is good to sing your praises, even when we do not feel like singing. It is good to declare your faithfulness when we have been unfaithful. It is good to give thanks, for when we do, we are reminded of the multitude of blessings we so often take for granted. Lead us in this time of worship. Amen.

CALL TO CONFESSION

Each of us has a mandate from God to give our best and bear fruit for God's realm. We who gather in God's house are called to be a faithful community in which all bow humbly before God, motivated by the love of Christ. This is a time to examine ourselves before our Creator.

PRAYER OF CONFESSION

God of all truth, who can stand before you? We judge by outward appearances, but you examine our hearts. We see what is on the surface, but you discern beauty deep within. We measure importance by paychecks, but you find value among those we deem lowly and insignificant. You offer us the deep and profound joy of living in your realm. We forget your promises and turn to pursuits that separate us from you and destroy community. We seek forgiveness and a new direction for our lives. Amen.

ASSURANCE OF FORGIVENESS

All of us must stand before the judgment seat of Christ, today and every day. When we come with true penitence, we can win a victory over sin. Christ died for us, that we might no longer live only for ourselves. In Christ, we no longer regard others from a human point of view. We are a new creation. The old has passed away; the new has come. We can live confidently, urged on by the love of Christ, to joyous, daring service.

COLLECT

Righteous God, whose works are greater than our wildest imagination and most sophisticated study, plant the seed of your Word among us today, and let each of us welcome the good news you would plant within us. Inspire in us deeper thinking and more open receptiveness. May our lives be the fertile ground in which your love bursts into life to nourish all whom we meet, in Jesus' name. Amen.

OFFERTORY INVITATION

God remembers our offerings of genuine thankfulness and regards with favor the sacrifices we make to extend God's realm. We give, not out of compulsion, but with joy. Whatever our age or circumstances, we have something to give. Let us give thanks as we present our tithes and offerings.

OFFERTORY PRAYER

All that we have is yours, O God. What we present for the church's use is no sacrifice. We are privileged to share good news in word and deed. May our common ministry be extended by the time and talents and treasure we invest. We would no longer live just for ourselves but for the realization of your reign among us. Let all things become new as we give our best. Amen.

COMMISSION AND BLESSING

Share your mustard-seed faith with the world.
God will make of it more than you can imagine.
> *We will dare to speak of God's love.*
> *We will seek to live out the love of Christ.*
In Christ, we are a new creation.
Our dried-up faith has received new life.
> *The mighty have been toppled from power.*
> *The humble and lowly have been lifted up.*
Walk by faith, not by sight.
God will add to your understanding day by day.
> *We will seek to view others as God sees them.*
> *We will claim them as sisters and brothers.*
Amen. **Amen.**

(See hymns 60, 61. Today's New Testament texts and different Hebrew Scripture readings are the basis for "Be Still and Know," *Whispers of God*, pp. 199–200.)

PROPER 7

I Samuel 17:(1a, 4–11,   (or Job 38:1–11   2 Corinthians 6:1–13
  19–23), 32–49   Psalm 107:1–3, 23–32)   Mark 4:35–41
Psalm 9:9–20 or I Samuel
  17:57–18:5, 10–16 and Psalm 133

CALL TO WORSHIP

Gather in awe before God, who laid the foundations of the earth.
Open your hearts to the steadfast love God offers.
The deeds of God are beyond our knowing.
Yet we catch glimpses of God's mercy and care.
God does not forsake us when we are dismayed and afraid.
Our Creator is with us in all times and places.
God is a stronghold for the oppressed and troubled.
The needy and the poor are not forgotten.
God is ready to listen to us in these moments together.
See, now is the acceptable time, the day of salvation.
Surely God will meet us here in our faith community!
How good it is when we sense our unity in Christ!

INVOCATION

We sing praises to you, O God, for you have been gracious to us amid the storms
of life. We do battle with many enemies within and among us, but you give us
confidence and courage to face them. Out of the whirlwind, you answer when we
call. We have gathered to listen for the voice we sometimes cannot hear in the daily
clamor of our lives. Help us to discard the excess baggage and unnecessary armor
that keeps us from the fullness of life you intend for us. Amen.

CALL TO CONFESSION

All of us have faltered before the lions and giants that seem ready to destroy us.
Life's storms overwhelm us, and fear takes a deadly toll. Sometimes we are snared
in the work of our own hands. We forget the greatest source of help and hope. In
these moments together, we lay aside our doubts and fear of judgment to open our
lives to God.

PRAYER OF CONFESSION

Help us, God, for we do not have the wisdom to help ourselves. When the good
we have known crumbles beneath our feet and we are mired down in hopeless-
ness and self-pity, we need you. When we cannot hide from the evil that is all
around us because some of it is also in us, we cry out for your saving mercy. We
confess that it is easier to see the problems than the promise. We have been more
ready to complain than to accept your help. O God, we open our hearts to you.
We want to be healed. Amen.

ASSURANCE OF FORGIVENESS

God has listened to us. In spite of all we have done or not done, God accepts us. This is a day of salvation, when brokenness is mended, problems are seen in a new light, and fierce winds are stilled. God does not forget the cry of the afflicted. God's affection for us is limited only by our failure to respond. Accept the gift of God's love, for it is everything we need.

COLLECT

Teacher, whose word rebuked the wind and stilled the sea, whose trust in all that is eternal transcended the betrayal of friends and the cruelty of enemies, speak to us here in the midst of our own particular needs, and let that word abide in us with a transforming sense of peace that we can share with others. Amen.

OFFERTORY INVITATION

God has lifted us up from the gates of death. We will praise God with all we have to give. Christ walks with us through difficult days and sleepless nights. We give thanks for the church that proclaims this good news. The Holy Spirit meets us in our weakness with a love that will not let us go. All this we want to share with the world. These moments of giving represent the commitment of our lives to God.

OFFERTORY PRAYER

Thank you, God, for meeting us in our need. We give that others in even greater need might not be forgotten. We are grateful for the trust you place in us. We give that others might respond to the good news of your love. We are hearing the word Jesus spoke in the midst of a storm: "Peace! Be still!" With fresh calm and confidence, we give ourselves that others might live. Thank you, God, for your steadfast love endures forever. Amen.

COMMISSION AND BLESSING

As servants of God, we commend ourselves in every way.
God has given us the ministry in which we serve.
We seek to be patient and kind with all people.
Our speech is truthful and our love genuine.
The grace of God rests on each one of us.
Holiness of spirit is God's gift to us today.
We feel empowered to endure all things.
God equips us to rejoice in all circumstances.
Let your faith grow and your trust expand.
Go into the world with confidence and courage.
We are not afraid, for we know God's presence.
We are alive to the possibilities before us.
Amen. **Amen.**

(See hymn 62.)

PROPER 8

Sunday between June 26 and July 2

| 2 Samuel 1:1, 17–27 | (or Lamentations 3:23–33 | 2 Corinthians 8:7–15 |
| Psalm 130 | Psalm 30) | Mark 5:21–43 |

CALL TO WORSHIP

Arise, people of faith, that Christ may give us life.
This is the day of meeting in Christ's name.
We reach out for health and wholeness.
We embrace one another with concern and care.
God is attentive to us and hears our cries.
God challenges us to eager engagement in life.
Like those who watch eagerly for the morning,
We wait in joyous anticipation of God's Word.
The word of life is ours to receive.
The good news is available to be shared.
We will sing praises to God's holy name.
We will tell of God's faithfulness day by day.

INVOCATION

We gather to thank you, gracious God, for those times when we have been lifted up by you and known your healing touch. You have clothed us with joy and filled us with hope. We are grateful that even in our days of deepest gloom and despair, you have surrounded us with a love stronger than all our pain and doubts and grievous losses. Come to us now that, together and individually, we may sense larger realities than the narrow focus of our daily concerns. We await your word. Amen.

CALL TO CONFESSION

Surrounded by the steadfast love of God, we gain courage to examine our lives and our relationships. Together we confess the sin that cuts us off from our Creator and separates us from one another.

PRAYER OF CONFESSION

God of peace, we confess that we have relied too much on the weapons of war. We are more ready to honor warriors than to give support to those who work diligently for justice and equality of opportunity. We extol our accumulation of gadgets over a balanced sharing of resources. We are more interested in securing your support for our desires than in conforming ourselves to your will. You have given us much, and we have misspent this abundance, creating idols and pursuing illusions of pleasure. O God, forgive us and re-center us in ways that really matter. Amen.

116 *Pentecost and the Season Following*

Assurance of Forgiveness

If God marked iniquities, who could stand? Yet there is forgiveness from the Source of Life. There is power to redeem us from the most grievous sin. God offers steadfast love to re-center our lives. When we revere God, all else in life is seen in a new light. What was dead in us is brought to new life. Our brokenness is healed. Our priorities are changed. Praise God!

Collect

Amazing God, whose love accomplishes more than all the armaments of an embattled world, and whose empowerment for abundant living we have barely tapped, we come with fear and trembling to reach out for help. We, who have created our own definitions of the abundant life, dare to seek your will for us as world citizens and bearers of your steadfast love. Amen.

Offertory Invitation

God's generous act in Jesus Christ invites our generosity. Identifying with our poverty, Jesus leads us to true riches. We are called to give according to our means, toward the goal of a fair balance among all God's children. May our offerings begin to answer that call.

Offertory Prayer

We pray that you will find our gifts acceptable, God. If we have not given according to what we have, we seek the courage to do so. May these gifts relieve suffering and reveal hope. May they give meaning to all who give and all who receive. We dedicate them, that those who have much may not have too much, and those who have little may not have too little. Amen.

Commission and Blessing

Continue to excel in everything.
Serve with eagerness, faith, and love.
>   *We seek to share the best that we know.*
>   *We want to pass on the love we have received.*
Dare to be generous with your time and resources.
The needs of others are not always apparent.
>   *We are eager to reach out helping hands.*
>   *We need strength and assurance to do so.*
Your faith is making you well.
God is healing and equipping you. Go in peace!
>   *Together, we have been empowered.*
>   *Apart, we will continue to feel God's touch.*
Amen. **Amen.**

(See hymn 63. See also "O Strong and Mighty God," *Whispers of God*,
pp. 201–2.)

PROPER 9

2 Samuel 5:1–5, 9–10   (or Ezekiel 2:1–5   2 Corinthians 12:2–10
Psalm 48   Psalm 123)   Mark 6:1–13

CALL TO WORSHIP

Great is our God and greatly to be praised.
Worship the One whose grace covers all our needs.
> **The God of hosts is with us here.**
> **We praise, with joy, God's holy name.**

Ponder God's steadfast love in the temple.
Practice sharing that love while we are together.
> **God's love is amazing, beyond our understanding.**
> **We seek to share the love we are receiving.**

We are here to be equipped for the journey of life.
We have gathered that our daily witness might be empowered.
> **Sometimes we are not strong enough to love.**
> **We pray that God will use our weakness for good.**

INVOCATION

God of faithful elders and lowly followers, our sure defense and faithful guide, we invoke your presence among us in this time of praise. Your name is proclaimed through all the earth, and by your hand we are made victorious over the unclean spirits and unbeliefs that stalk our paths. When we ponder your greatness, we are filled with awe. When we come to your holy mountain, we are amazed. Who are we to approach your majesty? How can we fulfill the covenant you offer us? Come, Spirit of truth, to show us the way. Amen.

CALL TO CONFESSION

Let us give voice to our anxiety before God. Let us bring to God the panic we feel when we measure our inner resources against the outward challenges of our frantic lives. Let us dare to confess the ways we fall short of God's expectations. God already knows them, but we need to face them.

PRAYER OF CONFESSION

When we ponder the vast universe at your command, O God, we are astounded. We are nothing, except that you have given us life. How often we have squandered that gift in meaningless pursuits, killing time we might have invested in honoring you! Instead we have belittled your prophets and made light of your commands. We alternate between boasting over our personal accomplishments and near-panic at our inability to cope with life's challenges. O God, we confess our desperate need for healing, forgiveness and a new perspective on life. Amen.

Assurance of Forgiveness

Rejoice in the judgments of God that are ever tempered with mercy. God understands our weaknesses and is acquainted with our needs. The grace of God is sufficient to cover our sin, for power is made perfect in weakness. When we recognize our weakness, God can strengthen us. When we accept the reign of love among us, we are empowered to be the church, reaching out to a sick and troubled world. Amen.

Collect

Mighty Ruler, Teacher of all who are willing to grow, let us hear enough of your Word to be astounded. Let us see as many of your deeds as will make us eager to join in outreach to people in need. Grant us enough of Christ's vision and compassion that our weakness may be useful to you in proclaiming your word, sharing your grace, and casting out demons. Amen.

Offertory Invitation

Some take offense when asked to give, but all of us are eager to receive. Jesus Christ turned these priorities around, giving thanks for the generosity of God's covenant with humanity, but finding greatest joy in the opportunity to share. In gratitude and joy, we bring our offerings.

Offertory Prayer

Thank you, God, for your steadfast love. We offer our praise; may it reach to the ends of the earth. We ask that our gifts empower ministry in this place and wherever our influence can reach. Let unbelief be turned to faith, ignorance to knowledge, sickness to health, brokenness to wholeness, both in us and in our neighbors near and far. Guide us, as we seek to invest our best for the sake of Christ. Amen.

Commission and Blessing

Go out into the world in the name of the carpenter.
Emulate Christ's deeds of compassion and power.
> *We face hardships and calamities with courage.*
> *Christ strengthens us when we are weak.*

In humility, reach out to help and to be helped.
Travel light, with your faith as your major resource.
> *We will trust God in our preparations and on the journey.*
> *We will give our best, relying also on God's grace.*

As disciples of Jesus Christ, you are blessed and empowered.
God's steadfast love surrounds you wherever you go.
> *Great is our God, and greatly to be praised!*
> *God will be our guide today and forever.*

Amen. **Amen.**

(See hymn 64.)

PROPER 10

Sunday between July 10 and July 16

2 Samuel 6:1–5, 12b–19   (or Amos 7:7–15   Ephesians 1:3–14
Psalm 24   Psalm 85:8–13)   Mark 6:14–29

CALL TO WORSHIP

Blessed be the God and parent of our Savior Jesus Christ!
Thank God for every spiritual blessing.
> *May the glory of God be known in this place!*
> *May God's peace dwell in this and every land!*

Who shall ascend the hill to reach for God?
Who shall stand in God's holy place?
> *Those who have clean hands and pure hearts,*
> *Those who are not false or deceitful.*

God speaks peace to those who are faithful.
Lift up your heads and your hearts to God.
> *We have come to hear the word of truth.*
> *We turn to God, eager to receive salvation.*

INVOCATION

Ruler of all worlds, whose glory surrounds our unseeing eyes, our muffled hearing and our dulled emotions, come to awaken us to the mystery of your will. Speak to us a word of truth that reveals our deceit and leads us away from falsehood. Touch us with healing grace that allows us to admit our woundedness and accept the comfort you offer. Let your Spirit move among us so we may recognize your presence in one another and in our own lives. May our response to you be faithful and our praise genuine. Amen.

CALL TO CONFESSION

God has chosen us to be holy and blameless in love before our Creator. In our hearts, we know we do not measure up to that high calling. We have built many barriers in our lives against true communion with God and honest community with one another. In our Prayer of Confession, we seek help to remove those barriers.

PRAYER OF CONFESSION

God of all hope and blessing, hear us as we turn to you with all our hearts. We have not been faithful to your word of love. We have hurt others and held grudges. We have been jealous and deceitful and ungrateful. We have turned from your Word and resisted the Holy Spirit. We have wanted our inheritance from you without the responsibilities that go with it. O God, we plead for your forgiveness and healing that we might respond with joy to the spiritual blessings you offer. Amen.

Assurance of Forgiveness

God's grace is freely given to us in Jesus Christ, through whom we are redeemed and forgiven. Let us set our hope on Christ, living each day for the praise of God's glory, ever seeking the truth that frees us to live fully and triumphantly. Join the dance of gratitude and joy, sharing with others the love God has poured into our lives.

Collect

Righteous and holy God, giver of life amid the hatred and cruelty that abounds among us when our rivalries get out of hand, let us hear your judgments as well as your promises, that our thoughts and actions may more nearly match your will for us and equip us to accomplish much good according to your counsel and to your glory. Amen.

Offertory Invitation

The earth belongs to God, and all that is in it. The world is God's creation, and so are we. All that we have is from the gifts of God, meant as a blessing for all to share. In these moments, we recognize our responsibility to manage these resources for the redemption of all God's people. Let us give with care.

Offertory Prayer

With joyous praise and dancing spirits, we dedicate this offering, acknowledging our covenant responsibility to share your word and love all your people. In gratitude for the gospel of salvation, we pledge our first loyalty and highest faithfulness as disciples of Jesus Christ. Thank you for the wisdom and insight we have received. Help us now to live according to the best we know, in Jesus' name. Amen.

Commission and Blessing

Remember each day that you are chosen by God.
Be open to the spiritual blessings available at all times.
We are cleansed and free, purified and made whole.
Great is our God and greatly to be praised!
Dwell in the mystery of God's will for you.
Dare to reach out in love to those who share your world.
We will seek God's counsel daily.
We will open our hearts to others' pain.
The Holy Spirit goes with you to empower you.
The love of Christ sustains you in all circumstances.
We have been blessed and fed in this place.
We will share with others the joy we have known.
Amen. **Amen.**

(See hymn 65.)

PROPER 11

Sunday between July 17 and July 23

| 2 Samuel 7:1–14a | (or Jeremiah 23:1–6 | Ephesians 2:11–22 |
| Psalm 89:20–37 | Psalm 23) | Mark 6:30–34, 53–56 |

CALL TO WORSHIP

Come away and rest for a while.
Leave behind your busyness to be fully present to God.
> *We have come for relief from life's turmoil.*
> *God gathers us as a shepherd gathers her sheep.*

God's steadfast love surrounds us here.
We are reminded of God's enduring faithfulness.
> *This is God's house, and we are God's children.*
> *God invites us to feel at home in this place.*

We have a covenant with our Creator.
This is a time for renewal of our promises.
> *God calls for righteousness and justice.*
> *God offers us goodness and mercy all our days.*

INVOCATION

Rock of our salvation, we have accepted the invitation of Jesus to gather as your beloved people. We have been far away from you in our thoughts and separated from you in much that we do. Now we are together, seeking reconciliation with you and one another. We call on your steadfast love for assurance and healing. We feel your compassion for us and for all your children. We sense your longing for our wholeness and renewed faith and trust. You call us to be saints and apostles and prophets. We are overwhelmed, even as you draw us close. Amen.

CALL TO CONFESSION

Alienated from our spiritual selves, we come to this time of confession seeking wholeness amid a fragmented world. The false promise of a good life, filled with things, has erected barriers among us. There are dividing walls of hostility separating God's people. We are called to admit our role in this brokenness.

PRAYER OF CONFESSION

God of all times and places, we confess that we have wandered after the false gods of this age. We have disobeyed your commandments, violated your covenant with us, and forsaken your ways. We have denied our need for you and mistreated those whom you have called us to love. We have become strangers and aliens, plagued by false values that squeeze life from our souls. Loving Parent, hear your penitent children, and let us come home, we pray. Amen.

ASSURANCE OF FORGIVENESS

We are no longer strangers and aliens but are citizens with the saints and members of the household of God, built on the foundation of the apostles and prophets with Jesus Christ as the cornerstone. We are the church, God's forgiven and forgiving people, becoming a temple in which God is pleased to dwell. Let us join our spirits and our voices in giving thanks for God's pardon and continuing offer of healing. Amen.

COLLECT

Healing God, whose touch we have sought and known and whose compassion has surrounded us like a good shepherd's care for wandering sheep, show us once more the dimensions of wholeness that can restore us to faithful living and fruitful service May we become reconcilers within and beyond the church. Amen.

OFFERTORY INVITATION

We bring a portion of all God entrusts to us to be used, not for our pet projects, but for the mission of the church, in this community, throughout our land and around the world. We express our gratitude for the gift of Jesus Christ and for the peace we know deep within when we become disciples and apostles. May we follow the model of God's generosity.

OFFERTORY PRAYER

Receive our best, gracious God, as we offer ourselves along with these tokens of thanks. Establish your rule in our midst so we may proclaim your reign in the world. Send us where you need us most. Use our gifts to reduce alienation and to build community. Be to us a watchful Parent, and teach us to live as sisters and brothers who find you in one another and respond in love to each other's needs. Amen.

COMMISSION AND BLESSING

Live with hope, for God is with us every day.
Live in peace, for God turns us from hostility.
We are one in Christ, who died for us.
We are one in the Spirit who creates community.
Renew your covenant vows with God and people.
Celebrate the oneness of humanity in Christ.
We have daily access to God our Parent.
We are citizens with the saints in God's family.
There are people in the marketplace awaiting good news.
Go to people you know who need your healing presence.
We seek to recognize the needs around us.
We commit ourselves to help as God give us strength.
Amen. **Amen.**

(See hymn 66. A hymn based on Eph. 2:11–22 may be found in *Whispers of God*, pp. 204–5.)

PROPER 12

2 Samuel 11:1–15   (or 2 Kings 4:42–44   Ephesians 3:14–21
Psalm 14   Psalm 145:10–18)   John 6:1–21

CALL TO WORSHIP

This is the hour to bend our knee before God.
This is a time to offer our best to our Creator.
> *We gather before God, who sees all our deeds.*
> *We open our hearts to One who knows all our thoughts.*

Fools say in their hearts, "There is no God."
We come together proclaiming, "God is with us!"
> *We come to be strengthened in our inner being.*
> *We seek to pattern our actions after Christ Jesus.*

God's presence evokes our joyous worship.
The Holy Spirit empowers our service.
> *To God be highest glory in the church.*
> *To God be endless adoration in the world.*

Amen. **Amen.**

INVOCATION

We are seeking after you, loving God, for you are our refuge. Your power is at work within and among us, even when we are unaware. We want to respond, not as fools, but as faithful friends of Jesus. We have come to discover the riches we did not know we possessed. We are here to offer our best for the good of all. Use us, we pray, to accomplish in and through this church, far more than we can ask or imagine. All glory be to you, amazing God, in this and every hour, forever and ever. Amen.

CALL TO CONFESSION

The psalmist asserted that all have gone astray, all are alike perverse; there is no one who does good—no, not one. We eat up people as bread and do not call upon God. Before we dismiss these claims as unwarranted exaggeration, let us examine ourselves before God.

PRAYER OF CONFESSION

O God, you know our secret hearts. You are aware of our distortions, our jealousies, our lust. You observe our unfaithfulness, our treachery, our unwarranted fears. We are corrupted by greed, self-indulgence, and desire to be entertained. We do not take responsibility for our misconduct, our abuse of power, our lack of trust in you. We have little sense of vision to see beyond immediate circumstances or to embrace new possibilities. We miss the signs of your grace and resist the empowerment of your Spirit. Mighty God, still the storms within us with your transforming peace and boundless forgiveness, in Jesus' name. Amen.

Assurance of Forgiveness

All who truly repent can know the love of Christ that surpasses human knowledge. We are rescued, delivered, and restored to fullness of life in God, our Creator. We are being rooted and grounded in love that we, in turn, might show love to others. We are invited to join the saints in realizing ever fuller dimensions of life centered in faith and trust.

Collect

Generous God, from whom comes every morsel we eat and every gift we are moved to share, test us, challenge us, feed us, that our eyes may be opened to realize the bounty we receive from your hand, our ears may be opened to hear the prophets' word, and our wills may be strengthened to follow fearlessly where Christ leads, to your glory, and for the benefit of all humankind. Amen.

Offertory Invitation

We have gladly taken more than our share of the world's good. Let us give in proportion to the blessings we have received. May the church be at the forefront of feeding, healing, caring for, and loving God's people. We are the church, the body of Christ, making a difference in the world.

Offertory Prayer

We join with Jesus in giving thanks for the little things we can see, that our eyes may be opened to the great possibilities we had not imagined. May our efforts be multiplied by your grace so there is more than enough for all—more comfort in sorrow, more relief from pain, more mercy to meet our treachery, more sense of presence amid our loneliness, more strength to overcome our weakness, more joy and enthusiasm to erase our apathy. Amen.

Commission and Blessing

Go out to share what you have received.
God will multiply the gifts that you give away.
> *We will turn away from fears of scarcity.*
> *We will celebrate and share our abundance.*
God meets you amid the storms of life,
God goes with you through the terrors of the night.
> *We are embraced by God's steadfast love.*
> *We will look up and not be afraid.*
May Christ dwell in your hearts through faith.
May the Holy Spirit strengthen your inner being.
> *To God be glory in the church forever.*
> *May Christ be honored in all we say and do.*
Amen. **Amen.**

(See hymn 67.)

PROPER 13

2 Samuel 11:26–12:13a   (or Exodus 16:2–4, 9–15   Ephesians 4:1–16
Psalm 51:1–12   Psalm 78:23–29)   John 6:24–35

CALL TO WORSHIP

Draw near to God, who has heard your complaining.
Come in the name of Jesus, who understands your need.
> *We have received manna in the wilderness.*
> *We have been offered the bread of life.*

Open your selves to God's steadfast love.
Be honest before the Holy One who knows all you do.
> *We are judged according to our deeds.*
> *Our secret sins are known to our God.*

The Holy Spirit has come to restore your joy.
God's presence is real to those who accept God's gift.
> *Whoever comes to Jesus will not be hungry.*
> *Whoever trusts in Christ will never be thirsty.*

INVOCATION

We hear you calling us, loving God, to a life of humility, gentleness, and patience.
Keep your call before us in this hour that we may recognize and celebrate our oneness in Jesus Christ. May your Spirit unite us in the bond of peace. Speak to us of
the Savior, who bore humanity's shame that we might learn to bear with one another in love. Draw us to a common faith, in spite of our differences. Lead us into
new depths of trust beyond our knowing, and along new pathways of service out-
distancing our fears. Amen.

CALL TO CONFESSION

We who are tossed about in a sea of competing images and priorities are summoned before God to be drawn back to a life centered by faith. Let us call upon
God's mercy and forgiveness.

PRAYER OF CONFESSION

O God, our transgressions are many. We have sinned against you and done evil in
your sight. We have wandered far from your truth. You alone know the extent of
our guilt. You are justified to pass judgment and sentence us. We are crushed by
the wrong we have allowed and the good we have avoided. We plead for mercy.
Wash us thoroughly and cleanse us deep within. Put a new and right spirit in us
and restore to us the joy of your salvation. Help us to lead lives worthy of your call
to us, in Jesus' name. Amen.

ASSURANCE OF FORGIVENESS

By God's grace, we are forgiven. In Christ, we are drawn together and entrusted with gifts for the good of all. We are knit into one body for mutual support, encouragement, and growth. Some of us are apostles, some prophets, some evangelists, some pastors, and some teachers. All of us have a part in building up the body of Christ and equipping the saints for the work of ministry. Give thanks for this opportunity!

COLLECT

Gracious God, from whom comes all the abundance of this earth, and who has given us the true bread from heaven, Jesus Christ, feed us again by your word of truth, that we may believe more deeply and trust more daringly, speaking the truth in love to our hurting world. Make your church be a transforming presence among all your children. Amen.

OFFERTORY INVITATION

From the abundance of our land, we have much to share. Yet often we benefit from economic policies that favor us over the poor of the world, whose meager resources put food on our tables and clothes on our backs. The church seeks to bring justice amid the world's inequities.

OFFERTORY PRAYER

We dedicate our offerings, not alone for the good they can accomplish and the mission they will support, but also because giving helps us to gain perspective on what really matters. We would stop working only for food that perishes, seeking for all the food that endures for eternal life. May our lives and all we give perform the works of God. Build us up in love for one another and for all your children everywhere.

COMMISSION AND BLESSING

Christ, the bread of life, sends you out to feed others.
Whoever comes to Christ will not be hungry or thirsty.
We will share our lives with brothers and sisters.
We seek to offer them the bread from heaven.
Join the saints in building up the body of Christ.
Seek to equip others for the work of ministry.
We find unity in our relationship with God.
We seek to grow toward the full stature of Christ.
The Spirit will go with you and dwell with you.
Receive with joy the salvation Christ offers each day.
We are being healed even as we serve.
We are empowered daily as we share love.
Amen. **Amen.**

(See hymns 68 and 69.)

PROPER 14

2 Samuel 18:5–9, 15, 31–33   (or 1 Kings 19:4–8   Ephesians 4:25–5:2
Psalm 130   Psalm 34:1–8)   John 6:35, 41–51

CALL TO WORSHIP

Wait for God, who deals gently with us.
Watch for God's appearance among us.
> *Out of the depths we cry out to God.*
> *Will God hear the voice of our supplications?*

In all times and places, we can rely on God.
We can know steadfast love, here and now.
> *We keep our morning watch together.*
> *We will support one another as we seek to know God.*

Find hope in God's power to redeem us.
Give thanks for the new day God promises to us.
> *Life's battles cannot destroy us.*
> *The losses we suffer are not the last word.*

INVOCATION

We come to you, holy God, with our many needs. Some of us are people in authority with weighty decisions to make. Some of us are fighting battles we cannot win. Some have faced unexpected losses that tear at the very fabric of life. There are broken relationships among us, feelings we do not want to admit, realities we do not want to face. There are also joys we have not really celebrated, reasons to give thanks to which we have never given voice. We come, O God, to be lifted out of our ruts and routines, seeking instead to find fullness of life with you. Amen.

CALL TO CONFESSION

If God should mark iniquities, who could stand? If God counted our sins, how would we ever find forgiveness? Yet, the attitudes and actions that build barriers among us and shut God out of our thinking and decision-making can be overcome. God is ready to help us.

PRAYER OF CONFESSION

O Holy Spirit, how we have grieved you! How often our words have been bitter, filled with malice and anger. How easily have we uttered lies of pretension and self-protection. How readily we take for ourselves the rewards of another's labor! Forgive all that is false and evil within us and among us. Free us from the self-justifying excuses that keep us from reaching out to one another. We want to believe, to trust, to live as imitators of Jesus Christ. Help us, gracious God. Amen.

Assurance of Forgiveness

God redeems us from our iniquities. Forgiveness is ours to receive and to share. God gives us the opportunity to become members of one another, speaking truth with our neighbors, working honestly with our own hands, building each other up and sharing with the needy. The gift of grace we have received grows larger in our lives as we extend it to friends and strangers we meet.

Collect

Bread of heaven, feed us. Word of truth, teach us. Author of life, fit us for eternity amid our days on this earth, that our deeds may honor you. Help us to be kind and tenderhearted to one another and to forgive one another as, in Christ, you have forgiven us. Amen.

Offertory Invitation

We who have accepted from God abundant gifts we did not deserve have the opportunity to express our thanks. We who have eaten manna in the wilderness are chosen to pass on the bread of life to neighbors in our own community and around the world. May our giving reflect the fragrant offering and sacrifice of Jesus Christ!

Offertory Prayer

Thank you, God, for your continuing providence, even when we complain. Thank you for the living bread, Jesus Christ, who feeds our spirits. In gratitude for undeserved grace and unlimited opportunity, we dedicate our offering and ourselves. Let our talk and our resources build up the body of Christ for greater service. May the needs of many be addressed in ways that bring hope, grace, and love to your children. Amen.

Commission and Blessing

The steadfast love of God goes with you.
The redeeming power of Christ sustains you.
> *We have been forgiven and renewed.*
> *We face another week with confidence.*
Be kind to one another, tenderhearted, and forgiving.
Live in love as Christ demonstrated God's love.
> *We want to share the gifts of God with others.*
> *We seek to build up the body of Christ.*
Jesus said, "Whoever believes has eternal life."
Whoever eats the living bread will live forever.
> *We have been taught to live as God's children.*
> *We can experience eternal life even today.*
Amen. **Amen.**

(See hymn 70. "O God, As We Come," *Whispers of God*, p. 208, reflects the Epistle reading for this day.)

PROPER 15

Sunday between August 14 and August 20

I Kings 2:10–12; 3:3–14	(or Proverbs 9:1–6	Ephesians 5:15–20
Psalm 111	Psalm 34:9–14)	John 6:51–58

CALL TO WORSHIP

God is gracious and merciful and trustworthy.
Let us join our voices in giving thanks.
> *The works of God are all around us.*
> *Those who share in God's work lack for nothing.*

We are called to faithfulness, as God is faithful.
We are people of the covenant, gathered to please God.
> *Holy and awesome is God's name.*
> *The fear of God is the beginning of wisdom.*

Come, then, as wise and faithful people.
Come as a beloved community of the redeemed.
> *We are amazed that God remembers us.*
> *We reach out to the God who cares for us.*

INVOCATION

God of steadfast love, your works delight our hearts and expand our thoughts. Your grace and mercy draw us together to praise you and to celebrate your wonderful deeds. Dwell among us today, and reign within the lives of each one gathered here, helping us to grow in discernment and understanding. Grant wisdom and courage that we may walk in your ways and keep your commandments. Amen.

CALL TO CONFESSION

There is much that is evil in our world today. There are many good things that are easily perverted. We live in a time when profligacy masquerades as progress and self-centered willfulness makes false claims to wisdom. We claim the authority of God in making our own authoritarian claims. Let us confess our sin.

PRAYER OF CONFESSION

O God, we confess that we have lived so comfortably in the abundance of our times that we have made things our gods. We spend our days dreaming of (and working for) possessions that cannot satisfy. The pursuit of riches replaces the quest for faith and faithful relationships. We do not know you, God, and our relationship with others is superficial at best. Redeem us, we pray, from our self-destructive ways and restore us to your covenant community. Amen.

Assurance of Forgiveness

We have received God's continuing offer to humankind of a lasting covenental relationship. God forgives and redeems the likes of us through Jesus Christ, the living bread, sent from heaven. Accept God's gift. Accept yourself, and know that this moment can mark a new beginning in faithfulness.

Collect

Bread of heaven, drink of eternal life, whose sacrifice for us calls forth a daring love of neighbor, feed us now and lead us to your Word every day, that our lives may be hymns of thanksgiving to our Creator, leading others to love and serve in your name. Amen.

Offertory Invitation

As we make melody to God with our hearts and voices, let our hands also be employed in service. We here offer ourselves and the fruits of our labor that God may bless and multiply the good to be accomplished through them and us. May our riches be employed for the common benefit of all God's children.

Offertory Prayer

Your generosity, O God, is beyond our deserving. You grant health to our bodies and minds. You surround us with vast resources and with people who love us. You allow us to make decisions about the use of our time and possessions and relationships. Thank you, God, for this opportunity to share with others some of what we have received. Help us to use all our gifts as you intend. Amen.

Commission and Blessing

Love God, and walk in the statutes that mark God's reign.
Let your worship continue throughout the week ahead.
We will remember God's steadfast love every day.
We seek to walk in faithfulness and uprightness of heart.
Live in awe before God, making the most of the time.
Shun destructive foolishness and ruinous excesses.
We aspire to better discernment between good and evil.
We ask for greater wisdom and understanding.
The grace and mercy of God go with you today.
God will keep covenant with you now and forever.
We accept the living bread that came from heaven.
We will walk with Christ through life's valleys.
Amen. **Amen.**

(See hymns 71, 72.)

PROPER 16

Sunday between August 21 and August 27

I Kings 8:(1, 6, 10–11),   (or Joshua 24:1–2a, 14–18   Ephesians 6:10–20
22–30, 41–43   Psalm 34:15–22)   John 6:56–69
Psalm 84

CALL TO WORSHIP

With profound happiness, we welcome one another.
How good it is to approach the courts of our God!
Happy are those who live in God's house!
Singing our praise to God fills us with joy.
Here we welcome both friend and stranger.
All peoples of the earth are God's children.
We greet one another by name in Jesus' name.
Together we extol the name of our God.
Open your hearts to receive new strength.
Open your lives to renewed understandings.
Surely God will equip us to face our world.
We will be ambassadors for God wherever we go.

INVOCATION

We come together in this house of prayer, trusting you, O God, to give us everything we need. As you provide for the birds of the air, you supply life's necessities
for your children to share. We choose to respond to your promises by identifying
ourselves as your servant people who seek to be guided by your word. We gather
to remember and reclaim your covenant with us. Fleeing from tents of wickedness, we gather to do the tasks you entrust to us here, praying for strength to do
our daily work as a ministry in your name. Amen.

CALL TO CONFESSION

God has called us, not to a set of beliefs but to a relationship of trust. We are drawn
to the Spirit whose will for us is life at its fullest, attuned to all that is good and
true. We are embraced by the gospel of peace. We come now to confess that we
have looked elsewhere for our salvation.

PRAYER OF CONFESSION

Alert us now, eternal Spirit, to your presence among us in this place. Together, we
confess that we have been busy with so many things that we have often forgotten
you. We have made little gods out of buildings and furnishings and programs.
Sometimes our pet beliefs and interpretations have been all-consuming as we do
battle to correct others and presume to defend you. We have forgotten that your
love is stronger than any force on earth. Forgive our mistrust of its power, and draw
us back into the company of disciples who are learning and growing in love. Amen.

Assurance of Forgiveness

Happy are those who daily find their strength in the living God, seeking to walk uprightly. Happy are those who trust in God, who sincerely and truthfully seek to serve where God needs them most. God redeems us, whatever our circumstances, lifting our spirits, even when our bodies are in chains. May we serve boldly as ambassadors for Jesus Christ.

Collect

Holy One of God, sent to live among us in faithfulness to God's loving intention for all humanity, lead our journey toward the truth that is eternal. Be to us the bread of life, a source of trust, a guard against misplaced loyalties and false assumptions, that we may live in harmony with all God's creation and relate to our brothers and sisters in ways that are pleasing to our Creator. Amen.

Offertory Invitation

The church is not a private club that we maintain for our own benefit. It is a mission outpost, constantly enlisting us and our resources for the spreading of good news and the increase of God's reign of love. Our offerings are one measure of how seriously we take our call as ambassadors for Christ.

Offertory Prayer

May our giving add strength to the witness of your church as we humbly seek your truth and lovingly share it. Ready us to proclaim the gospel of peace in our homes, in our places of work and leisure, throughout our community and the world. Keep before your people the awesome mystery of faith. May its power overcome the cynicism of our skeptical, self-serving age, uniting us in disciplines that are freeing and discipleship that is amazingly fulfilling. Amen.

Commission and Blessing

Take a prayerful spirit into your everyday world.
God will listen and respond to your prayers.
> *We pray for all God's saints engaged in ministry.*
> *All of us are ambassadors for Jesus Christ.*

You have good news to share with a needy world.
God will open up to you the mystery of the gospel.
> *We trust in God to lead and guide us in truth.*
> *Happy is everyone who trusts in God.*

Happy are those who look to God for strength.
All who dwell with God will go from strength to strength.
> *God grants abundant life to humble doorkeepers.*
> *We will do our part to extend God's reign.*

Amen. **Amen.**

(See hymns 73, 74.)

PROPER 17

Song of Solomon 2:8–13   *(or Deuteronomy 4:1–2, 6–9*   James 1:17–27
Psalm 45:1–2, 6–9   *Psalm 15)*   Mark 7:1–8, 14–15, 21–23

CALL TO WORSHIP

Come to listen for all God seeks to teach us.
God has given us birth by the word of truth.
> *We are drawn to God as to a lover.*
> *We leap for joy when we know God's care.*

Every perfect gift comes to us from God.
God's image is a part of each one of us.
> *God's grace has been poured into our lives.*
> *Wisdom and understanding are offered to us.*

Who will dwell on God's holy hill?
Those who walk uprightly and speak the truth.
> *We will honor God by honoring our neighbors.*
> *We will act toward them as we wish to be treated.*

INVOCATION

Our hearts overflow with longings too great for words, gracious God. You have been so good to us, yet we are dissatisfied. We have many things to enjoy, but seldom have we found our home with you. Meet us here to anoint us with the oil of gladness. Awaken us with singing and speak your truth to draw us away from the lure of wickedness. May this time of worship help us to become a wise and understanding people, eager to live as the body of Christ, making a difference in the world as Jesus did so long ago on the Galilean shore. Amen.

CALL TO CONFESSION

How easily we notice the sins of others, finding ways to criticize what they do or do not do. How much harder it is to believe that we are sinners needing to repent of habits that separate us from God and set us against neighbors who are different from us. Let us seek forgiveness.

PRAYER OF CONFESSION

O God, we admit that all is not well with us. We are easily angered and slow to forgive. We speak without listening and pretend to listen without really hearing. Our tongues become weapons rather than instruments of healing. We are more critical than helpful toward the poor in our midst. Hidden in our hearts are the attitudes that produce avarice, deceit, and violation of our promises to you and to one another. Turn us around so we can accept your forgiveness and learn to love ourselves as you want us to be, through Jesus Christ. Amen.

Assurance of Forgiveness

God frees us from our human bondage to live by commandments that build up rather than destroy. God offers us boundaries that liberate us from licentiousness, greed and false pride. Our Creator draws us close that our hearts may find their true home. Praise God for the grace that saves us from our self-deceit and lifts us up to bear good fruit.

Collect

God of all truth, whose reality is far beyond the religion we profess, and whose ways are broader than our flawed human precepts, we would honor you with our lips and our lives, worshiping you above all else in life and welcoming your transforming presence within us, that we might become doers of the Word who offer healing to the world. Amen.

Offertory Invitation

Let us not forget that the bounty we enjoy is only loaned to us for a little while, to be managed to the glory of God. Every generous act of giving is prompted by God's own generosity toward us. We are invited to return the first fruits of our labors that, through the outreach of our church, God may accomplish much good for those who most need to know that someone cares.

Offertory Prayer

Our hearts overflow with thanksgiving for all the bounty you entrust to our stewardship, O God of light. You have reached into the shadows, where we often flee, to rescue us and give us your work to do. As you have freed us from the chains of sin, we seek to offer healing to others as we listen and share and do. Bless our offering of self and substance, we pray. Amen.

Commission and Blessing

God offers to each of us deep inner cleansing.
We can become whole people, unstained by the world.
>*In the world around us, life is cheap.*
>*Violence destroys what is valuable to God.*
We are called to challenge this destruction.
We are to love righteousness and turn from wickedness.
>*We want to witness to the power of love.*
>*We believe people can change and turn from evil.*
God's Word transforms all who hear and heed it.
God blesses those who are doers of the Word.
>*God anoints us with the oil of gladness.*
>*Our hearts overflow with God's good gifts.*
Amen. **Amen.**

(See hymn 75.)

Proverbs 22:1–2, 8–9, 22–23   (or Isaiah 35:4–7a   James 2:1–10, (11–13), 14–17
Psalm 125   Psalm 146)   Mark 7:24–37

CALL TO WORSHIP

> Listen! God is welcoming us to this time of worship.
> Young and old, rich and poor, all are welcomed.
>> *This is a place where all belong.*
>> *This is a time when all are accountable to God.*
> The Maker of all seeks our common good.
> The God of Mercy calls on us to be merciful.
>> *We are not judges over our sisters and brothers.*
>> *We are called to love our neighbors as ourselves.*
> Come to sing praises and put your trust in God.
> Come to prepare yourself to serve in Christ's name.
>> *We bring all our needs to God, our hope.*
>> *We want to share faith and hope with others.*

INVOCATION

Author of all humankind, come to lift us up to our full humanity as we worship you in this hour. You surround us on every side and are acquainted with all our ways. You know our shallow motives and our deepest thoughts. You are aware of the distinctions we make and the favoritism we express. Yet you welcome us, not as strangers but as heralds of your reign. We want to worship you and to represent you well. Come among us now with your transforming power. Amen.

CALL TO CONFESSION

The Holy One—who opens eyes and ears, makes the mute to speak, and delivers the tormented from demons within—invites us to seek the healing we need. God reigns in spite of us but longs for our participation in faith-filled ministries. Let us confess our estrangement from the One who offers us true freedom.

PRAYER OF CONFESSION

O God, we confess that our good intentions have gone astray. We favor the people who are like us and honor those we deem to be important. We dishonor the poor, write off those with whom we disagree, excuse our self-serving behavior, and sow injustice on every hand. It is so much easier to give advice than to do good. We would rather point fingers at others who are unfair than to give up our own advantages. O God, we plead for your forgiveness and for a depth of faith that will make a difference in us and in our world. Amen.

Assurance of Forgiveness

When we show mercy, we are able to accept God's mercy, which triumphs over judgment. God can turn our waywardness upside down and set us on the path of true community with those whom we have disdained or ignored. God opens our minds and hearts to hear and understand those who need our help. God empowers our response.

Collect

Inclusive God, ever available to all who truly seek you, come to us now through all we read and speak, that the messages your people hear may become your word to us, a word that transforms, makes whole, and unites us in mutual learning and service, for the sake of all your children. Amen.

Offertory Invitation

Hear again the proverb: "Those who are generous are blessed, for they share their bread with the poor." What a joy we can know when our thankfulness exceeds our acquisitiveness, and our concern for others outweighs our greed! We are invited to share what we have received.

Offertory Prayer

We give because you have been generous to us, gracious God. We give because we need to give in order to realize your image within us. We give to feed the hungers of body and soul that are all around us and deep within. May the ministries of this church meet the needs of our members, our community, and our world. Help us to love our neighbors as ourselves. Amen.

Commission and Blessing

We are commissioned as carriers of love.
The attention we give to others is contagious.
> *We seek to honor all people by listening to them.*
> *We want to provide practical help to those in need.*

We are sent out to do good and to be merciful.
Our trust is in God, who equips us to serve.
> *We seek to minister impartially.*
> *Both friends and strangers are our concern.*

Be strong, fear not, for God will save.
Those who trust God will realize God's blessing.
> *God has blessed us with a good name.*
> *We are heirs of God's dominion forever.*

Amen. **Amen.**

(See hymns 76, 77.)

PROPER 19

Proverbs 1:20–33   (or Isaiah 50:4–9a   James 3:1–12
Psalm 19   Psalm 116:1–9)   Mark 8:27–38

CALL TO WORSHIP

Come away from dullness and complacency.
Wake up! God is calling us to listen and learn.
The heavens are telling the glory of God.
The firmament proclaims God's handiwork.
How long will we refuse the wisdom God offers?
How long will we ignore God's counsel and reproof?
The law of God is perfect, reviving the soul.
The decrees of God are sure, making wise the simple.
Our waywardness separates us from God.
Then, when we call on God, we hear no answer.
We gather to renew our relationship with God.
We seek enlightenment and the revival of our souls.

INVOCATION

God of all wisdom, renew our sense of awe and wonder as we gather before you,
the Source of all knowledge. Make your Word known to us, and stretch out your
hand to touch us. Draw us away from our own devices that we may truly listen to
the witness of all creation speaking of wonders we have ignored. Give us eyes to
see beauty in all around us. Align us with truth and righteousness. Quiet our scoff-
ing and awaken our trust. Show us the disciplines we need to stay in touch with
you each day. Amen.

CALL TO CONFESSION

People of God, the scriptures remind us that we are accountable to our Creator.
Instead, in our times of panic, we put God on trial, wondering why we cannot
find the help we seek. Shutting our eyes and ears to God becomes a habit we cannot break in times of desperation. That is why, together, we come to God, asking
to be cleared of secret faults and to detect the error of our ways in time to turn
around, letting God's Word reach our hearts.

PRAYER OF CONFESSION

God of all worlds, we confess our arrogance in turning away from the knowledge
you offer and the relationship with us that you desire. We make light of your commandments and scoff at discipline and boundaries as if they did not apply to us.
Our tongues reveal our ignorance before the vastness of your truth. The words we
speak in error spread poison that cannot be contained. Our waywardness is de-

stroying us. Our complacency before evil, within us and all around, threatens life itself. O God, we cry out for forgiveness. Amen.

ASSURANCE OF FORGIVENESS

We eat the fruits of our way and are sated with our own devices. Words of confession are not enough to break the patterns of complacency and self-justification that separate us from God. Thankfully, our Creator knows our honest intent. If we truly turn from our insolent, undisciplined ways, a new way is opening up for us, and God welcomes us as partners in the gospel. In keeping God's ordinances, there is unexpected reward.

COLLECT

Reigning God, whom we have glimpsed in creation and in the life of one who shared our common lot, help us to acknowledge the Messiah, not in empty words, but in self-emptying service that risks life for the sake of love. May we come to be so attuned to your precepts that the song of our hearts becomes a contagious attraction, transforming the groups of which we are a part. Amen.

OFFERTORY INVITATION

The ways we use the wealth entrusted to us teach even more than our words. What messages do our offerings send to the world? Do they communicate our delight in knowing God and following the Christ?

OFFERTORY PRAYER

We offer the treasures of this world as a way of recalling all of us to a right relationship with you, O God, the source of all wisdom and truth. Your design for life is more to be desired than the finest gold. To learn from you and to serve you is our highest joy. May our offerings and our daily lives communicate this message. Amen.

COMMISSION AND BLESSING

Let your words this week proclaim God's love.
May your hearts' meditations be acceptable to God.
> *We seek to let God guide our tongues.*
> *We want to speak without arrogance or false pride.*
Listen for the wisdom God wants you to know.
Seek God's counsel and reproof each day.
> *We will look for God in the midst of creation.*
> *We will seek God's face in the people around us.*
The heavens are telling the glory of God.
God's hand is outstretched to touch and heal you.
> *How good it is to sense God's guidance!*
> *How exciting it is to follow where Christ leads!*
Amen. **Amen.**

(See hymns 78, 79.)

Proverbs 31:10–31	*(or Jeremiah 11:18–20*	James 3:13–4:3, 7–8a
Psalm 1	*Psalm 54)*	Mark 9:30–37

CALL TO WORSHIP

Draw near to God, and God will draw near to you.
Happy are those who find delight in God's law.
God is always nearer than our next breath.
We gather to become more aware of that presence.
Knowledge of God is a delight to the righteous.
They seek to grow in wisdom and understanding.
There is always more to discover than we know.
God is our teacher and helper and judge.
Put your trust in God as you prepare to serve.
Learn to be peaceable, gentle, and merciful.
We seek to do good and not harm all our days.
We would open our hands to the poor and needy.

INVOCATION

You watch over us, O God, and show us the way to prosper in life, not so much in things as in relationships that contribute to our wholeness and well-being. Thank you for meeting us here and helping us to deal with our selfish ambition, disorder, and conflicts. We submit ourselves to you for instruction. Help us to be honest with ourselves and with you, voicing our doubts as well as our faith, our hypocrisy along with all that is deeply genuine. Create in us a space for quiet listening and thoughtful meditation. Amen.

CALL TO CONFESSION

We are called to resist evil and to purify our hearts. Often our need for such cleansing is not apparent to us. We are hard pressed to find anything bad that we need to confess, and we take real delight in the good we have done. Yet the peaceful community God seeks, the serving church that embodies Christ, the spirit-filled company we are meant to be, are not yet realized. Our Prayer of Confession is for the whole people of God, including ourselves.

PRAYER OF CONFESSION

Forgive us, God, for our complacent attitudes and self-serving comforts. We do not relish the thought of sacrificing for some larger good we cannot see, for people with whom we find it difficult to identify. We compare ourselves favorably against many who seem less attuned to your purposes than we, forgetting that our true standard is Christ Jesus. We ask you to take from us all the bitterness, envy, and anger that stands in the way of your reign. May all we ask of you be for the common good of all your children. Amen.

Assurance of Forgiveness

God, who tries our hearts and minds, judges righteously, hears our prayers, and forgives and upholds us. In our daily meditation, God meets us, and in our encounters with one another, God's presence is revealed in unexpected ways to those who are alert and receptive. Nourished by the streams of living water which our God provides, we will prosper in the work God gives us to do.

Collect

Gracious God, revealed to us as we welcome children in the name of Jesus, grant us childlike openness and honesty to explore your word. Teach us as Jesus taught the disciples that we may not so much aspire to greatness as to faithfulness, counting service in Christ's name a joyous privilege. Amen.

Offertory Invitation

With free-will offerings, we will sacrifice to God, giving thanks for mercies too abundant to count. We want to share all that has been entrusted to our keeping, that God may be praised, and peace may come to all God's people.

Offertory Prayer

We who have spent much on our own pleasures are pleased to share that others may obtain the necessities of body and spirit. Thank you, God, for this opportunity to support the ministry and mission of our congregation. May there be a harvest of righteousness among us, shown in the peaceful handling of disputes, in mutual love and support, and in courageous outreach to people near and far who need the help we can give. Bless each gift and giver. Amen.

Commission and Blessing

Go forth, trusting God and one another.
Live each day seeking to be trustworthy.
We seek to do well the tasks set before us.
We commit ourselves to quiet times for meditation.
The rhythms of prayer and service enrich our lives.
A gentle spirit and good fruits are the result.
We seek the wisdom God imparts.
We aim to serve without partiality or hypocrisy.
God is watching over you and caring for you.
In God's hands, your hearts are being purified.
We put our trust in the God who loves us.
Our strength and dignity find renewal in Christ.
Amen. **Amen.**

(See hymn 80. "Why Did We Talk of Rank?", *Whispers of God*, p. 213,
reflects today's Gospel reading.)

Esther 7:1–6, 9–10,   *(or Numbers 11:4–6, 10–16, 24–29*   James 5:13–20
   9:20–22   *Psalm 19:7–14)*
Psalm 124   Mark 9:38–50

CALL TO WORSHIP

Come one and all to meet God here.
Let all who are suffering find hope in this place.
> **We have come that God might raise us up.**
> **Our only hope is in the Maker of heaven and earth.**

Come, all who are weary and oppressed.
God offers relief and enlists our mutual helpfulness.
> **God hears our prayers and answers us.**
> **God equips us to be helpful to one another.**

Come together to sing songs of praise to God.
Give thanks for God's wondrous deeds.
> **God's glory abides in this place of worship.**
> **God's presence and help are real.**

INVOCATION

May all your people find favor with you this day, God of majesty and power. Turn our sorrow into gladness and our mourning into a holiday, a holy day, in which to praise you and find ways to help those less fortunate than ourselves. Lift us from our daily preoccupations that we may pray with earnest intent, both to thank you and to be changed by you. Let our prayers be powerful and effective. May our worship be alive and life-changing. May the service we extend find favor in your eyes, blessed God. Amen.

CALL TO CONFESSION

Confess your sins to one another, and pray for one another, so you may be healed. Prayers of the righteous are powerful and effective. We seek that right relationship with God that empowers our prayers and our service.

PRAYER OF CONFESSION

All-powerful God, we confess our devious ways. Even when prayers for others are on our lips, we seek ways to secure our own advantages. We put our trust in things we can accumulate rather than aligning ourselves with your will and way. Our behavior creates enemies and multiplies divisions among your people. Then we want you on our side against those who are different from us. We confuse our preferences with your intentions. O God, we need healing, but we are afraid to lose the illusions of control that are so much a part of us. We fear the very changes that would give us integrity. Help us, gracious God.

Assurance of Forgiveness

The snares that entrap us are broken. Our help is in the name of God, who made heaven and earth. Prayers of faith make a difference. They are powerful and effective. We are changed in the hands of a loving God. We have much to give, beginning with the simplest of gifts, like a cup of cold water offered to one who is thirsty. Praise God, who is transforming us.

Collect

Reigning God, whose dominion is over all worlds, and whose witnesses come from many places and points of view, expand our knowledge of your truth and our appreciation of diversity so we may find common ground with others rather than being stumbling blocks in their way. Show us how to be at peace with one another and faithful to you. Amen.

Offertory Invitation

Like salt that enhances the flavor of food, Christians are called to share the joy and gladness we are discovering in our relationship with Jesus Christ. The good news is extended through our support of the church and its ministries.

Offertory Prayer

We dedicate ourselves and our offerings to the work of your church. For those who are sick, who are suffering, who are grieving, who are lost, we have words of hope and acts of caring. We stand with all who face discrimination, oppression, and confusion, seeking to work with them for justice and a meaningful existence. As you have accepted us, we reach out to include all your children in the family of mutuality, self-revelation, and growing in love. Amen.

Commission and Blessing

God sends us out with courage to face life's evils.
We have insight to name the enemies we encounter.
>   *Sometimes we are our own worst enemies.*
>   *Sometimes perceived enemies can become friends.*
We are called to care in an uncaring world.
We are commissioned as lovers among the indifferent.
>   *As Christians, we cannot be apathetic.*
>   *The people we encounter are brothers and sisters.*
God is our helper, and Christ is our teacher.
Our prayers and our efforts will make a difference.
>   *God is with us wherever we go.*
>   *The maker of heaven and earth cares for us.*
Amen. **Amen.**

(See hymn 81.)

PROPER 22

Sunday between October 2 and October 8

Job 1:1; 2:1–10
Psalm 26

(or Genesis 2:18–24
Psalm 8)

Hebrews 1:1–4; 2:5–12
Mark 10:2–16

CALL TO WORSHIP

God's Word has been lived among us!
We gather in the name of Jesus Christ.
>*Christ is a part of God's ongoing creation.*
>*We gather before the One who is heir to all things.*

Long ago, God spoke to our spiritual ancestors.
Today, God continues that revelation through Jesus.
>*Who are we that God is mindful of us?*
>*Yet God crowns us with glory and honor.*

Jesus has named us as brothers and sisters.
We are called to recognize all humanity as children of God.
>*The realm of God is for all people.*
>*God's dominion is over all creation.*

INVOCATION

We have trusted in you, eternal God, and that trust brings us to this time of worship. In this place, your steadfast love becomes evident again as we sing our songs of thanksgiving and tell of your wondrous deeds. We are grateful for the life and witness of Jesus, whom you sent among people to make possible our reconciliation and healing. For the saving grace available wherever you reign, we give thanks. Help us to be childlike, to receive your blessing, and to welcome your embrace. Take us into your arms, we pray. Amen.

CALL TO CONFESSION

At our best, we seek to be upright and blameless, people of integrity who live with unwavering trust in God. We aspire to live as brothers and sisters of Jesus Christ, faithful and responsive to our Creator. But, in truth, we forget God in our hectic busyness, and we turn from the way of love in our relationships with others. There is much for us to confess.

PRAYER OF CONFESSION

All-seeing God, we would like to wash our hands in innocence, but we cannot escape from the guilt we carry. We compare ourselves favorably with people we label worthless or hypocrites, but that very judgment breaks faith with you. We avoid bribery and other evil devices, yet we would still like to have advantages for ourselves over others. We are not bloodthirsty, but we have not yet adopted the way of peace. We humbly seek forgiveness as little children in need of your welcoming love. Amen.

Assurance of Forgiveness

When we come as children, acknowledging our dependence on God for life and all that sustains it, we recognize that loving arms surround us, and hands of blessing rest on our lives. We are sisters and brothers of Jesus Christ, who is not ashamed to claim us and to walk with us through life. Rejoice that God tests our hearts and minds and helps us grow.

Collect

God of our ancestors, whose dominion is over all time and space, we thank you for receiving us as your children, for melting the hardness of heart that locks us into our own narrow point of view, and keeps us from sharing our lives fully with partners who are different from us. We ask you now to touch us in ways that heal, address our fears, awaken hope in us, and open us to self-giving love. We long to live in a world refreshed by mutual caring and honest commitment. Teach us, that we might fulfill our role toward this vision.

Offertory Invitation

Look around you with a sense of awe and wonder. Even in the most difficult circumstances of life, we can find beauty and integrity and places where God's abiding glory is evident. Let us give thanks for God's imprint on our lives, for the sustaining word that gives purpose to our days, and for the ministry in which we are engaged together, as we present our offering.

Offertory Prayer

As long ago you spoke through the prophets, speak now through us and through the fruits of our labor which we share. We dedicate to your service all the good things we have received from your hand. May we proclaim your name to our brothers and sisters in this congregation. May our gifts carry the good news throughout our community, making a difference in the quality of life experienced by many, near and far. Amen.

Commission and Blessing

For this little while, we have been in the arms of God.
Hands of blessing have rested lightly on our heads.
> **We have recognized one another as children of God.**
> **Our rivalries are turned to awe and wonder.**
We have brought our pain to the suffering Savior.
Christ has welcomed us as sisters and brothers.
> **We are united in love that lasts for eternity.**
> **The reign of God has already begun here and now.**
Walk with integrity through the storms of life.
God crowns you with glory and honor.
> **The imprint of God's love is on our lives.**
> **It is a privilege to reflect God's glory each day!**
Amen. **Amen.**

(See hymn 82. See also "Grant Sabbath Rest," *Whispers of God*, p. 215.)

Job 23:1–9, 16–17   (or Amos 5:6–7, 10–15   Hebrews 4:12–16
Psalm 22:1–15   Psalm 90:12–17)   Mark 10:17–31

CALL TO WORSHIP

Come, all who look for God with unseeing eyes.
Come, all who listen for God but hear nothing.
> *Oh, that we knew where to find God!*
> *We want to hear and understand God's Word.*
The word of God is living and active.
It pierces and judges and opens us to God's grace.
> *We cannot hide from God who knows us.*
> *God understands our thoughts and intentions.*
Leave everything to follow Jesus in this hour.
This is the time to embrace new ways.
> *Here we set the patterns for everyday life.*
> *Here we are strengthened for every day's challenges.*

INVOCATION

We seek to gather as children of your realm, reigning God. This is the time and place of your dominion. We recognize that you, not we, prescribe the rules under which life can be rich and full and free. Help us in this hour to embrace the best we know. Open our thoughts and feelings so we may learn better ways. We approach you with boldness, daring to question and make requests, knowing that your grace and mercy exceed our wildest imagining, and your guidance is ever available to those who ask. Amen.

CALL TO CONFESSION

The Word of God is living and active, sharper than a two-edged sword, able to judge the thoughts and intentions of our hearts. We cannot hide from God, but must render an account to our Creator. Come, then, to confess the sin and doubts that cripple your life.

PRAYER OF CONFESSION

Almighty God, hear us if you can. Know that many times we feel forsaken and terrified more than supported and comforted. We cry out and hear no answers. We suffer and find no relief. We are tempted to blame you even though we are the ones who cut off communication. We complain in the midst of plenty and groan over imagined slights. When we feel mocked and scorned and despised, we turn inward with the hurt instead of opening ourselves to your healing touch. Have mercy on us, and help us in our time of need. Amen.

ASSURANCE OF FORGIVENESS

Remember that Jesus shared our common lot and is able to sympathize with our weakness. The Man of Nazareth was tempted as we are tempted. Our confessions, both those spoken and those without voice, are no surprise to the Christ, who is our great high priest. Yet we are counted as brothers and sisters in the faith and offered abundant grace and mercy. For God, all things are possible. We are forgiven!

COLLECT

Eternal God, before whom our human systems and distinctions amount to nothing, and in whose love the last are often first, grant teachings that will astound us, your presence to transform us, and courage to witness with all we have and all we are to the good news of your love and the promise of eternal life. Amen.

OFFERTORY INVITATION

Jesus said to the young questioner who asked about eternal life: "You lack one thing; go, sell what you own, and give the money to the poor, and you will have treasure in heaven; then come, follow me." As long as our reliance is on things we have accumulated, our Christian discipleship is threatened. We give out of thanks to God and concern for our neighbors.

OFFERTORY PRAYER

Thank you, God, for the wealth you have entrusted to us. As we share a portion of that wealth, we pray that it may never become the object of our affection. Keep our focus on people and relationships and lasting values, rather than on the possessions we can accumulate. We dedicate our time, money, and ourselves to the reign of God among us, praying that all whom our gifts may reach may receive mercy and find grace to help in time of need. Amen.

COMMISSION AND BLESSING

The God whom we have met here is with us every day.
Be open each day to what God would say to you.
> *The Word of God is living and active.*
> *It is sharper than a two-edged sword.*

God's Word provides judgment on our thoughts.
It reveals the intentions of our hearts.
> *The scriptures lead us to Jesus, our Teacher.*
> *In Christ, we find support and encouragement.*

The word of God will guide you in all truth.
It will assure you of God's saving grace.
> *With God, all things are possible.*
> *From God, we seek to know eternal life here and now.*

Amen. **Amen.**

(See hymns 84, 85. See "What Shall We Do, O Christ?", *Whispers of God*, p. 216, which reflects today's Gospel reading.)

PROPER 24

Job 38:1–7, (34–41)	(or Isaiah 53:4–12	Hebrews 5:1–10
Psalm 104:1–9, 24, 35c	Psalm 91:9–16)	Mark 10:35–45

CALL TO WORSHIP

Let your minds ponder the manifold works of God.
Let your spirits soar amid the wonders of creation.
There is pulsating life all around us.
The earth is full of God's creatures.
Sun and rain proclaim God's infinite imagination.
Moon and stars sing the glory of the Eternal One.
It is God who shares with us wisdom and understanding.
We depend on God for the gift of life.
We gather to worship and praise the God of all people.
We come to learn from the God we only dimly perceive.
We reach out for answers to our questions
We long to find meaning and purpose for our days.

INVOCATION

Source of all things, how can we approach glory so vast that all space and time is surrounded by you? We cannot comprehend the marvels of the earth. How shall we honor your majesty? You are so unknowable, yet evidence of your work is on every hand. The mystery of life in all its many forms, the discoveries we are allowed to make, the sweep of knowledge entrusted to our use, the amazing resources of this planet—all speak of a God who cares, who honors us, who provides for our salvation. Let this time of meeting honor you and equip us to do your will. Amen.

CALL TO CONFESSION

In the poetry of the book of Job, God addresses the complainers of every age: "Who is this that darkens counsel by words without knowledge? Where were you when I laid the foundations of the world? When the morning stars sang together and all the heavenly beings shouted for joy?" In awe before God, we confess our ill-fated attempts to play God.

PRAYER OF CONFESSION

Reigning God, we confess that we, like the disciples James and John, seek places of honor, privilege, and reward. We succumb to the temptation to compare ourselves with others to our advantage. We want privilege without pain, greatness without the grind of hard work. We expect rewards for our efforts. We talk about serving you, but we do not want the rank of servant. We have lots of ideas about what you might do to intervene in the world and little commitment to what we might do in your name. Forgive us and help us, gracious God.

Assurance of Forgiveness

The tears and prayers of Christ are for us. The gift of the Holy Spirit re-creates us for ministry. Bless and thank our God for the manifold works which have sustained our lives and given them meaning. God deals gently with the ignorant and wayward. God is patient with our pretensions, seeking always to welcome us home to true community. Praise God!

Collect

In the name of Jesus Christ who came not to be served, but to serve, and to give life itself for us, we approach your Word with awe. We live in different times but in the same world in which Jesus ate and drank, lived, and died. We share the same baptism and have the same opportunity to know your love and serve you. Help us dare to believe and trust and live our days returning your love through the neighbors near and far who need to know your care. Amen.

Offertory Invitation

For Jesus, a life lived for others was the only life consistent with God's reign. The church exists to increase among us the love of God and neighbor, and to build within us the deep conviction that we are beloved, valued, people of worth. It is to this high mission that we devote our offerings for ministry in this community and throughout God's world.

Offertory Prayer

We give with joy, loving God, in thanks for all you have allowed us to experience. By your love, we have survived and learned and grown. We dedicate these gifts that more people may be brought to the feet of Jesus, who is the eternal source of salvation. Equip us to be an inviting, caring community in which all your ignorant and wayward people find a genuine welcome and are lifted up to new understanding and joy. Amen.

Commission and Blessing

You are clothed with honor and wrapped in light.
Bless God and proclaim God's greatness to the world.
In Christ, we are growing in wisdom and understanding.
How manifold are the works of God!
God has chosen us to be priests to our neighbors.
Deal gently and lovingly with the children of God.
We will daily turn to God in prayer and supplication.
With reverent submission, we will seek to do God's will.
There is glory in humble tasks done in God's name.
Abounding joy awaits you in God's service.
We face another week of living, with hope.
God is strengthening all of us as loyal servants.
Amen. **Amen.**

(See hymns 86, 87.)

PROPER 25

Sunday between October 23 and October 29

Job 42:1–6, 10–17   (or Jeremiah 31:7–9   Hebrews 7:23–28
Psalm 34:1–8, (19–22)   Psalm 126)   Mark 10:46–52

CALL TO WORSHIP

God is gathering us from many different places.
No one is worthy, but all are invited.
> *God lifts us up when we stumble and leads us back.*
> *God cares for us amid our pain and losses.*

We are delivered from our fears and saved from trouble.
Happy are those who take refuge in a loving God.
> *Our lips pour forth laughter and joyous singing.*
> *We join in shouts of praise to God Most High.*

Taste and see how good God is.
Trust in the One who awakens joy in place of tears.
> *We will bless our God in all times and places.*
> *Let us exalt God's name together!*

INVOCATION

All-powerful God, we invoke your presence among us, for we need the knowledge and energy you alone can provide. Your ways are wonderful beyond our understanding. When our strength is spent, our vision clouded, and our hope gone, you reach out to us in ways we often fail to discern. We take heart to think that you are calling us to yourself, opening our eyes to see your wonders as if for the first time. We want to be a part of your faithful remnant in a world that too often loses sight of the holy. Help us, we pray. Amen.

CALL TO CONFESSION

We who are called to be a servant people have often forgotten what it means to sacrifice ourselves for others. Success becomes more attractive than service, and so we focus on getting ahead, which often means leaving behind those who cannot keep up. This is a time to confess selfish motives and hurtful actions.

PRAYER OF CONFESSION

We confess, O God, that our lives have made of you a distant deity. We listen to what others say about you, but we have seldom glimpsed for ourselves who you are. We are dominated by our doubts instead of by our practice of prayer. We are not ready to repent in dust and ashes, but we do ask for mercy as we face up to sins we have not recognized and wrongdoing we have tried to ignore. Instill in us a new appreciation of righteousness, and help us to grow in the way you would have us go. Amen.

Assurance of Forgiveness

Our God, who has reached out to us in love, welcomes even our timid answers. God is most generous in blessing us and lifting us beyond our losses and our fears. In Christ, we are linked with God's saving grace for all time and eternity. Let us praise God, recognizing that faith has power to heal.

Collect

Amazing God, whose claims on us are as old as creation and as new as this very moment, help us to hear you calling us, not alone that we may be healed, but that we might become instruments of healing in a hurting world. Restore to us that sight that is beyond seeing, so your church may respond with joy to the great high priest, in whose name we pray and carry out our ministry. Amen.

Offertory Invitation

Our offerings are to magnify God's name and to express our deep sense of thanksgiving. They are also an expression of empathy and concern for sisters and brothers who struggle to find life. Giving reorients our lives to what is of lasting value and importance. Let us give as we are able—with joy!

Offertory Prayer

Hear our prayer for all who may be helped by what we give. We offer more than money; we offer ourselves. May the sympathy and comfort we share with people in need serve to draw them closer to you. Keep us strong, that this church may give radiant witness to truth, constructive opposition to evil, and merciful redemption to those caught up in the wickedness of our times. Amen.

Commission and Blessing

Take heart; your faith is making you well.
You will know wholeness and peace beyond your suffering.
We have witnessed miracles of transformation.
Christ grants insight and deep inner healing.
You are chosen as disciples and apostles of good news.
You have gathered to learn; now go out to witness.
It is hard to share good news that people resist.
We fear we do not know enough to defend our views.
God needs no defense from us but welcomes our thanks.
We can tell others about our own journey with God.
Our gladness and our humility are genuine.
We pray that God will work in and through us.
Amen. **Amen.**

(See hymn 88. See also "O, Sing Aloud," *Whispers of God*, pp. 217–18.)

Ruth 1:1–18   (or Deuteronomy 6:1–9   Hebrews 9:11–14
Psalm 146   Psalm 119:1–8)   Mark 12:28–34

CALL TO WORSHIP

Listen and hear, all you people of the book!
There is one God who created all time and space.
>   *Our hope is in God who made heaven and earth.*
>   *All creatures of the land and sea come from God.*

You shall love God with all your heart and soul.
You shall honor God with all your mind and strength.
>   *We will praise God as long as we live.*
>   *We will sing of God's glory all through our lives.*

A second commandment is like the first:
You shall love your neighbor as yourself.
>   *God watches over strangers and widows and orphans.*
>   *We honor God by honoring these, our sisters and brothers.*

INVOCATION

Reigning God, we have viewed the work of your hands. Where there is justice for the oppressed, we sense your presence. Where the hungry are fed, we know the providers are working with you. You set prisoners free and open the eyes of the blind. You lift up those who are bowed down and sustain the righteous with your love. We worship a God who is living and active. We give thanks that you call us to join the action, to love you and one another more than the rituals of our religion or the satisfaction of our successes. Focus us now on all that is worthy of our praise. Amen.

CALL TO CONFESSION

God alone deserves our trust and loyalty. Yet we have not trusted, and our faithfulness is in question. This time of confession offers the opportunity to unburden our conscience, to experience forgiveness, and to renew our covenant with the Eternal One.

PRAYER OF CONFESSION

We have not kept faith with you, righteous God. There are so many distractions that occupy our time! There are so many groups to claim our loyalty. There are so many activities that bid for our attention. Even the church involves us in busyness that keeps us from matters of greater importance. In these moments, we seek to know you and to be known by you, that in an honest exchange our relationship with you and with the people around us might be strengthened. In your name, and joining with you, we seek justice for the oppressed, food for the hungry, and healing for all. Amen.

ASSURANCE OF FORGIVENESS

We can count on God's active presence when all other hope is gone. Let us respond in gratitude to the One who deals kindly with us and whose will for us is love and joy and peace. Happy are those whose help and whose hope is in the one true God, who reigns for all generations and beyond time.

COLLECT

God of Israel, God of all nations, God of all worlds, known to humankind in many forms, yet far beyond our knowing, we seek to love you with our hearts and our understanding and our strength, that our thoughts and motives and energies might be devoted to serving you through the people and circumstances we encounter day by day. Reign within us and among us, today and always. Amen.

OFFERTORY INVITATION

Our energies and our resources are claimed by whatever is truly most important to us. If God is at the center of our lives, that will be apparent in what we give. From God we have received love so amazing that a lifetime of thanks is inadequate response.

OFFERTORY PRAYER

Receive from us, O God, the best we have to give. All we have comes from you. We return a portion with joy to accomplish the work we intend to do together in your name. We bring ourselves as well, to be blessed by you, so that while we are apart our words and deeds will continue to be a significant offering. May our lives praise you! Amen.

COMMISSION AND BLESSING

Find your direction in life as you follow Christ.
Find in your neighbor a brother or sister in Christ.
We are all children of the one God.
We are all beloved, honored, and set free.
Our freedom allows for full commitment.
Because we are free, we can choose to be loyal.
We will worship God together and alone.
We will be present for one another when needed.
Surely God will bless our journey.
Go in peace, confident of God's abiding grace.
We will dwell in God's love day by day.
God reigns in every place we go.
Amen. **Amen.**

(See hymns 89, 90.)

Ruth 3:1–5; 4:13–17   (or I Kings 17:8–16   Hebrews 9:24–28
Psalm 127   Psalm 146)   Mark 12:38–44

CALL TO WORSHIP

Come, all who are anxious or burdened.
This is a time to experience good news.
> **This is God's house, and we can meet God here.**
> **We are brought together in the family of God.**

Come with expectancy and anticipation.
God is present to greet you and change your life.
> **We are here to remember the ministry of Jesus.**
> **We have come to be equipped for our ministry.**

In our eager waiting, there is fullness of joy.
In our preparation for worship, we discover life.
> **Unless God is the shaper of our lives, we live in vain.**
> **Unless we view our city as God's own, there is emptiness here.**

INVOCATION

In the security of your love, mighty God, it is well with us. Our work is fulfilling, our relationships reflect your faithfulness, and our ability to trust is strengthened. We are here, seeking an extra measure of reassurance, the restoration of our best selves and the clarification of our responsibilities. You are the builder in whose hands the church can become a community of joy and fulfillment. You keep watch over us, strengthening us to be the church wherever we live and serve. Be known to us now and save all who eagerly await your word. Amen.

CALL TO CONFESSION

At our best, we long to be whole people whose words and deeds are a reflection of the truth within us. We want to be free of pretense and alive to the wonders that we encounter in other people and in all of God's creation. God is ready to cleanse and heal us as we confess our sin.

PRAYER OF CONFESSION

All-wise God, you know how much we enjoy being honored above others, and how often we resent the special respect others receive. You are aware of the short-cuts we take for our own advantage. You see the ways we pretend to be more than we are. You observe not only our actions but our motives as well. We need your help to put away all that is false and to discover our true identity as your children. Lift us up in your forgiving love, we pray. Amen.

Assurance of Forgiveness

Those who truly repent of the lies they have lived are welcomed as next of kin by Jesus Christ. The authentic, self-giving spirit of one who was fully human is ours to embrace. The witness of a life lived for the common good inspires us to rise up to the best we can be. We are forgiven, freed from the burden of our sin.

Collect

Gracious God, whose favor rests on those who are poor as much as on those who possess many things, and whose attention is drawn to our simple petitions more than to long, eloquent prayers that seek to impress, we ask in these moments to lay aside our anxiety that we might hear and respond to your word and be empowered to live by it. Amen.

Offertory Invitation

We are privileged to contribute out of our abundance that the Christian message might be proclaimed among us and to our children. We are challenged to give all that we have—our time, our talents, our work, and our leisure as witness to the love of God. The extent to which we invest ourselves is a measure of our commitment.

Offertory Prayer

We give in the spirit of Jesus, whose whole life was committed to proclaiming your love, gracious God. May our lives give evidence that we understand the care and compassion you have for all people, near and far, attractive and offensive, rich and poor. Our offerings today are a token of all the gifts we now invest in the work of your realm that is forever, with beginnings among us now. Amen.

Commission and Blessing

Lay aside the bread of anxious toil.
Give your best with joy, with Christ as your partner.
> **Our lives are restored to the balance God intends.**
> **Our work and our play become offerings to God.**
What God builds among us is of lasting value.
In the love of God, we guard the best that is in us.
> **Our prayers keep strong our connection with God.**
> **They are not empty words for the sake of appearance.**
Salvation is here for those who are eager to receive it.
Forgiveness and healing are freely given to us.
> **We are thankful for the days God gives us.**
> **We rejoice in the good things we are receiving.**
Amen. **Amen.**

(See hymn 91.)

I Samuel 1:4–20　　　　(or Daniel 12:1–3　　Hebrews 10:11–14, (15–18),
I Samuel 2:1–10　　　　　　Psalm 16)　　　　　　　　　　　　　19–25
　　　　　　　　　　　　　　　　　　　　　　　　　　　　Mark 13:18

CALL TO WORSHIP

　　Come, let us present ourselves before our God.
　　Bring all your troubles and anxiety to God in prayer.
　　　　Surely God knows our thoughts and hears our prayers.
　　　　We find strength for living as we praise God.
　　Lay down your arrogance and false pride.
　　Admit your needs as you seek God's favor.
　　　　We pour out our souls before the living God.
　　　　We do not withhold from God our misery and distress.
　　God grants our petitions and gives us peace.
　　The counsel of our God gladdens our hearts.
　　　　In God's presence there is fullness of joy.
　　　　As we meet together, we are encouraged and comforted.

INVOCATION

Our hearts exalt in you, O God. All knowledge has its origin in you. Our deepest hungers are satisfied as you give counsel and instruct our hearts. Be known to us now, that our covenant with you may be strengthened. Give confidence to all who enter this sanctuary, that our faith may grow, our love expand, and our hope find fulfillment. Show us the path of life, and grant us courage to walk in your ways. Amen.

CALL TO CONFESSION

Let us approach our God in all truth, confessing the deeds and distractions that have kept us from honoring God and have divided us from other human beings. We cannot undo all the wrong we have done, but we can be cleansed from an evil conscience to live a more wholesome and joyous life.

PRAYER OF CONFESSION

Mighty God, we confess the arrogance of our doubts and the falsehood of our denials. We have neglected to pray and have forgotten to give thanks. Many activities have become more important to us than gathering for worship. Our busyness crowds out times of private prayer. We shake our heads at the evil around us but do little to witness to a better way. Your law is seldom consulted, and your pathways of self-sacrificing love rarely explored. Turn us around, God. Only you can meet our need. Amen.

ASSURANCE OF FORGIVENESS

The Holy Spirit renews in us the covenant we have made with our God, offering us forgiveness and assuring us that our lawless deeds will be remembered no more. The law of God is planted in our hearts and written on our minds so love and good deeds may become second nature to us. We are set free to express gladness and to encourage one another.

COLLECT

Source of all wisdom, who in Jesus Christ offers to teach us the way of love, we have asked for signals and signs of your presence and your leading but have often been led astray by our own desires and interpretations. Testify to us now that we may hear your counsel above the clamor of other voices and, hearing, respond as you intend. Amen.

OFFERTORY INVITATION

We are encouraged to give as God has blessed us, bringing our offerings, not to win God's favor but to express our thanks, not out of habit but as a caring community that provokes one another to love and good deeds.

OFFERTORY PRAYER

Our hearts are glad and our souls rejoice in the opportunity to share. Here are the fruits of your generosity and our hard work. In thanks for the perfect offering of Jesus Christ, we bring ourselves with our gifts. Show us how to combine our efforts to build wholesome relationships, extend your church, and minister in your name throughout the world. Amen.

COMMISSION AND BLESSING

Go forth in confidence that God remembers you.
Go in peace, knowing you will find blessings in abundance.
> *God is with us wherever we go.*
> *We seek to recognize the blessings we have ignored.*
Live your lives in a continuing relationship of prayer.
Listen for the counsel God offers every day.
> *There is a word for us in every situation.*
> *God is always ready to guide our decisions.*
A new and living way opens before us.
We are learning to encourage our sisters and brothers.
> *We seek to provoke one another to good deeds.*
> *Love for one another will be our highest motive.*
Amen. **Amen.**

(See hymns 92, 93.)

PROPER 29 (REIGN OF CHRIST)

Sunday between November 20 and November 26

2 Samuel 23:1–7   (or Daniel 7:9–10, 13–14   Revelation 1:4b–8
Psalm 132:1–12, (13–18)   Psalm 93)   John 18:33–37

CALL TO WORSHIP

Rejoice in the light of the morning!
Give thanks for the sun's energy, even through clouds!
> **God has spoken to us and meets us here.**
> **We live in covenant with the Eternal One.**

Gather in the spirit of Jesus, whose name we bear!
Thank God for truth that lives in spite of death!
> **We celebrate the faithful witness of Jesus Christ.**
> **We seek to share the good news that Christ reigns.**

The Spirit encounters us here that we might learn.
The Spirit inspires us that we might serve.
> **God anoints us for ministry, giving us tasks to do.**
> **God's word is on our tongues, that the world may believe.**

INVOCATION

Speak to us, eternal God, through the representatives you anoint to proclaim your
Word. Grant that all in authority will speak truthfully, rule justly, and serve self-
lessly. Find your dwelling place today, not just in this sanctuary, but in our hearts
and lives—and not just today, but every day. Clothe your priests with faithfulness
and all your faithful people with garments of joy. May we know your grace and
peace as we honor your majesty, bowing in awe before the one who was, and is,
and is to come. Amen.

CALL TO CONFESSION

Do our lives reflect the love of God revealed in Jesus? Is the rule of Christ among
us our central concern? Do we daily join in ministry, following in the footsteps of
Jesus Christ? This is our call and our duty, for which we must give account.

PRAYER OF CONFESSION

Loving God, we confess that we have been more like thorn bushes than oaks of
righteousness. We sometimes repel rather than attract others to the gospel. Pride
and deceit fill our days more than grace and peace. We tire of satisfying the poor
with bread and upholding the covenant and decrees you have offered us. We turn
away from your anointed one, questioning his role in history and his relevance for
us. We admit that our inner faith battles are often the screen we use to keep from
facing our sin, admitting our guilt and seeking reconciliation. Open our eyes, heal
our open wounds, and embrace us in your love that we might be forgiven. Amen.

ASSURANCE OF FORGIVENESS

God is Alpha and Omega, the source and the ending of all that is and yet will be. You are known. You are loved. You are forgiven. Enter the realm which is not of this world, the community that acknowledges God's rule in all things. Know that you belong to the truth that comes from God.

COLLECT

Alpha and Omega, whose creative energy through untold billions of years has brought us to this time of encounter, we rejoice in the ministry of Jesus that revealed your love and provided for us forgiveness of sin and fullness of life. May we embrace that reign which is beyond the standards of this world, testifying to your truth by our words and deeds, that others may learn to trust your love. Amen.

OFFERTORY INVITATION

We decry the godlessness of our day. We mourn the loss of values that our faith has taught. Together as a church, we can address the world with good news that uplifts lives from self-serving, self-destructive ways. Our offerings are one way we make our witness.

OFFERTORY PRAYER

Our offerings measure our faithfulness to you, mighty God. They witness to the importance we place on sharing your Word, ministering to one another, and reaching out to make a difference in your world. As we have been influenced by your love in Jesus Christ, help us to communicate that love by what we do and say. Let us become as lamps brightening a cloudy day, as light breaking forth at dawn. To that end, we dedicate ourselves with our gifts. Amen.

COMMISSION AND BLESSING

Grace to you and peace from God Almighty.
May love and freedom be yours in Jesus Christ.
> *We receive the gifts of God's grace and peace.*
> *We rejoice in the freedom to love as Jesus loved.*
Let the Spirit of God speak through you today.
Let God's word be on your tongue through the week.
> *We are not ashamed to share the gospel.*
> *We want to be caring and kind in all our talk.*
Live the good news that you have received.
Be guided by the One who rules for all eternity.
> *We are here to testify to truth in word and deed.*
> *We will listen to God's Word for our instructions.*
Amen. **Amen.**

(See hymn 94.)

SPECIAL DAYS

ALL SAINTS' DAY

(November 1 or First Sunday in November)

Isaiah 25:6–9   Revelation 21:1–6a
Psalm 24   John 11:32–44

CALL TO WORSHIP

How often have we imagined the ruler of glory far off?
God is not in some remote heaven but here.

> *We wait in silence for God's appearing.*
> *Come, Holy One, to wipe away our tears.*

Stretch out your hands and open your hearts.
Purify your lives from all deceit and falsehood.

> *God reaches out to comfort and cleanse.*
> *We can sense God's hand of blessing resting on us.*

The earth and all things in it are God's.
The world and all its people belong to God.

> *We are God's people, called and saved by Christ.*
> *We are the saints who share in Christ's ministry.*

INVOCATION

Creator of all life, who could dare to stand before you were it not for your vindication of us? You are the Alpha and the Omega, the beginning and the end of all things. You take away our disgrace and restore us to wholeness. You swallow up death in the larger reality of life eternal. You grant hope for a new heaven and earth even in the midst of our present struggles. Surely you will bless us in this time of worship, unbinding us from our dull routines and freeing us to worship in spirit and in truth. Amen.

CALL TO CONFESSION

We have hidden our soiled hands and impure hearts from one another, but we cannot hide from God. We are dead in our sin, yet Christ reaches through the stench to offer new life, not just a few little adjustments, but a transformed outlook and purpose. If we want to be healed, we are invited to a time of confession.

PRAYER OF CONFESSION

We are unprepared to meet you, mighty God, but we cannot put off this encounter. You continue to summon us to the mountaintop, there to feel your presence and respond to your Word. You invite us to lift up our heads and to see the ruler of glory but we have stubbornly refused to acknowledge your work among us or to see any purpose emerging from the depths of our despair. We fear death. We shrink from life. This is our greatest sin, cutting ourselves off from you. God help us! Amen.

ASSURANCE OF FORGIVENESS

God is ready and able to help us when we welcome the Ruler of glory into our lives. God's home is among us and within us. We know that when we take time to be aware. Every place we go is a holy place because God is there. All our denials do not change that. Our defacement of the holy is not the last word. God is Alpha and Omega, the beginning and the end. God is here in these moments to fill us with a sense of forgiveness and to free us from our sin. Praise God!

COLLECT

God of the living, whose will for us is the experience of steadfast love in all our relationships, and in whose hands death is but an entry into new dimensions of life, keep us, we pray, from denying life, either by avoidance of involvement that may bring loss and pain, or by inflicting on others suffering at our hands. Allow us a role in unbinding those who find themselves in the clutches of death in the midst of life. Amen.

OFFERTORY INVITATION

As God wipes away our tears, we are called to be tissue-bearers to the world. When there is pain and suffering, the church has a healing mission. Where there is doubt and despair, we offer hope's embrace. Much of this ministry we offer personally, but our outreach is extended by the material offerings we give. May this be a time of generous sharing!

OFFERTORY PRAYER

The earth is yours, O God, and all that is in it. We have received untold blessings from your hand. You set before us the vision of a new heaven and a new earth, inviting us to share in its formation. May the love of Jesus be expressed to others by our sharing of gifts, both person-to-person and through the investment of dollars to support the ministries of others. This offering of service and sacrifice is the high point of our worship. Amen.

COMMISSION AND BLESSING

People of God, come out of your past.
Embrace the future God offers us today.
> *The bindings of sin are removed, and we are free.*
> *The chains of fear are broken so we can live.*
The world awaits the good news you may bring.
Your sisters and brothers need your healing touch.
> *The home of God is in our midst.*
> *We will live as members of the household of God.*
Lift up your heads, and be lifted up.
Open your doors to the ruler of glory.
> *We welcome the God who welcomes us.*
> *We rejoice in the One who is making all things new.*
Amen. **Amen.**

(See hymns 95, 96.)

All Saints' Day   163

THANKSGIVING DAY

(Fourth Thursday in November—U.S.)

(Second Monday in October—Canada)

Joel 2:1–27   I Timothy 2:1–7
Psalm 126   Matthew 6:25–33

CALL TO WORSHIP

Be glad and rejoice, for God has done great things.
Our mouths are filled with laughter and shouts of joy.
A harvest of abundance surrounds us.
We will eat in plenty and be satisfied.
Praise God for all the bounty we enjoy.
Give thanks for every good and perfect gift.
We lay aside our worries and our fears.
God has dealt wondrously with us, and we rejoice.
Seek first God's realm of righteousness.
Let God reign in all your thoughts and relationships.
We know God is with us here.
We trust God to supply what we most need.

INVOCATION

How good it is to join in prayers of thanksgiving and songs of praise! You have
been good to us, gracious God! For sunshine and rain, for the labors of all who
harvest the grain, we pour out our gratitude. You have dealt wondrously with us
so that we have more than we need. Dwell with us now that we may not only be
inspired to share but also prompted to work for a more just world in which all your
children have enough to eat and reasons for joy. Amen.

CALL TO CONFESSION

The lilies of the field and the birds of the air offer their praise to God in beauty
and in song. We have been more ready to complain than to praise. Plants and an-
imals offer up their lives that we might be fed. We have received these gifts with
little awareness of the sacrifices others have made for us. We have enjoyed them
without asking how we might share the benefits. Surely we have much to confess.

PRAYER OF CONFESSION

You know the truth about us, O God, better than we know ourselves. We have
gathered the bounty of your earth to fill our bank accounts, struggling to get ahead,
blinded by greed. We have not stopped to gaze with wonder at the birds of the air
or the flowers of the field. We have not paused to listen to one another or to walk
with Christ among outcasts and sinners. We turn away from the prompting of the
Holy Spirit, choosing to worry rather than to praise. Turn us around, we pray, that
we might receive forgiveness and enter into a time of true thanksgiving. Amen.

ASSURANCE OF FORGIVENESS

God does not put us to shame but deals wondrously with us, restoring our fortunes and blessing us with peace. God desires our salvation, our healing, our embracing of truth. Therefore, we are not to worry. The gifts of God are known to all who first seek God's reign.

COLLECT

Caring God, whose attention is given impartially and completely to each and all of your children, and whose love is ever available, make yourself known to us now. Clothe us with faith, fill us with knowledge of your truth and lift us up to new heights of godliness and dignity, that our thanksgiving might be generously shared and joyously celebrated. Amen.

OFFERTORY INVITATION

Let our offerings be a joyous outpouring of thanksgiving to God, who deals wondrously with us. Out of gratitude, we respond to the needs of people nearby and far away who long for a crust of bread and a cup of pure water.

OFFERTORY PRAYER

We have bread, so we will share. We have pure water, so we will give to dig wells for others. We have faith, so we will tell others of the great things you have done, O God. These sacred moments of giving acknowledge your ownership of all our possessions. We seek to answer your call to responsible stewardship and faithfulness in mission. We are your heralds and apostles. Thank you, God. Amen.

COMMISSION AND BLESSING

Let thanksgiving continue every day you live.
Find joy in the wonder of God's generosity.
> *We will be glad and rejoice in our God.*
> *We seek to follow in the footsteps of Jesus.*
Christ leads us toward knowledge of God's truth.
Our worth is affirmed in the joy of discipleship.
> *Our prayers of thanksgiving will continue.*
> *We will lift up our intercessions for others.*
All humankind dwells as God's family on earth.
All creation partakes of the abundance God provides.
> *We are stewards of all these blessings.*
> *We seek justice that all might benefit.*
Amen. **Amen.**

(See hymn 97.)

Related Hymns

THE ADVENT SEASON

1

Restore Us, God of Hosts

First Sunday of Advent
Lavon Bayler

10.10.9.10.10.10.
(Veni Emmanuel) (was 8.8.8.8.8.8.)

Restore us, God of hosts, and come to save
Your people for the better life we crave.
We long to be as clay in your hand;
O Potter, fashion us as you have planned.
Restore, restore your people, God of hosts,
That we may serve with deeds, not idle boasts.

The mountains quake and nations shudder now
Before your anger which we disavow.
We tremble, quite aware of our sin,
Denying in ourselves its origin.
Restore, restore your people, God of hosts,
That we may serve with deeds, not idle boasts.

Give ear, O Shepherd, to your hurting flock.
Receive our earnest prayers and hear us knock
On heaven's door when we have transgressed.
Forgive, and help us learn to do our best.
Restore, restore your people, God of hosts,
That we may serve with deeds, not idle boasts.

O Hidden One, reveal yourself once more;
Surprise us with your presence, we implore,
That we may gladly do what is right,
And call upon your name both day and night.
Restore, restore your people, God of hosts,
That we may serve with deeds, not idle boasts.

(Psalm 80:1–7, 17–19, Isaiah 64:1–9)

2

Faithful God, We're Watching

First Sunday of Advent
Lavon Bayler

6.5.6.5.D.
(Lyndhurst)

Faithful God, we're watching,
Knowing you will bless.
Grace and peace you've promised
In our dark distress.
As we face our suffering,
Glory intervenes
In our Savior's coming
To our human scenes.

Heaven and earth may falter,
Yet your word is true,
Granting strength and guidance,
Making all things new.
Jesus is revealing
Gifts that you impart,
Drawing us together,
Claiming every heart.

Wide awake and watchful,
We prepare the way
In this Advent season
For that glorious day
When you claim all people
For your very own,
When the Christ is honored,
And your will is known.

(Mark 13:24–37, I Corinthians 1:3–9)

3

Comfort My People

Second Sunday of Advent
Lavon Bayler

6.6.8.6.D. (S.M.D.)
(Diademata)

Comfort my people now;
Speak tender love and grace
To those who fear God's ruling might
Or doubt God's strong embrace.
Prepare the way for Christ
To make God's pardon known.
In desert places, high and low,
God's glory will be shown.

Look for the word of God
That constant will remain,
When grasses wither, flowers fade,
And some deny God's reign.
Cry out God's promises,
Good tidings to proclaim;
Lift up your voices to announce
Forgiveness in Christ's name.

Come, Holy Spirit, come;
Baptize your church with power
To stand against all evil ways
That injure and devour
Your children, great and small,
Both innocent and strong.
Come, feed your flock and gather us
To sing your Advent song.

(Isaiah 40:1–11, Mark 1:1–8)

4

Come, Speak to Us

Second Sunday of Advent
Lavon Bayler

7.6.7.6.D.
(Lancashire)

Come, speak to us, Creator;
Renew your promises.
The earth awaits Christ's coming,
When no one perishes.
We beg for your forgiveness,
Repenting of our sin,
While seeking peace among us,
And righteousness within.

Your steadfast love has led us,
Your faithfulness inspires
Our answering devotion
And holier desires.
Our lands have yielded increase;
You give us what is good.
Your saving grace assures us
That we are understood.

Fill earth and heaven with newness;
Restore your favor here.
Disclose your truth among us,
That we no more may fear
To hear what you would teach us
To live as you direct.
Our hearts behold your glory
As you our lives perfect.

(Psalm 85:1–2, 8–13, 2 Peter 3:8–15a)

5

Come Home with Praise

Third Sunday of Advent
Lavon Bayler

8.6.8.6.D. (C.M.D.)
(Carol)

Come home with shouts of joyous praise;
Let now your weeping cease.
Good news will come to broken hearts,
Good news of love and peace.
Proclaim God's favor every day,
And comfort those who mourn.
Oppressed will hear of liberty,
And hope will be reborn.

God's justice reigns in spite of wrong;
God's covenant endures.
Beyond deserving, we receive
A gift that saves and cures.
Our fainting spirits are revived,
God's glory to display,
And we become a faithful flock,
Our Shepherd to obey.

True freedom comes when we commit
Our lives to God's intent,
When we are oaks of righteousness,
Prepared and confident.
When wrong no longer reigns within,
And selfish pride is gone,
We reap the joy of lives in tune
With God's approaching dawn.

(Psalm 126, Isaiah 61:1–4, 8–11)

6

Make Straight the Way

Third Sunday of Advent
Lavon Bayler

8.6.8.6.6.8. (C.M. Ref.)
(Antioch)

Make straight the way for Christ to come;
Bear witness to the light.
Not one of us is worthy yet
His sandals to untie,
His sandals to untie,
His sandals, sandals to untie.

We do not know the One who comes;
We only glimpse the Word,
Made flesh among our humankind,
In hopes that we have heard,
In hopes that we have heard,
In hopes, in hopes that we have heard.

Let us rejoice that God has called,
And chosen us to be
A church of prayer and thankfulness,
God's gracious will to see,
God's gracious will to see,
God's gracious, gracious will to see.

Cry in the wilderness today,
While holding fast to good.
Test every act by God's intent
To build true neighborhood,
To build true neighborhood,
To build, to build true neighborhood.

(John 1:1–6, 19–28, I Thessalonians 5:16–24)

7

Welcome God's Word

Fourth Sunday of Advent
Lavon Bayler

7.7.7.7.7.7.
(Dix)

Welcome God's incarnate Word;
Come, explore the mystery.
Test the truth that we have heard:
Christ is lord of history.
In a humble child, behold,
One whose advent was foretold.

Crown the Coming One with strength
To fulfill God's high intent.
All, throughout earth's breadth and length,
Bow in awed acknowledgment:
Christ is coming soon to reign,
Sent to make God's mercy plain.

Souls that magnify the Lord
Find their spirits lifted high,
Offering praise with one accord,
For God's gifts that satisfy;
Pardon, faith and bread to share
Demonstrate God's gracious care.

Will we build, at God's command,
Genuine community,
Not the structures of our hands,
But a deeper unity?
God's vast love empowers our quest,
As, in Christ, our lives are blessed.

(2 Samuel 7:1–11, 16, Luke 1:47–55, Romans 16:25–27)

THE CHRISTMAS SEASON

8

A Child Is Born

Christmas Eve/Day (Proper I)
Lavon Bayler

8.8.8.8. (L.M.)
(Von Himmel Hoch)

A child is born; the light has come!
Good news for people bound by fears,
For in a new life's mystery,
We find a hope that lifts and cheers.

Amid the darkness we have known:
Defeat, oppression, and distress,
Our God surprises with a gift
That promises to change and bless.

This child will grow and justice claim,
That we from sin may find release,
Wonderful Counselor, Mighty God,
One who will serve the cause of peace.

Say to the nations: "God will reign,"
Who judges us in righteous ways.
Let heavens be glad, let earth rejoice;
God's majesty can fill our days.

O sing to God a song of joy.
Ascribe to God the glory due
The name of One who saves and frees.
Give thanks for love alive and true.

(Psalm 96, Isaiah 9:2–7)

9

Blessed Hope

Christmas Eve/Day (Proper I)
Lavon Bayler

6.6.7.7.5.5. Irregular
(Stille Nacht)

Blessed hope, now fulfilled:
Grace of God has appeared
With salvation God has willed
For the penitent who feared.
God in Christ has come.
God in Christ has come.

Blessed peace, come to earth
In a child, humbly born,
Who redeems, proclaims our worth,
Comforting the ones who mourn.
God in Christ has come.
God in Christ has come.

Blessed joy, known and shared
As our praise glorifies
God who intervened and cared
For a people some despise.
God in Christ has come.
God in Christ has come.

Blessed light shines around
All who dare see and hear
Miracles in mangers found,
Telling God is always near,
God in Christ has come.
God in Christ has come.

(Luke 2:1–20, Titus 2:11–14)

10

See Salvation Coming

Christmas Day (Proper II)   6.5.6.5.D.
Lavon Bayler   (Cranham)

See salvation coming;
Let the earth rejoice.
God redeems the people,
Giving hope and voice.
In a lowly manger,
Christ is born today;
In this child of promise,
We discern God's way.

Hear the songs of angels,
Bringing joyous news:
God has sent a Savior,
Evil to diffuse.
Shepherds, watching, wond'ring,
See the glorious light,
Hasten to the manger,
Marvel at the sight.

Let us pause to welcome
Love in human form,
Taking time for wonder,
Letting hope transform,
Giving faithful service,
As our souls, renewed,
Live by grace and promise
At the manger viewed.

(Psalm 97, Isaiah 62:6–12, Luke 2:8–20, Titus 3:4–7)

11

Listen! Good News!

Christmas Day (Proper III)　　　　　　　　　　7.6.7.6.6.7.6.
Lavon Bayler　　　　　　　　　　　　　　(Es Ist Ein' Ros')

Listen, good news is coming
From messengers of peace.
God's light and love, returning,
Proclaim that gloom shall cease.
Will we believe good news?
Will we receive a Savior?
Will we God's ways now choose?

Long, long ago the prophets
Spoke judgment on the earth.
Now Christ has come to claim us,
Proclaiming human worth.
Sing to our God a song;
Make joyful noise together!
Night cannot last for long.

Comfort and hope surround us,
Word taking flesh and space.
Christ who, from the beginning,
Reigned, full of truth and grace,
Now seeks to meet us here
To claim us as God's people:
Loved, rescued, saved, brought near.

(Psalm 98, Isaiah 52:7–10, John 1:1–14)

12

Praises We Sing

First Sunday after Christmas
Lavon Bayler

11.10.11.10.
(Morning Star)

Praises we sing to the God of creation,
Praise from the heavens and praise from earth's heights.
Praise for the love that has offered salvation.
Praise for the sun, moon, and stars, God's great lights.

Praise we will offer for glorious redemption.
Praise fills our lips for the One we adore:
Praise from God's children, made whole by adoption,
Praise that in Christ we are heirs evermore.

Praise for the freedom to offer our praises,
Praise that our slav'ry has ended in joy,
Praise for good gifts by which God still amazes,
Praises will ever our voices employ.

Praise in the temple, and praise in the market
Praise in our youth, and when older we grow,
Praise when our hearts are pierced through like a target,
Praise, 'mid our grief, to the God whom we know

Praise God, rejoicing, with glad adoration.
Praise God for faithfulness, though we rebel.
Praise God, assembled, a great congregation.
Praise God who calls us to do all things well.

(Psalm 148, Isaiah 61:10–62:3, Luke 2:12–40, Galatians 4:4–7)

13

How Majestic!

Holy Name (January 1)   8.7.8.7.8.7.
  Lavon Bayler   (Regent Square)

How majestic, Gracious Sovereign,
Is your name in all the earth!
All the heavens reflect your glory;
Moon and stars proclaim your worth.
What are we that you would claim us,
Children whom you bring to birth?

You have crowned our lives with honor;
We are creatures of your care.
You have given us dominion
Over land and sea and air.
In your name, we act as stewards
Who will nurture and repair.

Babes and infants bring renewal,
Speaking truth that we resist.
You would reconcile avengers
At a lowly manger tryst.
Enemies are stilled before you
As their best you, God, enlist.

Bless and keep us in your service.
Shine your light along our way.
You have made us heirs of promise,
Gracious mercy to convey.
We would glorify and praise you,
Sharing good news every day.

(Numbers 6:22–27, Psalm 8, Luke 2:15–21, Galatians 4:4–7)

14

Live for Christ

New Year's Day (January 1)
Lavon Bayler

6.6.7.7.7.8. Ref. (Irregular)
(In Dulci Jubilo)

Rejoice in this new year!
Look forward without fear.
Everything will have its time,
Whether common or sublime.
There's a season to be born
And days will come when we must mourn.
Seek to know God's way;
Live for Christ each day.

Enjoy God's majesty!
Give thanks for all you see.
God who made the heaven and earth
Gives each person special worth,
Grants dominion to our hands,
And bids us love as Christ commands.
Seek to know God's way;
Live for Christ each day.

Accept eternity
As where you want to be.
Even now, within this land,
Learn to live as God has planned,
Serving each and every one
As if, for Christ, 'twas being done.
Seek to know God's way;
Live for Christ each day.

(Psalm 8, Ecclesiastes 3:1–13, Matthew 25:31–46)

15

Word for All Times

Second Sunday after Christmas
Lavon Bayler

10.10.10.10.10.10.
(Yorkshire)

Word for all times, return to us, we pray;
Bring life and light to all who seek Christ's way.
We have been blessed, adopted, and redeemed,
Yet life is not transformed as we had dreamed.
We are not centered in the faith we claim.
Our choices are not made in Jesus' name.

Forgive the doubts we hide behind today,
Recall us when we coldly turn away.
Save us from sins that fragment and destroy;
Help us to find in faithfulness our joy.
Heal us of brokenness we now confess,
That deeds may match the faith that we profess.

Teach us your truth, and lead us in this hour
To live within your grace and claim the power
Granted your children, saved and born anew.
Strengthen the disciplines that we pursue.
Plant in our hearts the peace of Christ, we pray,
That we may, joyously, your word obey.

Singing with gladness songs of faith and praise,
We recommit ourselves to Jesus' ways.
Radiant with hope, we gather to the light
People who want to grow and do what's right.
Lead us in paths made straight by God alone,
And raise us to the best that Christ has shown.

(Psalm 147:12–20, Jeremiah 31:7–14, John 1:1–18, Ephesians 1:3–14)

EPIPHANY AND THE SEASON
FOLLOWING

16

Rise Up and Shine

Epiphany
Lavon Bayler

6.8.6.8. (C.M.)
(Winchester Old)

Rise up and shine; your light has come.
God's glory fills the earth,
And darkness disappears before
The humble Savior's birth.

Behold the star that leads the way:
Your radiant eyes uplift
As trav'lers from afar present
Each strange and precious gift.

In faithfulness they traveled far,
The holy child to greet.
Then, warned by God in dreams, they blocked
King Herod's grim deceit.

The search continues to this day
To find God's gift of life,
To learn the ways that Jesus trod
Amid earth's pomp and strife.

Christ offered hope to needy ones;
The poor, now unafraid,
Could challenge violent control
And seek a Savior's aid.

We, too, are called to witness now
Against oppressor's might.
As saints of God, we're called to change
The world's vast wrongs to right.

(Psalm 72:1–7, 10–14, Isaiah 60:1–6, Matthew 2:1–12, Ephesians 3:1–12)

17

Ascribe to God

First Sunday after Epiphany (Baptism of Jesus)
Lavon Bayler

7.6.7.6.D.
(Angel's Story)

Ascribe to God, O heavens,
The glory due God's name.
Ascribe all strength and splendor,
And shout your glad acclaim.
God's voice, from the beginning,
Created day and night,
And still God is creating
And showing us the light.

O worship God in splendor,
In truth and holiness.
God sends us mighty waters
To baptize and refresh.
In majesty and power,
God reigns through time and space,
And holds the whole creation
Within a warm embrace.

May God give strength to people,
And grant to them true peace.
May those who hear God's message
Continue to increase.
Sing glory, glory, glory
To praise God's majesty.
Awake, O earth, and ponder
New wonders yet to be.

(Genesis 1:1–5, Psalm 29)

18

We Celebrate Baptism

First Sunday after Epiphany (Baptism of Jesus)   8.6.8.6. (C.M.)
     Lavon Bayler   (Serenity)

We celebrate what God has done,
Creating life anew.
You, child, are God's beloved one.
God's favor rests on you.

You have not earned this holy rite
That God is pleased to grant,
But you are precious in God's sight,
And held in covenant.

Our church receives you in its care,
As we our sins confess.
We have not always been aware
Of needs that you possess.

We make our promises today
That we will do our parts
To lead you into Jesus' way
And hold you in our hearts.

We welcome you with arms held wide,
With thanks that God has blessed
The family where you abide,
And places where you rest.

In Jesus' name we greet you now
And seek the Spirit's power,
That God will strengthen every vow,
And bring our faith to flower.

(Mark 1:4–11, Acts 19:1–7)

19

Hear Now the Voice

Second Sunday after Epiphany
Lavon Bayler

10.10.10.10.
(Toulon)

Hear now the voice that calls you from your sleep.
Listen for messages profound and deep.
Open your ears, for God may call your name,
Seeking your full abilities to claim.

God, who has searched you, measures every deed,
Noting if thought and actions match your creed.
You are God's temple, valued, loved and known,
As if God's favor were for you alone.

Live, then, as people who have passed the test,
Guided by Christ to always give your best,
Holding as sacred: body, soul, and mind,
Seeking God's will for all of humankind.

Called as ambassadors for Jesus Christ,
Who, in the cause of love, was sacrificed,
We boldly tell what we have seen and heard,
Sharing with all the world God's holy word.

We are the word that Jesus speaks today.
We are appointed keepers of Christ's way.
Unless the church is faithful in this role,
Many will miss the joy that makes life whole.

(I Samuel 3:3–20, Psalm 139:1–6, 13–18, John 1:43–51, I Corinthians
6:12–20)

20

God, Our Refuge

Third Sunday after Epiphany
Lavon Bayler

8.7.8.7.D.
(Austrian Hymn)

God, our refuge and salvation,
Be to us a fortress strong.
When our world is stressed and shaken,
Save us from the grip of wrong.
Help us listen; help us ponder
Ways that you would have us go.
We await your word in silence,
Seeking now your will to know.

Jesus Christ once called disciples,
Saying, "Come, and follow me."
As we hear that word of challenge,
We are drawn to ministry.
Yet, we hesitate to follow,
Fearing we will not be heard.
How can we announce your judgment?
How can we proclaim your word?

With your steadfast love, surround us.
In your service, help us find
Ways to speak your word of warning
For the sake of humankind.
In this world of passing values,
We your way would represent.
Trusting in your grace and mercy,
We will go where we are sent.

(Psalm 62:5–12, Jonah 3:1–5, 10, Mark 1:14–20, I Corinthians 7:24–31)

21

Raise Up Your Prophets

Fourth Sunday after Epiphany　　　　　　　　14.14.4.7.8.
　　　Lavon Bayler　　　　　　　　　　　　(Lobe den Herren)

Raise up your prophets, O God, to confront our pretensions;
Challenge excuses, to heal and transform our intentions.
Teach us your word,
That your desires may be heard
Now, in their fullest dimensions.

May what we learn today be to us all so enthralling,
That we will dare to respond with delight to our calling.
As we are taught,
Shape every action and thought,
Your perfect wisdom installing.

Hear now our thanks as we gather as your congregation,
Joining our voices in joy, and in great exultation,
Praising your deeds,
Knowing you meet all our needs,
With your divine affirmation.

Living in covenant, given a good understanding,
We will rejoice in the faithfulness you are commanding.
Let what we say
Never lead others astray,
As you their trust are expanding. Amen.

(Deuteronomy 18:15–20, Psalm 111, Mark 1:21–28, 1 Corinthians
8:1–13)

22

Have You Not Known?

Fifth Sunday after Epiphany
Lavon Bayler

8.6.8.6.D. (C.M.D.)
(All Saints New)

Have you not known? Have you not heard?
Our God reigns over all!
This life, created by the Word,
Is subject to God's call.
No weariness will overtake
The One who knows us well,
And God will nevermore forsake,
But lead us to excel.

All praise to God, we sing today,
As by a healing touch,
Our wickedness is wiped away,
And we are given much.
We will not boast in what is ours,
But share it with the rest,
Extolling Jesus' saving powers
And giving of our best.

Commissioned to proclaim and teach
The gospel we have heard,
We pray you, God: inspire our speech
And let our hearts be stirred.
Teach us the discipline of prayer,
That we may be prepared
To pass along the love and care
That you, in Christ, declared.

(Psalm 147:1–11, 20c, Isaiah 40:21–31, Mark 1:29–39, 1 Corinthians
9:16–23)

23

We Cry for Help

Sixth Sunday after Epiphany
Lavon Bayler

8.8.8.8. (L.M.)
(Canonbury)

We cry for help, O God, to you,
For you have healed and made us whole.
Restore us to a larger view
When we have failed to meet your goal.

You teach us simple ways to cleanse
The stains of sin that we may live
As members, not as aliens,
Among the people you forgive.

When we reject what you command,
Recall us to your better way,
That we may hear and understand,
Accept your leading, and obey.

We seek to run the race of life,
With discipline and self-control.
You overcome our pain and strife;
May we your glorious name extol.

We'll sing your praise and spread the word
Of wholeness that your love imparts.
We'll share good news that we have heard
And raise to you our thankful hearts.

(2 Kings 5:1–14, Psalm 30, Mark 1:40–45, 1 Corinthians 9:24–27)

24

Your Chosen People

Seventh Sunday after Epiphany   7.6.7.6.D.
Lavon Bayler   (Aurelia)

Your chosen people praise you,
O God of all the earth.
We worship and adore you
For showing us our worth.
Your love protects and heals us
When we are sick and lost.
You challenge us to service,
Whatever that may cost.

Your faithfulness has led us;
Your Spirit fills our hearts.
Your love sustains us daily,
And hopefulness imparts.
You call our lives to newness;
You give us strength to face
Life's trials with assurance
That foes cannot erase.

We bring our friends to meet you,
To find your healing power,
To know their sins forgiven,
Their virtues brought to flower.
May all of us together
Link efforts, in your name,
To bring your new day closer
And celebrate your reign. Amen.

(Psalm 41, Isaiah 43:18–25, Mark 2:1–12, 2 Corinthians 1:18–22)

25

Jesus Said, Follow Me

Eighth Sunday after Epiphany
Lavon Bayler

6.4.6.4.D.
(Bread of Life)

Jesus said, "Follow me,"
Go where I go.
Question and learn from me,
God's way to know
I welcome one and all,
Calling by name
All who, in covenant,
God's will proclaim.

Sinners were welcome where
Jesus was guest.
All those who needed help,
By Christ were blessed.
Ones who professed their need,
Though they had strayed,
When Jesus touched their lives,
Found hope and aid.

Jesus still calls today,
"Come, follow me!"
Be my disciples now;
Help others see.
Mercy and grace abound
Within God's care.
We are Christ's letters now,
God's truth to share.

(Psalm 103:1–13, Mark 2:13–22, 2 Corinthians 3:1–6)

26

This Sabbath Day

Ninth Sunday after Epiphany
Lavon Bayler

8.4.8.4.8.4.
(Wentworth)

This Sabbath day we gather here
To praise your name.
We sing aloud to God our strength,
With glad acclaim.
All power comes from you alone,
Through years the same.

We raise our songs with voices full
Of love and joy
That persecution, pain, or death
Cannot destroy.
The trumpet, harp, and tambourine
Our praise employ.

The rules we make are in your hands,
And you alone
Can judge and measure faithfulness,
And how we've grown.
We want to follow in the way
That Christ has shown.

Go with us to our journey's end
And fill our days
With glory in the face of Christ
To teach love's ways.
May we be lights to all we meet,
Their spirits raise.

(Deuteronomy 5:12–15, Psalm 81:1–10, Mark 2:23–3:6, 2 Corinthians
4:5–12)

27

In Dazzling Array

Last Sunday after Epiphany (Transfiguration)
Lavon Bayler

11.11.11.11.
(St. Denio)

In dazzling array, Christ is lifted above
Life's everyday sojourn to dwell in God's love.
Disciples see visions of prophets, long known,
As Jesus, transfigured, is viewed as God's own.

Elijah and Moses share wisdom and light
With Jesus, soon hidden by clouds from friends' sight.
Another voice summons their listening ears:
Give heed to my Chosen Ones; lay aside fears.

Transformed by their vision, yet told not to speak,
Christ's followers climbed down the mountain to seek
New meaning and purpose in each day's events,
As doubts and resistance became more intense.

The mantle would fall on their shoulders one day,
To share with the world the intent of Christ's way.
The light they had seen would empower them to lead
A movement of love that would grow and succeed.

And so we are gathered in covenant grace,
Appointed as leaders now setting the pace
For churches to grow in response to God's care,
While sharing the Gospel's good news everywhere.

(2 Kings 2:1–12, Psalm 50:1–6, Mark 9:2–9, 2 Corinthians 4:3–6)

THE LENTEN SEASON

28

Merciful and Loving One

Ash Wednesday
Lavon Bayler

7.8.7.8.8.8.
(Liebster Jesu)

Merciful and Loving One,
God, whose search for us is endless:
We confess the wrong we've done
And the ways that we are careless.
Wash away our great transgression
In this holy Lenten season.

We have broken faith with you,
Lied to self and cheated others.
Cleanse our hearts and make us new,
Reconciled as sisters, brothers.
Come among this congregation
With the joy of your salvation.

Heal us as your grace imparts
Truthfulness within our being.
Teach us wisdom in our hearts
To discern the love we're seeing.
All around, your Spirit meets us,
Reconciles and warmly greets us.

Guide us in self-discipline
That will draw us ever nearer
To our Holy Origin,
Making your intention clearer.
We would fast and pray, while giving
All our best in gracious living. Amen.

(Joel 2:1–2, 12–17, Psalm 51:1–17, Matthew 6:1–7, 16–21,
2 Corinthians 5:20b–6:10)

29

To You, O God

First Sunday in Lent
Lavon Bayler

10.10.10.10.
(Morecombe)

To you, O God, we lift our souls in trust.
Make us to know your ways as we repent.
Your love is steadfast and your judgments just.
Lead us along your paths of truth this Lent.

We have been tempted in the wilderness,
Wandering far from all the best we've known.
You have observed the ways that we transgress;
Our many sins are known to you alone.

Make your salvation real to us again.
Help us to face the wrong that we have done.
We are, in Christ, no longer alien,
And, by your grace, our healing has begun.

On every hand are symbols of your care.
All living creatures join in songs of praise.
After the clouds and storms, your bow is there,
Lifting our hopes for all our nights and days.

Living by mercy in your covenant,
We seek to learn and do what's good and right.
Baptized and blessed, we ask you now to grant
Life in it fullness in your realm of light.

(Genesis 9:8–17, Psalm 25:1–10, Mark 1:9–15, 1 Peter 3:18–22)

30

Praise God Almighty

Second Sunday in Lent
Lavon Bayler

8.8.8.8.8.8.
(Melita)

Praise God Almighty, who has blessed
Earth's people, troubled and oppressed.
God welcomes into covenant
Each seeking, searching supplicant.
All families of the earth, rejoice,
And worship God with heart and voice.

Fear God who rules, and pay your vows,
For we are heirs whom God endows
With promises and grace to stand
Against the sins that mark our land.
Grow strong in faith and fruitfulness,
And live for God, in righteousness.

God feeds our lives with bread and hope
That satisfies us as we cope
With suffering, death, and deep regrets,
Forgiving us our many debts.
We'll walk with God, and not deny
The One whose name we glorify.

We'll set our minds on following
The Savior, through whose suffering,
We learn the love you seek to teach
With deeds, not just through facile speech.
No longer swayed by fears of loss,
For Christ, we dare to risk the cross.

(Genesis 17:1–7, 15–16, Psalm 22:23–31, Mark 8:31–38,
Romans 4:13–25)

31

The Heavens Shout

Third Sunday in Lent
Lavon Bayler

6.6.8.6.S.M.
(Festal Song)

The heavens shout your praise
And glory, night and day;
The firmament, O God, proclaims
Your true and righteous way.

The sun its journey takes
Across the heavens above,
Like those who run their course with joy,
And celebrate your love.

There is no speech nor words,
And yet their voice goes out
Through all the earth to every land,
Addressing fear and doubt.

Your perfect love, O God,
Revives our hearts and souls.
Your precepts make the simple wise,
And redefine our goals.

Reveal our hidden faults,
And help us recognize
The clear intent of your commands,
Enlightening our eyes.

May all our thoughts, O God,
And words that we express
Be blameless and acceptable,
As you redeem and bless.

(Psalm 19)

32

Celebrate God's Power

Third Sunday in Lent   7.7.7.7.7.7.
Lavon Bayler   (Redhead No. 76)

Celebrate God's power to save
Through the message of the cross,
Where the guidance Jesus gave
Seemed at first a bitter loss.
What appears as foolishness
Has the strength to free and bless.

Take away the market place
And the money changer's stalls.
Let them not Christ's church disgrace;
Listen as the Savior calls.
This shall be a house of prayer,
Spreading justice everywhere.

We may struggle and debate;
We may look for signs and proof.
But it is on Christ we wait;
We cannot remain aloof.
There are choices to be made,
Actions we cannot evade.

What seems weakness on the cross,
Still the power of love contains.
Evil always leads to loss,
While God's foolishness remains.
There is life in sacrifice
Jesus gladly paid the price.

(John 2:13–22, I Corinthians 1:18–25)

33

Giving Thanks

Fourth Sunday in Lent
Lavon Bayler

8.7.8.7.D.
(Beecher)

Giving thanks, redeemed from trouble,
We, your people, gather here.
With your steadfast love, surround us,
God, whose care is ever near.
You have fed us, healed our sickness,
Met us in our deep distress,
Save us now from self-destruction;
Draw us near to calm and bless.

We admit our grim impatience
When the wilderness seems long,
When we wander, drained of purpose,
Facing days and nights of wrong.
Following the world's distractions
Brings no comfort that abides.
Dead through sin, we reach for mercy
That your love in Christ provides.

May your light expose the evil
That so often lurks within.
Come, forgive us, and deliver
All your children from their sin.
We would sacrifice to thank you,
As your peace expands our powers.
Raise us up with Christ in glory;
Let eternal life be ours. Amen.

(Numbers 21:4–9, Psalm 107:1–3, 17–22, John 3:14–21,
Ephesians 2:1–10)

34

Living in Covenant

Fifth Sunday in Lent
Lavon Bayler

6.4.6.4.6.6.6.4.
(Bethany)

Living in covenant,
God's law within,
We come for mercy, and
Pardon from sin.
Wash our iniquity;
Heal each infirmity.
Purge us and make us clean,
Freedom to win.

Your judgments, God, are fair
And justified.
Yet, you forgive and bless,
Cleansing inside.
No longer crushed by sin,
Freed from the guilt within,
We seek your presence now;
With us abide.

We seek to know you, God,
Deep in our hearts.
Teach us the truth, we pray,
That Love imparts.
Let joy and gladness reign,
Our willing spirits sustain,
As your salvation grants
Life-giving starts.

(Psalm 51:1–12, Jeremiah 31:31–34)

35

Draw Us Closer

Fifth Sunday in Lent
Lavon Bayler

8.7.8.7.
(Galilee)

Draw us closer to your glory,
Jesus Christ, that we may see
Truth that we have long excluded
From our daily registry.

In your prayer and supplications,
Through your tears and cries of pain,
You persisted on life's journey,
Confident that God will reign.

You have taught a simple gospel:
Only grains that fall to earth
Know that death is not an ending
But a glorious new rebirth.

Help us view obedient service
As the path you chose to take.
Putting love before your safety,
You have suffered for our sake.

We would follow where you lead us,
In your service find our way,
Risking all for love of neighbor,
Your example to obey.

Grant us life in all its fullness,
As we glorify God's name
May your church reflect your spirit,
And your purposes proclaim. Amen.

(John 12:20–33, Hebrews 5:5–10)

36

Prepare Us, God

Sixth Sunday in Lent (Passion Sunday)   8.6.8.6.D. (C.M.D.)
          Lavon Bayler   (Old 22nd)

Prepare us, God, for Holy Week,
To walk with Christ each day.
We trust in you to give us strength
To follow Jesus' way.
Whether anointed or betrayed,
Your Chosen One was true;
May we in covenant abide,
And worship only you.

We break the bread and share the cup,
Rememb'ring all Christ gave.
As we partake, we give you thanks
That Jesus came to save.
When we desert and run away,
And focus on our loss,
Lead us to stay awake and pray,
Lest we reject the cross.

Grant us the courage to resist
The pow-ers that deny.
Keep us from shouting with the crowd:
"Condemn and crucify."
When darkness comes, and all is still,
And Jesus breathes his last,
Fill us with hope that overcomes
Death's cruel and evil blast. Amen.

(Psalm 31:9–16, Mark 14:1–15:47)

37

We Sing Hosanna

Sixth Sunday in Lent (Palm Sunday)
Lavon Bayler

7.6.7.6.D.
(Webb)

We sing our loud hosannas
To welcome Christ today.
God's steadfast love surrounds us
Each step along the way.
The gates are flung wide open
As crowds their tribute raise:
"Hosanna in the highest!"
Our Savior's name we praise.

A lowly, peaceful donkey
Bears Jesus through the throng
Of joyous, shouting people
Who sing their vict'ry song:
Rejoice in God's anointed
Who claims us as God's own,
And offers us salvation
Through Christ, the cornerstone.

May we who seek to follow
Be emptied of false pride,
And take the form of servants,
With boundless love supplied.
Throughout our lives, rejoicing
In days that God provides,
We give our humble thanks, and
Obey, as Jesus guides. Amen.

(Psalm 118:1–2, 19–29, Mark 11:1–11, Philippians 2:5–11)

38

Fountain of Life

Monday of Holy Week
Lavon Bayler

8.8.8.8. (L.M.)
(Maryton)

Fountain of life, we see your light,
Shining in Christ, our souls' delight.
Teach us to follow Jesus' way
That leads from night to endless day.

How precious is your steadfast love,
That opens eyes to things above,
That sets imprisoned people free
And lets us all your glory see.

Your righteousness, like mountains high,
Judgments in depths that clarify
Meanings beyond our human reach,
We seek to emulate and teach.

Keep us in covenant, made new
In Christ, whose love was ever true.
Whose spirit was not crushed by pain,
But firmly cried: Let justice reign!

Come, Great High Priest, and take our hands.
Lead us to witness through the lands,
Giving our best, whate'er the cost,
To share your word and find the lost.

(Psalm 36:5–11, Isaiah 42:1–9, John 12:1–11, Hebrews 9:11–15)

39

The Message of the Cross

Tuesday of Holy Week
Lavon Bayler

8.7.8.7.D.
(Bishopgarth)

The message of the cross is heard
As foolishness to many.
They perish in their doubts and fears,
Or arrogance or envy.
How oft' are we among their ranks,
Avoiding change or danger!
Incline your ear and rescue us,
Lest we meet Christ as stranger.

The message of the cross is power
To those whom God is saving.
God's foolishness seems wise to them;
God's presence they are craving.
We wish to join them in their quest
To find a rock and fortress.
Deliver us from vanity,
Lest we remain in darkness.

The message of the cross conveys
Christ's sweeping invitation:
Come, follow now, and serve with me,
Whate'er your race or nation.
Continue walking in the light,
Lest enemies alarm us.
Come, live with hope that conquers death,
For evil cannot harm us.

(Psalm 71:1–14, Isaiah 49:1–7, John 12:20–36, I Corinthians 1:18–31)

40

Wakened by Your Word

Wednesday of Holy Week
Lavon Bayler

8.7.8.7.
(Rathbun)

Wakened by your word of comfort,
We are open to receive
Truth that challenges and strengthens
Our intentions to achieve.

We would challenge those who question
How the cross can be our friend,
For the sin that clings so closely
Finds in Christ its welcomed end.

Look to Jesus, who is faithful,
Pioneering ways that win.
As we run the race before us,
Jesus guards our path from sin.

Christ is making haste to help us,
Saving lives along the way,
Lifting up each weary traveler,
Leading toward life's better day.

Let us, therefore, stand together
Through these days of suffering.
Come, rejoice, in spite of troubles.
Bring to Christ your offering.

(Psalm 70, Isaiah 50:4–9a, John 13:21–32, Hebrews 12:1–3)

41

Christ Invites

Holy Thursday
Lavon Bayler

6.6.8.6.D. (S.M.D.)
(Leominster)

The love of Christ invites
Our presence at the feast.
Come, lift salvation's cup tonight,
That faith may be increased.
Receive what God supplies
And let no one betray.
Receive instead transforming power
That leads to God's new day.

As Jesus washed the feet
Of followers and friends,
We're taught humility and care
That God in Christ intends.
To take the servant role
Will help us understand
The way that loving sacrifice
Embraces heart and hand.

At table with the Christ,
We wait for bread and cup.
A new life-giving covenant
Now beckons us to sup.
We seek, as we are fed,
To live by Christ's command
To love, in full discipleship,
As God in Christ has planned.

(Psalm 116:1–2, 12–19, John 13:1–7, 31b–35, I Corinthians 11:23–26)

42

Come to the Garden

Good Friday
Lavon Bayler

8.6.8.6. (C.M.)
(Beatitudo)

Come to the garden where Christ prayed;
Meet the disciples here.
Watch while the Savior is betrayed
And friends escape in fear.

Notice as soldiers and police
Bind and arrest their prey.
No one remains to seek release
As Christ is led away.

Stand by the fire to overhear
Peter deny the claim
That he is one whom Christ holds dear,
The rock of faith, by name.

Share Peter's guilty memory,
Hearing the rooster crow,
Facing the growing certainty
Of no safe place to go.

Pilate has asked, "Are you a king?"
And Jesus testifies
Of realms beyond our reckoning
That God alone supplies.

Finally the hill where all seems lost,
And Christ is crucified,
Challenges us to face the cost
Of human sin and pride.

(John 18:1–19:42)

43

Life Ebbs Away

Holy Saturday
Lavon Bayler

4.8.4.8.
(Golgotha)

Life ebbs away;
We meet in sad distress today.
All mortals die,
Including One they crucify.

Fear seals the tomb,
Since many have for Christ no room.
Jesus is dead,
Yet there is hope for those he led.

Suff'ring for us,
Christ Jesus raises consciousness.
Love is the way,
The only way to God's new day.

Save us, we pray;
Incline your ear to us today.
Our time is yours,
And what is done for Christ endures.

Let hope abound;
The acts of God will yet astound
All gathered here.
Christ will arise! Our help is near! Amen.

(Job 14:1–14, Psalm 31:1–4, 15–16, Matthew 27:57–66, I Peter 4:1–8)

THE EASTER SEASON

44

At the Tomb

Easter Sunday
Lavon Bayler

8.7.8.7.D.
(Hymn to Joy)

Join us at the tomb this morning,
Seeking Christ, the crucified.
Pay respects to One who loved us,
Honoring the One who died.
Feel amazement as you enter,
For the stone is rolled away.
Sitting there is one who tells us:
Jesus lives! Rejoice today!

Filled with terror and amazement,
We know not what we should do,
No disciples will believe us.
How can we believe it's true?
Dare we wipe our tear-stained faces,
Filled with faith that changes lives?
Has God swallowed death forever?
Will we all in Christ arise?

Turn us to the light, dear Savior,
That our joy may be complete.
In our fellowship with Jesus,
Let us every neighbor greet.
All the world is your dominion;
All have sinned and need your grace.
You are faithful to forgive us,
As we enter Love's embrace.

(Isaiah 25:6–9, Mark 16:1–8, 1 John 1:1–2:2)

45

Worship the Risen Christ

Easter Sunday
Lavon Bayler

6.6.8.6.D. (S.M.D.)
(Diademata)

Worship the Risen Christ
Who calls each one by name.
Give thanks to God who loves us all,
And chooses to reclaim
Our loyalty and trust,
And joyous servanthood.
This is the day that God has made,
And we have found it good.

We will believe and trust
The message we receive.
Refit us for apostleship,
That may, in Christ, achieve
Glad victories of love
That cause the world to sing.
O, help us grow in faithfulness
And patient shepherding.

God is our strength and might;
Salvation is God's gift.
God's work in Christ is marvelous,
Our spirits to uplift.
God's grace is not in vain,
For we are filled with power
To heal and witness in Christ's name,
Beginning in this hour.

(Psalm 118:1–2, 14–24, John 20:1–18, Acts 10:34–43,
I Corinthians 15:1–11)

Hymns for the Easter Season

46

We Celebrate Tonight

Easter Evening
Lavon Bayler

11.10.11.10.9.11.
(Tidings)

We celebrate tonight in awe and wonder,
Singing the songs of joyous victory.
You, God, have given much for us to ponder,
As we remember Jesus' ministry
Hearts burn within us; feelings are stirred,
As Christ awakens our int'rest in your word.

Many a question fills our conversation;
We are surprised by all that we have heard.
After the agony of crucifixion
Spirits were crushed, and vision badly blurred
Then came the news that all was not lost;
Love won a vict'ry that sin could not exhaust.

You have removed the shroud of death and evil,
Wiping our tears, and lifting our disgrace.
Jesus has conquered every human peril,
Giving us courage for the tasks we face.
May your salvation fill us with joy:
Springs overflowing that nothing can destroy.

We have not seen, and yet we trust the message:
Christ is alive and walking with us still.
Whether alone or in a vast assemblage,
We can draw close and seek to know your will.
Free us from malice day after day,
That truth may triumph in all we do and say.

(Psalm 114, Isaiah 25:6–9, Luke 24:13–49, 1 Corinthians 5:6b–8)

47

Behind Locked Doors

Second Sunday of Easter
Lavon Bayler

10.10.10.10.10.
(Old 124th)

Behind locked doors, disciples met in fear.
Mourning the leader who had brought God near.
Then Jesus came and stood among them there,
Calming their dread and making them aware:
Death cannot void the ways that love makes clear.

Fear not, for I have come to bring you peace.
Let all dissension still among you cease.
As God has sent me, I commission you:
Go to the world to tell of love so true
That you, from sin, may find a sure release.

Joy was contagious, yet some lived in doubt.
They had not seen what others talked about,
Nor were we there to see the Risen One.
Shall we believe what God in Christ has done?
Jesus invites us to a life devout.

Those who believed became one heart and soul;
Living for Jesus Christ became their goal.
Blessed in their new-found unity, they shared
All that they owned with those for whom they cared.
Like them, we pray that God will make us whole.

(Psalm 133, John 20:19–31, Acts 4:32–35, I John 1:1–2:2)

48

Holy and Righteous One

Third Sunday of Easter
Lavon Bayler

6.5.6.5.6.6.6.5.
(St. Dunstan's)

Holy and Righteous One,
Jesus, our Savior,
Pardon what we have done;
Turn our behavior
Toward honest faithfulness
That will your name confess,
Knowing how much you bless
Us with your favor.

Come to us when we fall,
Needy and goal-less;
Answer us when we call
In stress and lowness.
We put our trust in you,
Knowing you'll see us through.
With love forever true,
Grant strength and wholeness.

When fears and doubts arise,
Stand here among us.
Come with your fresh surprise
Where life has flung us.
Children of God, we reach
For love and peace you teach.
Live now, with all and each,
To energize us. Amen.

(Psalm 4, Luke 24:36b–48, Acts 3:12–19, 1 John 3:1–7)

49

You Follow Us, God

Fourth Sunday of Easter
Lavon Bayler

12.11.12.11.
(Kremser)

You follow us, God, with your goodness and mercy.
Each day of our lives we are under your care.
You lead by still waters the ones who are thirsty.
You show us steadfast love and make us aware.

Your people are scattered, in need of a shepherd,
For we have not followed the paths you provide.
We dwell in our sickness; our deep wounds have festered.
Come now to bring us healing; stay by our side.

You bind up our wounds as we pass through dark valleys.
You keep us from evil that threatens our days.
When we are discouraged, Christ heartens and rallies
Our courage to rebound, our boldness to raise.

Receiving whatever we ask is the promise
To all who would follow your loving commands.
When we seek to please you, with Christ our accomplice,
You dwell within our hearts; our service expands.

In Christ, we are gathered for learning and action
To listen for truth reassuring our hearts.
Together, away from life's daily distractions,
We seek to grow in love your Spirit imparts.

(Psalm 23, John 10:11–18, Acts 4:5–12, 1 John 3:16–24)

50

Beloved of God

Fifth Sunday of Easter
Lavon Bayler

8.6.8.6.D. (C.M.D.)
(St. Matthew)

Beloved of God, redeemed and healed,
Come now to sing your praise.
Come, pay your vows and grow in trust,
For God will guide your ways.
Seek now the word of truth and power
That brings good news to birth.
Let justice reign and peace expand
To cover all the earth.

Each generation claims anew
The promises fulfilled
In Christ who came to earth to save,
Community to build.
Let congregations near and far
Know love that casts out fear,
That we may claim our kinship ties
And know that God is near.

Christ is the vine from whom we take
Our energy and zeal.
We are the branches, bearing fruit,
That will our faith reveal.
Disciples we are called to be,
To glorify God's name.
May we abide in Jesus' word
By making love our aim. Amen.

(Psalm 22:25–31, John 15:1–8, Acts 8:26–40, I John 4:7–21)

51

Holy Spirit, Come

Sixth Sunday of Easter
Lavon Bayler

8.7.8.7.8.8.7.7.
(Darmstadt)

Holy Spirit, come among us;
Lift our hearts in joyous song.
We would join the heavenly chorus,
Praising you the whole day long.
You are ever our defender,
And in steadfast love remember,
All your children everywhere
Who receive your watchful care.

Every nation is included
In the love that you command.
No one is to be excluded
From the joy that you have planned.
We will celebrate with singing
Righteous judgments you are bringing.
We'll raise trumpets, sound the horn;
May your love in us be born.

We are servants of the Savior,
Who has called us friends instead,
Showing love in our behavior,
That your reign may grow and spread.
We are chosen and appointed
To bear fruit as your anointed
Messengers with truth to share,
That we lovingly declare.

(Psalm 98, John 15:9–17, Acts 10:44–48, I John 5:1–6)

52

In Awe before God

Ascension Day (or Seventh Sunday of Easter) 8.8.8.8.D. (L.M.D.)
Lavon Bayler (He Leadeth Me)

In awe before our God Most High,
We gather here to make reply
To all that you, O God, have done
To give us hope and make us one.
We'll clap our hands and shout for joy,
Our thoughts and energies employ,
In thanking you and giving praise,
While practicing your loving ways.

We pray for wisdom to discern
The truth that you would have us learn.
Speak to our minds and warm our hearts
With fervor that your love imparts.
With eyes enlightened, strength renewed,
Our doubts allayed and fears subdued,
We seek, as saints in Christ, to do
Those things that will our faith renew.

Instruct us now to heed your word,
That we may share the things we've heard.
Direct us by your Spirit's power
That this may be a healing hour.
Establish in our church your reign,
That we may live as you ordain.
Your witnesses we seek to be,
That all may know your sovereignty. Amen.

(Psalm 47, Luke 24:44–53, Acts 1:1–11, Ephesians 1:15–23)

53

Happy Are the Chosen

Seventh Sunday of Easter
Lavon Bayler

7.7.7.7.D.
(Spanish Hymn)

Happy are the chosen ones
Who decide to concentrate,
Day and night upon God's law,
Taking time to meditate.
Like a tree by quiet streams,
They are fed by waters pure,
Yielding fruits of righteousness
That will prosper and endure.

Evil counsel and deceit,
They avoid with firm intent,
Turning from the scoffer's seat,
Knowing they by God are sent.
Never, as the wicked, blown
Like the chaff upon the wind,
Their delight is serving God,
Off'ring grace to those who sinned.

When, on judgment day, they stand
Confident and unafraid,
They will know their greatest joy,
Praising all that God has made.
As God watches over them,
They will prosper on their way,
Living resurrection faith,
Hearts united as they pray. Amen.

(Psalm 1, John 17:18, Acts 1:21–26)

54

Make Us One

Seventh Sunday of Easter
Lavon Bayler

11.10.11.10.
(Cushman)

Make us one, Jesus; let us be disciples,
Finding eternal life in serving you.
We would be learners, studying our Bibles,
Searching to know the ways forever true.

Make us believers, in your spirit growing,
Finding new ways to trust what we have heard.
We would bear witness to the love you're showing.
Grant us a ministry, in deed and word.

Make us apostles, who will tell the story,
Finding the ageless truths that set us free.
We would be open to the signs of glory,
Ever around us when we dare to see.

Make us examples of the faith we're sharing,
Finding the best in us, despite our sin.
We would extend to everyone your caring,
Seeking their trust and loyalty to win.

Make us true heralds of your resurrection,
Finding new life, O Christ, in every day.
We would be leaders, under your direction,
Giving our best, compassion to display. Amen.

(Psalm 1, John 17:6–19, Acts 1:15–17, 21–26, 1 John 5:9–13)

PENTECOST AND THE SEASON FOLLOWING

55

Pour Out Your Spirit

Pentecost
Lavon Bayler

7.6.7.6.D.
(St. Theodolph)

Pour out your Holy Spirit,
O God, on all who wait,
Here gathered in your presence,
The Church to celebrate.
With tongues of fire descending
And resting over all,
We stand amazed and joyful,
As we your truth recall.

Send hope to meet our doubting,
Your breath to bring us life.
Our bones are bleached and empty,
Dried out by fear and strife.
Your winds around us blowing
Bring promise to inspire
Fresh dreams and stirring visions
That set our hearts on fire.

How manifold the blessings
You give with open hand.
You feed us with abundance
That echoes through the land.
May all we do be pleasing
To you; come search each heart,
And guide our thoughts and actions
By wisdom you impart. Amen.

(Psalm 104:24–34, Ezekiel 37:1–14, John 16:13, Acts 2:1–21,
Romans 8:22–27)

56

Holy, Holy, God of Glory

Trinity Sunday (First Sunday after Pentecost)   8.7.8.7.D.
Lavon Bayler   (Hyfrydol)

Holy, Holy, God of glory,
We, your children, bow in prayer,
Filled with awe before your splendor,
Sensing we are in your care.
Strength and majesty surround us;
Wind and flame declare your power.
Speak your word that we may listen;
Let this be a holy hour.

Born of flesh, with selfish interests,
We confess our guilt and sin.
We are lost in our distractions,
Self-absorbed, unclean within.
Touch our lips and cleanse our spirits;
Put to death our fear and strife.
Take away our slavish passions;
Grant us strength and give new life.

Born of water and the Spirit,
Cleansed and freed, we join in song:
Triune God, our host and savior,
All our lives to you belong.
We will go where you will send us;
We will do what you command.
May our witness bless your people,
Bringing peace to every land.

(Psalm 29, Isaiah 6:1–8, John 3:1–17, Romans 8:12–17)

57

Great Are Your Thoughts

Proper 4
Lavon Bayler

6.6.8.6. (S.M.)
(Trentham)

Great are your thoughts, O God,
By which we've fully known.
You search our paths and see our ways,
And call us as your own.

Before we drew a breath
Our times were in your hands.
Wonderful are your works, O God,
And fair are your demands.

Speak to us, God, today;
We seek to listen well,
And we would praise your holy name,
Your faithfulness to tell.

Lead us to know your light
In Jesus Christ, we pray.
All power on earth belongs to you,
And we are made of clay.

When suff'ring comes our way,
We are not crushed by pain.
When persecuted or struck down,
We do not trust in vain.

We serve the One whose love
Reached out to heal and save.
We seek to follow where Christ leads,
Returning what you gave. Amen.

(1 Samuel 3:1–10, Psalm 139:1–6, 13–18, Mark 2:23–3:6,
2 Corinthians 4:5–12)

58

Out of the Depths

Proper 5   6.6.6.6.8.8.
Lavon Bayler   (Arthur's Seat)

Out of the depths, O God,
We cry with heart and voice.
Give ear to us, we pray,
And help us to rejoice.
Your steadfast love and faithfulness
Reach out each day to save and bless.

Yet often we will flee,
Remorseful and afraid,
Aware of your commands
That we have disobeyed.
But you mark not iniquities
When we repent and seek to please.

Your name we will exalt;
Your glory we will sing.
Your purposes we praise,
As thankfulness we bring.
Our joy abounds and faith expands,
Receiving bounty from your hands.

As we await your word
With hope, throughout our days,
You give us strength of soul
And set our hearts ablaze.
For, through our troubles, you preserve
And bless our lives that we may serve. Amen.

(Genesis 3:8–15, 1 Samuel 8:4–20, Psalms 130 and 138)

59

God, We Believe

Proper 5
Lavon Bayler

10.4.10.4.10.10.
(Sandon)

God, we believe; help now our unbelief,
And hear our cries.
Raise us with Christ, your presence here to know;
Lift up our eyes.
We would behold your glory all around,
That thankfulness may everywhere abound.

We seek your pardon for our blasphemy;
Forgive our sin.
Tend to the broken fragments that reside
So deep within.
Let no divisions in our lives remain
To cramp our health or cause another pain.

Knit us together in your family,
Eternally,
That when we look into another's face,
There Christ we'll see.
Living by grace, we'll seek while life shall last
To live as kin, not noting race or caste.

Wasting away, afflicted and oppressed,
We'll not lose heart.
God will renew our inner nature yet,
And strength impart.
And when this earthly tent in which we live
Remains no more, a new home God will give. Amen.

(Mark 3:20–35, 2 Corinthians 4:13–5:1)

60

Peaceably, We Come

Proper 6
Lavon Bayler

7.7.7.7.
(Seymour)

Peaceably, O God, we come,
Here to worship and adore.
May we view, through eyes of faith,
Truth you ask us to explore.

We have seen, with partial sight,
That which outwardly appears.
You know what is deep within:
Sin and goodness, hopes and fears.

We confess our faithlessness,
Taking pride in things we own,
Worshiping our own success,
Turning from your love alone.

God, forgive our foolish ways,
And receive our sacrifice.
May we feel at home with you,
Daily seeking your advice.

Grant us now those hearts' desires
That your purposes fulfill.
May we please you day by day,
Seeking first your holy will.

All that we regarded once
From a human point of view:
How to live and ways to serve,
Are, in Christ, created new. Amen.

(1 Samuel 15:34–16:13, Psalm 20, 2 Corinthians 5:6–17)

61

We Seek to Know

Proper 6
Lavon Bayler

8.6.8.8.6.
(Rest (Elton))

We seek, O God, to know your reign
Among us here and now.
Plant seeds that burst to life, like grain
In your good soil and sun and rain.
New life in us endow.

We thank you, God, for Christ, who died
That we might truly live.
Before love's judgment seat, we're tried,
That Christ may in our lives abide
And show us how to give.

We walk, O God, by faith not sight,
For everything is new.
The confidence that you invite
Will lead your church to take delight
In Jesus' point of view.

We serve you, God, with thanks and praise;
In steadfast love, we're clad.
May we bear fruit through all our days,
As you continue to amaze.
Your work has made us glad. Amen.

(Psalm 92:1–4, 12–15, Mark 4:26–34, 2 Corinthians 5:6–17)

62

Trust and Hope

Proper 7
Lavon Bayler

11.10.11.10.10.
(Langham)

God, our Creator, helper of the needy,
We sing your praise and celebrate your deeds.
When, in life's storms we call, your help is speedy,
Bidding us follow where your Spirit leads.
We put our trust and hope, O God, in you.

Jesus, our Teacher, by your incarnation,
Sharing our lives and tempted as are we,
Here in God's presence, filled with adoration,
We turn from fear to seek your peace so free.
We put our trust and hope, O Christ, in you.

Come, Holy Spirit, source of inspiration,
Granting endurance, holiness, and grace.
Hear our petitions and our aspiration,
Now to be truthful, all our sins to face.
We put our trust and hope, O Spirit, in you.

Now is the time, the day of our salvation.
Hearts open wide, your healing touch to know.
We are expectant, seeking transformation.
Fill us with faith, that we in love may grow.
We trust and hope in you, O Triune God.

(Psalm 9:9–20, Mark 4:35–41, 2 Corinthians 6:1–13)

63

Rejoice in Faith

Proper 8
Lavon Bayler

8.8.8.8. (L.M.)
(Duke Street)

Rejoice in faith that makes us whole,
Filling with hope each waiting soul.
In steadfast love, we're lifted high
By gifts of grace we cannot buy.

Who will forgive the wrong we've done?
One who, through death, our pardon won.
Jesus the Christ for us was poor,
That our enrichment might be sure.

Let our abundance be for all,
Resource and help for those who call,
Seeking new life, set free from sin.
Come, Holy Spirit; reign within.

We seek the peace that you provide,
God, when our hearts in Christ abide.
Filled with amazement and with joy,
We give ourselves to your employ.

Called to excel in eagerness,
In faith and knowledge to express,
Genuine love and depth of care,
We will, O God, our witness bear.

(Psalm 130, Mark 5:21–43, 2 Corinthians 8:7–15)

64

We Bring Our Weakness

Proper 9
Lavon Bayler

8.6.8.6.D. (C.M.D.)
(Ellacombe)

We bring our weakness, God, to you,
For you can make us strong.
Our needy boasting you subdue,
And turn us from our wrong.
Accept, we pray, our urgent plea
For grace amid our trials.
And, in our blindness, help us see
Beyond the world's denials.

We gather to express our praise,
For you are great and good.
Your works continue to amaze,
Where love is understood.
Our guide and shepherd you have been,
Through journeys that you grant.
Your word equips us deep within
To live in covenant.

You send us out, good news to share
With all the doubting world,
For Christ has taught us how to care
Despite invectives hurled.
We seek not honor or acclaim
But only to extend
The service done in Jesus' name,
More broken lives to mend. Amen.

(2 Samuel 5:1–5, 9–10, Psalm 48, Mark 6:1–13, 2 Corinthians 12:2–10)

65

Lift Up Your Heads

Proper 10
Lavon Bayler

10.10.10.10.
(Langran)

Lift up your heads to see God's glory here.
Be lifted up to know that help is near.
God, our Creator, meets us on this day,
And dwells where'er we go along life's way.

All of the earth is God's, and all within
Receive God's blessing still, in spite of sin.
Come, for salvation waits for those who yearn
Daily Christ's new and better ways to learn.

Cleanse now our hands and purify our hearts,
God, our Creator, as your love imparts
Pardon and promise and your governance
Within the pledge of our inheritance.

We are God's people, chosen and redeemed,
Loved and forgiven, counseled and esteemed.
Within the myst'ry of your holy will,
We set our hope in Christ, among us still.

Joining in songs of longing and of praise,
We seek to share your word through all our days.
Fill us with truth, your gospel to proclaim,
Sending us out to serve in Jesus' name. Amen.

(Psalm 24, Ephesians 1:3–14)

66

Come Rest Awhile

Proper 11
Lavon Bayler

7.6.8.6.8.6.8.6.
(St. Christopher)

Come, rest awhile with Jesus;
Come, take the time to pray.
We gather here to worship one
Whose word we would obey.
God's steadfast love and faithfulness
Upholds us day by day.
We celebrate the covenant
That leads us in truth's way.

Come, build the church with Jesus
Who bids our conflicts cease.
We work to end hostility
And form a world at peace.
Christ came to reconcile us all
To God, and friends and foes.
We are no longer strangers here
As hope within us grows.

Come, join the saints in service
To all humanity.
Go out to share good news of Christ
That makes for unity.
Live out the reign of righteousness,
God's goodness to unveil.
God sends us forth to teach love's way,
That justice may prevail. Amen.

(2 Samuel 7:1–14a, Psalm 89:20–37, Mark 6:30–34, 53–56,
Ephesians 2:11–22)

67

To God Be Glory

Proper 12
Lavon Bayler

6.6.6.6. Ref.
(Need) (was 6.4.6.4. Ref.)

We bow our knees before
The One whom we adore,
For God, our origin,
Now strengthens us within.

Refrain
To God be all the glory,
In our work and worship
We thank the One who offers
Us partnership.

While foolish ones proclaim,
"There is no God to name.
It does no good to pray."
We here rejoice to say:
Refrain

We ask that you will feed
And heal us in our need.
Forgive and purify,
Our gifts to multiply.
Refrain

Come, dwell within our hearts
With love your grace imparts
Give power to comprehend
The messages you send.
Refrain

(Psalm 14, John 6:1–21, Ephesians 3:14–21)

68

O God of Mercy

Proper 13
Lavon Bayler

8.6.8.6.D. (C.M.D.)
(Geneve)

O God of mercy, meet us here,
As we confess our sin.
According to your steadfast love,
Come, wash us deep within.
Against you only have we sinned
In harming self and friends.
Our self-indulgence and deceit
Your righteous will offends.

Create in us clean hearts, O God,
And let your Spirit reign.
Blot out our grave iniquities
And make us whole again.
Restore the joy that once we knew
Within our secret hearts,
And plant your truth in every life
As selfishness departs.

Before your presence, we rejoice
That love is paramount
As you forgive and rescue us,
Yet call us to account.
You teach your wisdom day by day
To those who listen well.
You help us do the good we know,
That we your truth might tell. Amen.

(2 Samuel 11:26–12:31a, Psalm 51:1–12)

69

Come, Bread of Life

Proper 13
Lavon Bayler

11.11.11.6.
(Integer Vitae (Fleming))

Come, bread of life, to feed our needy spirits.
Give us the food and drink that marks your visits.
Transform our thinking and our daily habits.
Grant us your grace, we pray.

Help us to lead lives worthy of your calling,
Growing in patience, gentleness installing.
May we, in love, bear one another's falling.
Grant us fresh hope, we pray.

Make us disciples, list'ning, learning, daring.
Make us apostles who your word are sharing.
May we be Christ-like in our daily caring.
Grant us true strength, we pray.

Make us one body, faithful in our service.
From fear or pridefulness, O God, preserve us.
Let no attack or trickery unnerve us.
Grant us humility.

Unite our spirits, growing in Christ's image.
Let not adversity our faith discourage.
One in our baptism, growing in your knowledge,
Grant us maturity. Amen.

(John 6:24–35, Ephesians 4:1–16)

70

Out of Our Need

Proper 14
Lavon Bayler

6.4.6.4.6.6.4.4.
(Love's Offering)

Out of our need, we cry, O God to you.
Hear voices lifted high, hope to renew.
Waiting and watching here,
Seeking to know you're near,
We cry to you. We cry to you.

If you, O God, should mark iniquities.
Who, God, could stand, or seek your ways to please?
But you forgive our sin,
Cleansing us deep within.
We cry to you. We cry to you.

Help us to speak the truth to friend or foe.
May we do honest work where'er we go.
Turning from bitterness
To tender-heartedness,
We praise your name. We praise your name.

Christ is the bread of life, in whom we trust,
Who for eternity dwells with the just.
Grant us such grace, we pray,
That each and every day
We may forgive. We may forgive. Amen.

(Psalm 130, John 6:35, 41–51, Ephesians 4:25–5:2)

71

We Thank You, God

Proper 15
Lavon Bayler

8.6.8.6. (C.M.)
(Winchester Old)

We thank you, God, with hearts made whole
Through love that you provide.
All life is under your control,
And we in you abide.

How great the works and wondrous deeds
That show your majesty!
You faithfully supply our needs
And teach us honesty.

You grant to us discerning minds
To know which deeds are right,
And here your church, in worship, finds
The precepts that unite.

We live within your covenant,
With wisdom you supply,
And riches more significant
Than things for which some die.

We have a goodly heritage
By which our days are blessed,
That even in this present age
Our lives can pass love's test.

(I Kings 3:3–14, Psalm 111)

72

Grant Us Bread

Proper 15
Lavon Bayler

6.4.6.4.6.6.6.4.
(St. Edmund)

Grant us the bread of life.
O God, we pray.
Feed us with Jesus' words
Day after day,
And, in the Word-made-flesh,
May we begin afresh,
Each morning to proclaim
Your holy name.

Help us to understand
Your perfect will,
That we may live with care,
Good to fulfill.
When evil stalks our days,
And sin denies your ways,
Lead us away from wrong
To sing your song.

Keep us from foolish ways
That may abuse
Gifts you have given us;
Help us to choose
Life that is Spirit-filled,
Thankful that you have willed
Our efforts to employ,
Sharing true joy. Amen.

(John 6:51–58, Ephesians 5:15–20)

73

By Your Word

Proper 16
Lavon Bayler

10.11.9.11.9.10.
(Harre Meine Seele)

By your word of promise, keep covenant,
God of all the nations, steadfast love to grant.
No house we build ever can contain
All your sacred truth or fully show your reign.
All earth and heaven rest in your care,
And your gracious presence is everywhere.

We, your servants, long to walk where you lead,
With our hearts wide open, your commands to heed.
Hear all our prayers, spoken or unsaid;
Grant us your forgiveness, saving us from dread.
In awe and wonder, we spread the word:
"God is ever faithful; our cries are heard!"

Happy are your servants, singing your praise,
Joyfully, together, as your deeds amaze.
Great is your name, and your mighty hand
Draws your wandering people to your promised land,
Where, in your arms, we find our abode
And the gentle Spirit that shares our load.

People faint with longing to know the joy
Of your gracious favor nothing can destroy.
We put our trust in your holy word;
May it spread forever, 'til good news is heard
In every corner where people dwell.
May we always honor and serve you well. Amen.

(1 Kings 8:22–30, 41–43, Psalm 84)

74

We Receive God's Promise

Proper 16   8.7.8.7.D.
Lavon Bayler   (Beecher)

We receive God's gracious promise,
As we put our armor on,
That we may withstand all evil,
Whether in the dark or dawn.
Gird the belt of truth around you;
Seek the reign of righteousness.
Take the shield of faith to guard you
Through life's journey perilous.

With the helmet of salvation,
And the Spirit as your sword,
Put on shoes to spread the gospel,
That God's peace may be restored.
Standing firm amid detractors,
Share the word you have received,
And with prayer and supplication,
Grow in all you have believed.

Take the bread and cup with pleasure,
That you may forever live,
Knowing Christ as friend and mentor,
Who will teach you to forgive.
Choose this day to serve with valor,
With the energy of youth.
God, who rescues you from bondage,
Grants sincerity and truth. Amen.

(Joshua 24:14–18, John 6:56–69, Ephesians 6:10–20)

75

Author of Lights

Proper 17
Lavon Bayler

8.8.8.8. (L.M.)
(Germany)

Author of Lights, your word abides
Where truth is held in rev'rent awe,
Where your commandments serve as guides,
And liberty is found in law.

Hearts overflow with gratitude
For your abiding presence here,
Where grace is giv'n and vows renewed,
And love erases hate and fear.

The oil of gladness overflows,
And music stirs our waiting souls.
We seek to do as you propose,
Not merely name some far-off goals.

Wipe out the evil deep inside
That may distort our high intent.
Remove our stubborn, selfish pride,
That we may go where we are sent.

We would arise to serve you well,
Bringing our best, first fruits to give.
As you our wrongful thoughts dispel,
We find in Christ the way to live.

(Psalm 45:1–2, 6–9, Song of Songs 2:8–13, Mark 7:1–8, 14–15, 21–23,
James 1:17–27)

76

God Our Maker

Proper 18
Lavon Bayler

7.8.7.8.7.7.
(Ratisbon)

God, our Maker, Healer, Guide,
With your gracious love surround us.
You we trust, in you abide,
For your peace and joy have found us.
You have saved from wickedness
Those who seek your righteousness.

We will work for justice here,
Doing good with hearts uplifted,
Seeking first to know you're near,
Then responding as we're gifted,
Fighting poverty and wrong,
Trusting you to keep us strong.

We would heed your full commands,
Keeping vows of faithful living,
Shrinking not from love's demands,
Gen'rous with our time and giving.
May our faith persist and grow,
As we seek Christ's way to know.

Free our tongues to sing your praise.
Let our inmost selves find healing.
When our eyes behold your ways,
And our ears hear those appealing
For the help that we can give,
Teach us to be sensitive. Amen.

(Psalm 125, Proverbs 22:1–2, 8–9, 22–23, Mark 7:24–37)

77

My Brothers and Sisters

Proper 18
Lavon Bayler

7.6.7.6.D.
(Tours)

My brothers and my sisters,
Who meet in Jesus' name,
Why do we choose as fav'rites
The ones with wealth and fame?
The poor receive God's favor,
For they have learned to trust.
Their faith is rich and growing;
They, more than we, are just.

By disregarding others
Whose ways are different,
We violate the mandate
That God, in Christ, has sent.
Love neighbors as yourself, and
Shun partiality.
Our sisters and our brothers
Are all humanity.

What good are words of faith that
Are empty platitudes,
That speak of warmth and peace, yet
Will offer no one foods
To fill their bodies' dire need
Or meet their spirits' thirst.
Forgive us, God, and help us
Put serving actions first. Amen.

(James 2:1–10, 14–17)

78

All Heaven and Earth

Proper 19
Lavon Bayler

10.10.11.11.
(Lyons)

All heaven and earth their Maker proclaim,
Through night and through day pour forth their acclaim.
Their witness is silent, yet rich and profound,
In tune with God's law, and with pow'r to astound.

God's wisdom confronts the scoffer and fool,
Whose busyness finds no time for God's rule.
Reproof goes unheeded, and truth is deplored,
While God's revelation and call are ignored.

When panic and stress bring anguish and fear,
The counsel of God will fail to appear
To those who, so long, have designed their own way
And, sated with self, do not know how to pray.

Our waywardness kills the best that we know.
Complacency hides the love God would show
To all who will listen and heed the commands
That offer us light which the heart understands.

We pray, then, that hidden faults may be cleared,
And insolent claims no more be revered.
Let words from our lips and our hearts' deep desire
Find favor with God, as to faith we aspire.

(Psalm 19, Proverbs 1:20–33)

79

You Are the Christ

Proper 19
Lavon Bayler

6.6.8.6.D. (S.M.D.)
(Terra Patris)

"You are the Christ of God!"
Is Peter's cry and ours,
For Jesus taught the way of love
That strengthens and empowers.
God calls on us to teach
The truth that we have found.
That words and deeds together may
God's gracious will expound.

The ones who teach are judged
More strictly than the rest.
Our daily lives and ways we speak
Are subject to God's test
Of faithfulness to truth
And purity of soul.
May our intent be true to Christ,
God's reign of love our goal.

We follow where Christ leads,
Denying selfish claims.
Our tongues are tamed and finely tuned
To speak of Godly aims.
The gospel bids us risk
Ourselves for Jesus' sake.
We celebrate God's glorious reign,
And joyously partake. Amen.

(Mark 8:27–38, James 3:1–12)

80

Draw Near to God

Proper 20
Lavon Bayler

8.6.8.6.D. (C.M.D.)
(Materna)

Draw near to God, and find delight
In wisdom God reveals.
Seek gentleness and righteousness
And purity that heals.
Be peaceable and merciful;
May true humility
And kindness mark our words and deeds
With strength and dignity.

We seek to turn from selfishness
And partiality,
From bitter envy and disputes
That mar integrity.
May jealous cravings be subdued,
Disorder overcome,
And wickedness of every kind
Be seen as burdensome.

Then, may we find true happiness,
O God, in serving you,
Witn open hands to help the poor,
True justice to pursue.
We ask to grow in childlike trust
That sees the good in all,
And welcomes them in Jesus' name,
Whatever may befall. Amen.

(Psalm 1, Proverbs 31:10–31, Mark 9:30–37, James 3:13–4:3, 7–8a)

81

Hear Us! Save Us!

Proper 21
Lavon Bayler

6.6.8.6.6.8.3.3.6.6.
(Arnsberg)

Hear us when we suffer;
Listen to our praying:
Keep our wounded lives from straying.
May we be forgiven
For the sins we carry,
Coming to this sanctuary.
Calm our fear; Keep us near,
God of strength and power;
Meet us in this hour.

Save us from oppression,
Help the sick and dying.
May our prayers be edifying.
Raise us up and heal us,
As we help each other,
Caring for each sister, brother.
May our youth Seek your truth,
Guard their feet from stumbling
When their world is crumbling.

Grant us strength to praise you;
Fill our hearts with gladness.
Take away our numbing sadness.
Give us faith to follow
Where the Teacher leads us,
As with lasting food Christ feeds us.
Salt and peace: We'll not cease
Serving where you send us.
May your love defend us. Amen.

(Esther 7:1–6, 9–10; 9:20–22, Psalm 124, Mark 9;38–50, James 5:13–20)

82

Upright and Blameless

Proper 22
Lavon Bayler

10.10.10.10.10.10.
(Song 1)

Upright and blameless, we would walk, O God.
Grant us integrity to keep your ways.
Your glory shines on paths that we have trod,
Sustaining us through good and evil days.
You carry us in times of pain and loss,
As you sustained our Savior on the cross.

Let us, as little children, come to you,
To hear your Word and feel your welcome touch.
In all the hurts and joys that we go through,
Your steadfast love is more than salve or crutch.
You give us life, with wonders that amaze,
And we are moved to join in songs of praise.

As once you spoke through prophets, speak to us,
And purify our lives through Jesus Christ.
To our best thoughts and deeds give impetus,
In light of all that Jesus sacrificed.
We cannot wash our hands in innocence,
But we can live our lives with confidence.

Come, test our hearts and minds, and help us trust,
That we may serve with faithfulness each day.
When ills and suff'ring seem to us unjust,
Keep us from bitterness, that when we pray
Your reign of love may help to keep us strong,
To live within your realm where we belong. Amen.

(Job 2:1–10, Psalm 26, Mark 10:2–16, Hebrews 2:5–12)

83

Celebration of Marriage

Proper 22
Lavon Bayler

6.6.8.6. Ref. (S.M. Ref.)
(Marion)

We celebrate the day
When two are joined as one.
When vows are said that promise life
In unity begun.
One flesh! Thank God!
For joining us in love.

We celebrate each day
The gift that we receive
When opening our hearts to love,
We turn from make-believe.
One flesh! Thank God!
For joining us in love.

We celebrate the years
Through which we live and grow,
While facing stress and sharing joys
That no one else may know.
One flesh! Thank God!
For joining us in love.

We celebrate the bonds
That none can separate,
For God, who loves us as we are,
Continues to create
One flesh! Thank God!
For joining us in love.

(Mark 10:2–12)

84

Why Have You Forsaken?

Proper 23
Lavon Bayler

11.11.11.11.
(Muller)

Why have you forsaken us, God, in our need?
Our cries are unanswered. Why do you not heed
Our bitter complaints and our desperate pleas?
Our praying seems lost in the fog and the breeze.

Our enemies mock us; our friends shake their heads.
Our thinking is scrambled by horrors and dreads.
Both terror and darkness have clouded the way,
And hearts that were stalwart are fainting today.

By night and by day, hear our groans; feel our pain.
Why must our petitions seem scorned and in vain?
Our case is before you; our troubles you know.
We seek the relief only you can bestow.

When reasoning fails us, we cling to the hope
That this, too, will pass, and you'll help us to cope.
Our faith is still stronger than doubts can devour.
We trust your compassion; we know your great power.

We look for deliv'rance; to you we commit
This day and our future. God, help us submit
Our worries and failures to your tender care,
In Christ, finding answers, and faith we can share. Amen.

(Job 23:1–9, 16–17, Psalm 22:1–15)

85

Good Teacher, Listen

Proper 23
Lavon Bayler

8.7.8.7.8.8.7.
(Nun Freut Euch)

Good Teacher, listen when we ask
To know of life eternal.
We want to master every task
To merit your referral.
We know the things that you command,
And on our record we would stand,
Reaching for joys supernal.

The word of God will be the judge
Of all who seek the kingdom.
It pierces hearts with more than nudge
Of mercy, grace, and wisdom.
No wealth can purchase us a place
In our Creator's warm embrace.
Christ Jesus paid our ransom.

The first are last, and last are first.
Come, curb your self-indulgence.
When we are at our best, or worst,
God's judgment cuts through pretense.
Salvation's joy we cannot earn;
God's gift of love we may discern
Through lives that share Christ's presence. Amen.

(Mark 10:17–31, Hebrews 4:12–16)

86

Out of the Whirlwind

Proper 24
Lavon Bayler

10.10.10.10.
(Field)

Out of the whirlwind, when we're overwhelmed,
Crushed and uncertain, suffering and afraid,
We hear a voice that heartens and confronts:
Where were you, child, when all the worlds were made?

Are you the only one in doubt and pain?
Can bitter words accomplish any good?
When have you tapped the wisdom God imparts?
When have you sought faith's depths and understood?

Have you not heard the heavens shout for joy?
Have you not sensed the majesty of life?
Each one contributes to the greater whole.
Meaning may yet be found beyond our strife.

Mountains and valleys each do have their place.
Out of the chaos, beauty may emerge.
God uses wind and rain as messengers,
And ministries of fire to cleanse and purge.

Let us, then, bless our God and lift our eyes,
Seeing the stars and joining in their praise.
O Lord, our God, how great are all your works.
Teach us to know your truth and love your ways.

(Job 38:1–7, (34–41), Psalm 104:1–9, 24, 35c)

87

Greatness Is Our Goal

Proper 24
Lavon Bayler

8.8.8.8. (L.M.)
(Federal Street)

Greatness, O Jesus, is our goal.
We want to be your special friends.
When your reign comes, we want a role
Within that realm that never ends.

Grant us to share your glory there.
We want to sit beside your throne
We can be priests who show your care,
Making your words and actions known.

Such talk of favors is profane.
It is divisive and unfair.
Here is Christ's cup of bitter pain
In which disciples often share.

All who would lead must sacrifice.
First shall be last, and last be first.
Those who are baptized learn the price
Of faithfulness when times are worst.

As Jesus came to love and serve,
We, too, are called to give our all.
Awed by salvation undeserved,
We humbly answer Jesus' call.

(Mark 10:35–45, Hebrews 5:1–10)

88

Sight and Hearing

Proper 25
Lavon Bayler

8.7.8.7.D.
(St. Asaph)

Sight and hearing Jesus offers
Those who seek and call today.
There is welcome for each beggar,
Searching for life's better way.
We can all take heart, rejoicing,
Knowing we are called by name.
We are touched and healed so deeply
We can never be the same.

Faith that we received from others
Only can become our own
When we reach for understanding,
Offered us by God alone.
In our struggles to be faithful,
Through our days of toil and stress,
God is with us as a refuge,
Promising to hear and bless.

Let the humble sing their praises
With a radiant confidence,
Serving in the name of Jesus,
With no arrogant pretense.
Magnify God's name together;
Taste and see that God is good.
Celebrating Christ's perfection,
Live today as Jesus would.

(Job 42:1–6, 10–17, Psalm 34:1–8 (19–22), Mark 10:46–52,
Hebrews 7:23–28)

89

Worship with Praise

Proper 26
Lavon Bayler

6.6.4.6.6.6.4.
(Italian Hymn)

Worship with songs of praise,
Echoing through the days,
Happy to trust
God, in whose love we dwell,
Even when we rebel.
God, let us serve you well
Through causes just.

Praising with every breath,
'Til we lie down in death,
We learn to cope,
Knowing that you sustain
People in want and pain,
Helping us live again
With radiant hope.

Great are your mighty deeds,
Meeting our deepest needs,
Help us, in turn,
To live with loyalty,
'Though we may disagree.
You set our spirits free
To grow and learn.

(Ruth 1:1–18, Psalm 146)

90

Eternal Spirit, Reign

Proper 26   11.10.11.10.10.
Lavon Bayler   (Peek)

Eternal Spirit, shown to us in Jesus,
Teach us the loving ways that you intend.
Break through our dull routines and weary rituals,
Bringing to life your reign that has no end,
Bringing to life your reign that has no end.

Help us to realize your rule among us,
Loving with all our heart and soul and mind.
Putting you first, O God, we bring our worship
That, in these moments, we your truth may find.
That, in these moments, we your truth may find.

You are beyond our widest understanding,
Yet, you are nearer than the air we breathe.
We want to live in harmony with others,
Letting our deeds reveal what we believe,
Letting our deeds reveal what we believe.

Help us to cherish life that you have given,
Loving ourselves as children of your grace.
We would extend that love to all our neighbors,
Family and friends of every age and race,
Family and friends of every age and race.

(Mark 12:28–34, Hebrews 9:11–14)

91

From Anxious Toil

Proper 27
Lavon Bayler

8.4.8.4.8.8.8.
(Thy Great Bounty)

From anxious toil, we turn, O God,
To meet you here;
From early morn 'til late at night,
We will not fear.
Your love is our security.
You let us know that we can be
Christ's next of kin, redeemed and free.

We want to pledge our hearts and hands,
Our loyalty.
For Christ has borne our many sins
With dignity.
In eagerness, we wait and pray,
Intent on learning Jesus' way.
May we, O God, your word obey.

Come, build with us, lest we become
So filled with pride
That we demand a special place
Where we preside.
Help us, instead, to give our best,
From our abundance to invest
Ourselves, our all, as we are blessed. Amen.

(Ruth 3:1–5; 4:13–17, Psalm 127, Mark 12:38–44, Hebrews 9:24–28)

92

O God of Hosts

Proper 28
Lavon Bayler

7.6.8.6.D.
(St. Christopher)

O God of hosts, remember
Your servants in distress.
Look on their great anxiety
And bitter cheerlessness.
When hearts are sad, and weeping
Continues night and day,
Hear everyone who calls your name
And answer when they pray.

When we are judged unfairly
And others doubt our worth,
May we find favor in your sight,
Experiencing rebirth.
In you we find our refuge,
In you we take delight.
You feed the hungers deep inside
And offer us new life.

You raise the poor to riches.
You lift us from the dust.
You guard the feet of faithful ones,
For you are strong and just.
Our sadness turns to praising
As hope and joy return.
Your peace, O God, now sends us forth,
Our Savior's ways to learn. Amen.

(1 Samuel 1:4–20; 2:1–10, Psalm 16)

93

Come, Holy Spirit, Come

Proper 28
Lavon Bayler

6.4.6.4.10.10.
(Sursum Corda (Lomas))

Come, Holy Spirit, come;
Write on our hearts
Laws of the covenant
That love imparts,
And fill our minds with thoughts that animate,
Hope, joy, and faithfulness to demonstrate.

We seek to be released
From chains of sin,
That our new life in Christ,
Strong may begin.
Hear our rejoicing that you still forgive,
Washing us clean with waters curative.

Bold in our confidence,
We seek to give
Fresh hope to friends and foe,
That all may live
By Jesus' new design, the living way,
That seeks to bring the world to God's new day.

Come, help us build, O God,
As you propose,
Not monuments of stone
With doors that close,
But open, sensitive community,
Living your truth, in love, with unity. Amen.

(Mark 13:1–8, Hebrews 12:11–25)

94

Our House with God

Proper 29 (Reign of Christ)   8.6.8.6.D. (C.M.D.)
Lavon Bayler   (Bethlehem (Seraph))

Is not our house like this with God:
A place of joy and light?
Like rising sun on cloudless days,
God brings the dawn of right.
An everlasting covenant
Is offered to us all,
And we, who seek to be the church,
Give answer to God's call.

We worship at the feet of Christ,
Whose reign we celebrate,
Whose realm endures beyond all time,
God's love to demonstrate.
We seek the truth that Jesus lived,
And listen for the voice
That bids us love as we are loved,
And moves us to rejoice.

The grace and peace of One who was,
And is, and is to come,
Is freely shared with all of us,
And makes us venturesome.
We dare to follow where Christ leads,
From sin and death set free.
O, teach us faithfulness that we
May true disciples be. Amen.

(2 Samuel 23:1–7, Psalm 132:1–18, John 18:33–37, Revelation 1:4b–8)

SPECIAL DAYS

95

The Earth Is God's

All Saints' Day   8.8.8.8. (L.M.)
Lavon Bayler   (Waltham)

The earth is God's, and all within
Are called to worship and adore.
Come purify your hands and hearts,
And lift your souls to dance and soar.

God wipes our tears and conquers death,
And takes away deceit and sin.
We wait, anticipating grace,
That heals and cleanses deep within.

God sets before us all a feast
Of food and wine to be enjoyed.
Yet, richer fare is ours as well:
Soul food that cannot be destroyed.

God feeds our spirits, blesses us
With saving love that helps us live,
No more in isolated fears
But sharing all we have to give.

God reigns in glory over all
The nations, whether small or great.
All worlds are subject to the rule
Of One continuing to create.

(Psalm 24, Isaiah 25:6–9)

96

God Grant Us Hope

All Saints' Day
Lavon Bayler

6.6.6.6. Ref.
(Come to the Savior)

God grant our hearts to know
A hope beyond our years.
Our spirits, touched by grief,
Are weighted down with tears.

Refrain
You are the first and last,
Beginning and the end,
Alpha, Omega, and
Our everlasting friend.

New earth and heav'n will come
When old things pass away,
And death will be no more
On that fulfilling day.
Refrain

Your voice assures us here;
We know your words are true.
We trust your promises
Of making all things new.
Refrain

Unbind us now, we pray,
And help us to believe,
That we, with all the saints,
Christ's blessing may receive.
Refrain

(John 11:32–44, Revelation 21:1–6a)

97

Do Not Fear

Thanksgiving Day
Lavon Bayler

8.7.8.7.7.7.
(Unser Herrscher)

Do not fear, O land and creatures;
Our Creator will provide.
God has done great things before us,
And among us will reside.
Bounteous orchards, fertile fields,
Trees and vines will give their yields.

Seeds were planted as we trusted
From our God would come the rain.
Now, with harvests overflowing,
Threshing floors are full of grain.
From this plenty we shall eat.
God supplies our fruit and meat.

Those who sowed in tears and sorrow,
Fearing armies that destroy,
Know again God's wondrous mercy
As they reap with shouts of joy.
Join in laughter, sing your praise;
God is good through all our days.

With thanksgiving and rejoicing,
We approach our God today,
Grateful for the many blessings
All around us on display:
Plenty meant for us to share,
That the world may know God's care.

(Psalm 16, Joel 2:21–27)

98

Thank You, God

Thanksgiving Day
Lavon Bayler

8.7.8.7.8.7.7.
(Cwm Rhondda)

Thank you, God; we sing your praises
For the ways that you provide
Life and beauty, strength and glory,
As we, in your love, abide.
Hear our prayers and supplications
For the rulers of all lands.
For the rulers of all lands.

We would intercede for justice,
Quietness and dignity,
For all humankind, your children,
That your people may be free,
Free to live your truth, while striving
For the reign of righteousness,
For the reign of righteousness.

We would work for peace and order
Knowing your desire to save
Every one whom you created,
High and lowly, free and slave.
As you feed and clothe your people,
We would ease their worried minds.
We would ease their worried minds.

Thank you, God, for Christ, our teacher,
Whose apostles we would be,
Reaching out to offer healing
Through a vital ministry.
May the riches of your Spirit
Come to all who seek your truth.
Come to all who seek your truth. Amen.

(Matthew 6:25–35, I Timothy 2:1–7)

99

Thank God for Pioneers

Retirement Celebration
Lavon Bayler

8.6.8.6.D. (C.M.D.)
(Materna)

Thank God for pioneers of faith
Who dare to blaze the way
For future generations' sake
By what they do today.
We thank you, God, for loving care
From one among us here,
Whose great concern for justice is
Compelling and sincere.

Thank God for years of ministry
To people far and near
Whose lives were touched by saving grace
Through words they came to hear.
Impassioned eloquence, they knew,
Would from the pulpit flow
When this, God's servant, rose to speak
Of ways that they might grow.

Thank God for one whose loyalty
To friends and family
Has modeled for the rest of us
What we, in Christ, can be.
Grant rest from toil and time for play,
And vigor to enjoy
Fulfillment in the days ahead
That nothing can destroy. Amen.

In honor of the Reverend Dr. W. Sterling Cary on his retirement as Minister of the Illinois Conference.

Related Hymns

100

Transform Us, God

Retirement Celebration
Lavon Bayler

10.10.10.10.10.10.
(Finlandia)

Transform our hearts, O God, in Jesus' name.
Let love be central to our words and deeds.
To follow Christ in all things is our aim,
To be responsive to our neighbors' needs.
Heal us within, and strengthen us to stand
For truth and justice in your promised land.

Transform our fam'lies, that your will may be
Worked out among us in our daily lives.
Help us to listen when we disagree,
And do those things on which affection thrives,
When anger flares, turn us away from wrong,
And let forgiveness make our union strong.

Transform our churches, that we may discern
The goals and dreams you want us to pursue.
Prompt us to grow in ways that help us learn
All that is good, acceptable, and true.
With joyous thanks, we worship and adore
One God whose love surrounds us evermore.

May we, together, be renewed this day,
And honor Christ in all we do and say,
That when we part our lives may still display
The joys of following your perfect way.
Conforming not to views the world may hold,
We seek for all the freedom of your fold. Amen.

(Romans 12:2, Colossians 3:17)

Written for the 1994 Nebraska Conference U.C.C. Annual Meeting in honor of "Clip" and Janice Higgins on his retirement as conference minister.

Indexes

ALPHABETICAL INDEX OF HYMNS

(by hymn number)

Topical Index of Hymns

INDEX OF SCRIPTURE READINGS

(The italicized scriptures indicate the alternate series of readings
for the Sundays following Pentecost)

Job

Psalms

Abundance
Easter 7
After Pentecost
Propers 12, 13, 15, 20, 27, 28
Thanksgiving Day

Abundant Life
Lent 4
After Pentecost
Proper 16

Acceptable Time
After Pentecost
Proper 7

Accountability
After Pentecost
Propers 5, 18, 19

Adoration
Epiphany
After Pentecost
Proper 12

Alienation
After Pentecost
Proper 11

Alpha and Omega
After Pentecost
Proper 29
All Saints' Day

Amazement
Epiphany
After Epiphany 1
After Pentecost
Propers 9, 24, 26

Ambassadors
After Pentecost
Proper 16

Anger
Holy Week—W, F
Easter 3
After Pentecost
Propers 14, 17, 20

Anxiety
Advent 1
After Pentecost
Proper 27, 28

Apathy
After Pentecost
Proper 12

Arrogance
After Epiphany 1
After Pentecost
Propers 19, 28

Assurance
Holy Week—S
Easter 4
After Pentecost
Proper 11

Atonement
Easter 5

Authority
Ascension Day
After Pentecost
Propers 9, 14, 15, 29

Awaken
Advent 1
Lent 6—Passion
Holy Week—W

Awe and Wonder
Advent 1
After Epiphany 4
Lent 3
Trinity Sunday
After Pentecost
Propers 7, 9, 15, 19, 22, 24, 29

Baptism
Advent 2, 3
After Epiphany 1, 6
Lent 1
Easter 5, 6
Ascension Day
Trinity Sunday
After Pentecost
Proper 24

Battles
After Pentecost
Propers 7, 14, 29

Bearing Fruit
Easter 6

Beauty
After Christmas 1
After Pentecost
Propers 19, 22

Belief
After Christmas 2
Holy Week—F
Easter 2
After Pentecost
Propers 14, 16, 24, 29

Betrayal
Lent 6—Passion

After Pentecost
Proper 7

Birds
After Pentecost
Proper 16

Birth
After Christmas 2
Trinity Sunday
After Pentecost
Proper 17

Blessing(s)
After Christmas 1, 2
January 1—Holy Name
Lent 2
Easter 5
Ascension Day
After Pentecost
Propers 10, 18, 22, 24, 26, 28
All Saints' Day

Blood
Easter 2
After Pentecost
Proper 9

Body of Christ
After Epiphany 4
Ascension Day
Easter 7
After Pentecost
Propers 12, 13, 17

Boundaries
After Pentecost
Proper 19

Bread
Easter Evening
After Pentecost
Propers 13, 14, 15, 16

Breath
Holy Week—M

Pentecost
After Pentecost
Proper 20

Brokenness
Lent 6—Passion
Holy Week—S
After Pentecost
Propers 4, 5, 7, 11, 14

Build
January 1—New Year
After Pentecost
Propers 13, 14, 17, 27

Burdens
After Epiphany 9
Lent 6—Passion
After Pentecost
Proper 27

Busyness
After Pentecost
Propers 16, 22, 26, 28

Call(ed)
Advent 4
After Epiphany 1, 2
Holy Week—Tu
Easter—7
After Pentecost
Propers 4, 13, 25, 29

Care(s), Caring
January 1—New Year
After Christmas 2
Holy Week—Th
Easter 4
After Pentecost
Propers 10, 12, 15, 22, 27, 28, 29

Center
Lent 4
After Pentecost
Proper 26

Celebration
Holy Week—Th
Easter Day
After Pentecost
Proper 15

Challenge
After Pentecost
Propers 9, 11, 17, 23

Change
After Christmas 2
After Epiphany 1, Last
Easter Day
Pentecost
After Pentecost
Propers 21, 27

Child(ren)
Christmas, Proper II
January 1—Holy Name
After Pentecost
Proper 20, 22

Children of God
Christmas, Proper III
January 1—Holy Name
Easter 3
Trinity Sunday
After Pentecost
Propers 11, 114, 15, 16, 18, 22, 23, 26

Chosen
Easter 6, 7
After Pentecost
Proper 10

Christ's Coming
Advent 1

Christ's Example
After Epiphany 1
Lent 2, 7
After Pentecost
Proper 9

Christ's Sacrifice
Lent 6—Passion

Church
Advent 3
Epiphany
After Epiphany 2, 4, 5
Easter 2, 5, 7
Ascension Day
Pentecost
Trinity Sunday
After Pentecost
Propers 9, 16, 17, 24, 25, 27,
    28, 29
All Saints' Day

Cleansing
After Epiphany 6
Ash Wednesday
Lent 5
Easter 3
Trinity Sunday
After Pentecost
Propers 4, 10, 13, 17, 20, 27, 28

Cloud of Witnesses
Holy Week—W

Comfort
Advent 2
Easter 4
After Pentecost
Propers 12, 20, 23, 28

Command(ments)
After Christmas 2
After Epiphany 1
Lent 4
Holy Week—Th
Easter 4, 6
After Pentecost
Propers 4, 5, 11, 15, 17, 19
Commission
Epiphany

After Pentecost
Proper 18

Commitment
Lent 2, 4
Easter 3, 7
After Pentecost
Propers 22, 24, 26, 27

Communicate
After Pentecost
Propers 19, 23, 29

Community
Lent 1
Easter 2, 5, 6, 7
After Pentecost
Propers 5, 11, 15, 18, 20, 24, 27,
    28, 29

Compassion
After Epiphany 8
Holy Week—Th, F
After Pentecost
Propers 4, 9, 11, 27

Complacency
After Pentecost
Propers 19, 20

Confession
Advent 2
After Pentecost
Propers 18, 20, 23

Conflict
After Pentecost
Proper 20

Confidence
Epiphany
Trinity Sunday
After Pentecost
Propers 7, 28

Counsel
After Pentecost
Propers 19, 28

Courage
Lent 2
Holy Week—Th
Easter 4
Trinity Sunday
After Pentecost
Propers 7, 20, 21, 23, 28

Courts of God
After Pentecost
Proper 16

Covenant
Advent 3, 4
After Epiphany 8
Lent 1, 2, 5
Holy Week—M
Easter 5
After Pentecost
Propers 9, 10, 11, 15, 26, 28,
    29

Create, Creation
After Epiphany 1, 2, 5
Lent 5
Pentecost
After Pentecost
Propers 10, 16, 19, 22, 24, 26, 27
All Saints' Day

Cross
Lent 4, 5, 6—Passion
Holy Week—Tu, W, Th, F
Easter Day

Crown
After Christmas 1
January 1—New Year
After Pentecost
Proper 22

Cynicism
After Pentecost
Proper 16

Dance
After Pentecost
Proper 10

Darkness
Lent 4
Easter 4
After Pentecost
Propers 4, 24

Dead Works
Holy Week—M

Death
Lent 4, 5
Holy Week—F, S
Easter Day, Evening
Easter 3, 7
After Pentecost
Propers 7, 29
All Saints' Day

Deceit
After Pentecost
Propers 10, 17, 29

Deliverance
Lent 6—Passion
Holy Week—W, F, S
After Pentecost
Proper 12

Denial
Lent 6—Passion
Holy Week—F
Easter 4
After Pentecost
Propers 11, 28
All Saints' Day

Despair
After Epiphany 9
After Pentecost
Propers 5, 19
All Saints' Day

Devotion
Lent 6—Passion
After Pentecost
Proper 26

Discernment
After Pentecost
Proper 15

Discipleship
After Epiphany 1, 3, 8
Holy Week—W, S
Easter Evening 5, 7
After Pentecost
Propers 10, 11, 16, 20, 23, 25

Discipline
After Pentecost
Propers 16, 19

Distortions
After Epiphany 2
After Pentecost
Proper 12

Distress
Easter 3
After Pentecost
Proper 28

Division
After Pentecost
Proper 5, 11

Doers
After Pentecost
Proper 17

Doorkeeper
After Pentecost
Proper 16

Doubt
Easter Day, Evening
Easter 2, 3
After Pentecost
Propers 7, 20, 23, 25
All Saints' Day

Dreams
Pentecost

Dry Bones
Pentecost

Dullness
After Pentecost
Proper 19
All Saints' Day

Empowerment
January 1—New Year
After Christ 2
After Epiphany 1, 8
Easter 4
Ascension Day
After Pentecost
Propers 4, 12, 13, 27

Emptiness
Palm Sunday
Pentecost
After Pentecost
Proper 27

Encouragement
After Pentecost
Propers 13, 23, 28

Endurance
After Pentecost
Proper 7

Enemies
January 1—Holy Name
Easter 5
After Pentecost
Propers 7, 21

Enlightenment
After Pentecost
Proper 19

Error
After Pentecost
Proper 19

Escape
Epiphany 9

Estrangement
After Pentecost
Proper 18

Eternal, Eternity
Christmas, Proper III
Epiphany
Lent 2, 4, 5
Easter 2, 7
Trinity Sunday
After Pentecost
Propers 13, 14, 15, 16, 22, 23, 24,
    25, 29
All Saints' Day

Evangel(ism) (ists)
After Pentecost
Proper 13

Evil
Lent 4, 6—Passion
Easter Evening
After Pentecost
Propers 7, 13, 14, 15, 16, 17, 19,
    20, 22, 25, 28

Eyes
January 1—Holy Name

After Pentecost
Propers 4, 12, 18, 19, 23, 25
    26, 29

Face of God
January 1—Holy Name
Pentecost
Faint
After Epiphany 5

Faith
After Christmas 2
Lent 2, 4
Holy Week—W, Th
Easter Day, 2, 3, 6
After Pentecost
Propers 5, 7, 9, 11, 12, 13, 15, 16,
    18, 20, 23, 25, 28

Faithfulness
Advent 1, 2, 3, 4
Christmas, Proper II
January 1—New Year
After Epiphany 4, 6
Lent 1, 2, 5, 6—Passion
Holy Week—W
Easter Day, 3, 6
Ascension Day
After Pentecost
Propers 5, 10, 11, 12, 15, 16, 20,
    21, 22, 25 26, 27, 29

Family
Lent 2
After Pentecost
Propers 5, 11, 27

Fasting
Ash Wednesday

Faults
After Pentecost
Proper 19

Fear(s)
Advent 3
Christmas, Proper I
Lent 6—Passion
Easter 2, 3, 5, 7
After Pentecost
Propers 7, 12, 13, 18, 22, 25
All Saints' Day
Thanksgiving Day

Feast
Easter Evening

Feeding, Food
January 1—New Year
Easter, Evening, 4
After Pentecost
Propers 12, 13, 15,26

Fire
Pentecost

Flesh
After Christ 2
Trinity Sunday

Follow
After Epiphany 1, 2
Lent 5
Holy Week—Tu, W
After Pentecost
Propers 12, 19, 23, 26

Foolishness
Lent 4
Holy Week—Tu
After Pentecost
Propers 12, 15

Foot-washing
Holy Week—Th

Forgiveness
Advent 2, 4

After Epiphany 3, 4, 6, 9
Lent 1, 5
Holy Week—F
Easter 2, 4, 7
After Pentecost
Propers 5, 10, 11, 14, 15, 17, 18,
19, 20, 22, 23, 26, 27, 28, 29
All Saints' Day

Fragmentation
After Pentecost
Proper 11

Free(dom)
Christmas, Proper I
After Epiphany 4
Holy Week—Th
Easter 3
After Pentecost
Propers 17, 18, 23, 26, 29
All Saints' Day

Friends
Easter 6
After Pentecost
Propers 12, 14, 16, 18

Fruitfulness
Lent 2
Holy Week—Tu
Easter 5, 7
Trinity Sunday
After Pentecost
Propers 11, 15 17, 19, 20, 22, 28

Generosity
After Epiphany—1
Easter 4, 6, 7 after Pentecost
Propers 11, 15, 17, 18, 24, 28
All Saints' Day

Gentleness
After Pentecost
Propers 13, 20, 24

Gift(s)
Christmas, Propers II and III
After Epiphany 1
Easter 7
Trinity Sunday
After Pentecost
Propers 12, 13, 14, 15, 17, 23, 24,
27, 28
All Saints' Day

Giving
Ash Wednesday
Easter 7
After Pentecost
Propers 16, 17, 23

Gladness
Christmas, Proper III
After Christmas 2
Lent 5
Easter Day, 2, 3,
After Pentecost
Propers 17, 21, 25, 28
Thanksgiving Day

Glory, Glorify
Christmas, Propers II and III
January 1—Holy Name, New
Year
Epiphany
After Pentecost
Propers 22, 26

God of Hosts
Advent 1

God's Call
Advent 4
January 1—New Year
After Epiphany 2, 3
Lent 1, 2
After Pentecost
Proper 4

God's Care
After Christmas—2
After Epiphany 2, 5
Lent 2
After Pentecost
Propers 15, 17, 20, 24, 25

God's Faithfulness
Advent 1, 3, 4
After Epiphany 2, 4, 6
Lent 1, 2, 6—Passion
Holy Week—S
Easter 2
After Pentecost
Propers 5, 11, 15, 27

God's Gifts
Advent 1
Christmas, Propers I, II, and III
January 1—New Year
After Epiphany 1, 8, 9
Lent 4
Easter 4, 7
Ascension Day
Pentecost
After Pentecost
Propers 9, 11, 13, 20
Thanksgiving Day

God's Glory
Advent 2
Christmas Propers I and III
After Christmas 1, 2
January 1—Holy Name, New Year
Epiphany
After Epiphany 2, 7, Last
Lent 2
Easter 5
Pentecost
Trinity Sunday
After Pentecost
Propers 4, 5, 10, 12, 17, 19, 22,
24, 26
All Saints' Day

God's Goodness
Lent 4, 6—Palm
Easter 3, 4
After Pentecost
Propers 11, 25

God's Greatness
After Pentecost
Propers 9, 10, 24

God's Guidance
Pentecost
After Pentecost
Propers 11, 16, 19, 23, 28

God's House
After Pentecost
Propers 16, 27

God's Law
January 1—Holy Name
After Epiphany 5
Lent 4, 5
Holy Week—F
After Pentecost
Propers 19, 20, 28

God's Leading
Lent 2
After Pentecost
Proper 15

God's Love
Christmas, Proper III
January 1—Holy Name, New
    Year
After Christmas 2
After Epiphany 2, 6, 7, Last
Ash Wednesday
Lent 2, 4, 5, 6—Passion
Holy Week—M, W, F
Easter Day, 3, 4 5, 6, 7
Ascension Day
Trinity Sunday
After Pentecost

Propers 5, 7, 9, 10, 11, 12, 13, 16,
    17, 19, 22, 24, 26, 27, 29

God's Majesty
January 1—Holy Name, New
    Year
After Epiphany 4
Trinity Sunday
After Pentecost
Propers 9, 21, 24, 29

God's Mystery
After Christmas 2
Epiphany
Palm Sunday
After Pentecost
Proper 10

God's Power
After Christmas 2
After Epiphany 1, 4, 5
Lent 4, 6, Palm
Holy Week—Tu
Ascension Day
Trinity Sunday
After Pentecost
Propers 12, 14, 16, 21

God's Presence
Advent 1, 3, 4
After Christmas 1
After Epiphany 1, 2, 6, 9, Last
Ash Wednesday
Lent 1, 2, 4, 5, 6—Passion
Easter Evening
After Pentecost
Propers 7, 9, 10, 11, 12, 13, 16,
    17, 20, 23, 25, 26, 27, 28, 29
All Saints' Day

God's Promises
Advent 2, 3, 4
After Christmas 1
After Epiphany 7
Lent 1, 2, 5

Ascension Day
After Pentecost
Propers 7, 10, 11, 16
Thanksgiving Day

God's Providence
After Epiphany 2
Easter 4
After Pentecost
Propers 14, 24

God's Purposes
Lent 1
After Pentecost
Propers 5, 20

God's Realm
January 1—New Year's
After Epiphany 3
Lent 1
After Pentecost
Propers 22, 23, 27, 29
Thanksgiving Day

God's Reign, Rule
Advent 1
Christmas, Propers II and III
Epiphany
After Epiphany
Lent 1, 2, 6—Palm
Holy Week—F
Easter 5, 6
Ascension Day
After Pentecost
Propers 5, 9, 11, 15, 16, 18, 19,
    20, 22, 23, 24, 26, 29
Thanksgiving Day

God's Saving Acts
Lent 4

God's Spirit
Advent 3
After Christmas 1
January 1—Holy Name

After Epiphany 8, Last
Lent 1, 6—Palm
Holy Week—M

God's Way(s)
Advent 1
Christmas, Proper III
After Epiphany 3, 7
Lent 1
Pentecost
After Pentecost
Propers 11, 15, 23, 15, 28

God's Will
Christmas, Proper III
January 1—New Year
Lent 2, 5
Holy Week—F
Easter 3
After Pentecost
Propers 5, 10, 15, 21, 24, 26
All Saints' Day

God's Wisdom
Lent 5
After Pentecost
Proper 24

God's Word
Advent 1, 2
Christmas, Proper III
After Christmas 2
After Epiphany 3, 4, 5, 6 8
Lent 4, 5, 7
After Pentecost
Propers 5, 10, 15, 18, 19, 23, 29
All Saints' Day

God's Work
January 1—Holy Name
Palm Sunday
Pentecost
After Pentecost
Propers 4, 5, 13, 15, 24, 25, 26, 28
All Saints' Day

Good News
Advent 2
Christmas, Propers I, II, and III
After Christmas 1
January 1—Holy Name
After Epiphany 6, Last
Lent 1, 4, 5, 6—Passion
Easter Day, 3, 5
Ascension Day
Trinity Sunday
After Pentecost
Propers 7, 9, 11, 16, 22, 25, 27, 29
All Saints' Day

Gospel
After Epiphany 5
After Pentecost
Propers 10, 16, 19, 29

Grace
Advent 1
Christmas, Propers I, II, and III
After Christmas 2
Epiphany
After Epiphany 1
Ash Wednesday
Lent 4
Holy Week—F
After Pentecost
Propers 5, 7, 9, 10, 12, 13, 14, 15, 17, 22, 23, 25, 26, 29

Gratitude
After Epiphany 1
Ascension Day
After Pentecost
Propers 10, 11, 14, 26
Thanksgiving Day

Greatness
After Pentecost
Proper 24

Greed
After Pentecost
Proper 18

Grief
Holy Week—S

Growth
After Epiphany 4
After Pentecost
Propers 9, 13, 16, 22, 24

Guidance
After Christmas 1
After Epiphany 4
Easter 6
Pentecost
After Pentecost
Proper 22

Guilt
Holy Week—F
Easter 3
After Pentecost
Propers 13, 22, 29

Habits
After Pentecost
Propers 17, 19

Hands
January 1—Holy Name
Easter 6
After Pentecost
Propers 4, 10, 14, 15, 19, 20
All Saints' Day

Happiness
After Pentecost
Propers 16, 20, 25, 26

Hardness of Heart
After Pentecost
Propers 4, 22

Harmony
After Pentecost
Proper 16

Haste
Holy Week—W

Healing, Health
After Epiphany 4, 6, 7
Lent 4, 5
Holy Week—F, S
Easter 3, 4
After Pentecost
Propers 4, 9, 10, 11, 12, 15, 17,
    18, 19, 21, 22 23, 25, 26,
    27, 29
All Saints' Day

Hearers, Hearing
After Epiphany 2, 3
Holy Week—Th
After Pentecost
Propers 4, 10, 14, 18, 23, 25,
    27, 28

Heart(s)
January 1—Holy Name
Epiphany
After Epiphany—Last
Ash Wednesday
Lent 2, 4, 5
Holy Week—Th
Easter 2, 7
After Pentecost
Propers 5, 7, 11, 12, 15, 16, 17, 18,
    19, 20, 22, 23 25, 26, 28, 29
All Saints' Day

Heaven(s)
Lent 1
Ascension Day
After Pentecost
Proper 19
All Saints' Day

Heir(s)
After Christmas 1
January 1—Holy Name
After Pentecost
Proper 22

Help(er)
After Pentecost
Propers 5, 14, 17, 18, 19, 20, 21,
    23, 26

Holy
After Epiphany 2
Trinity Sunday
After Pentecost
Propers 5, 10, 15, 17, 21, 25
All Saints' Day

Holy Spirit
Christmas, Proper II
After Christmas 1
January 1—Holy Name
Easter 2, 6
Ascension Day
Pentecost
Trinity Sunday
After Pentecost
Propers 5, 7, 10, 11, 14, 18,
    29

Honesty
After Pentecost
Propers 20, 22

Honor
January 1—New Year
Lent 5, 6—Passion
After Pentecost
Propers 17, 28, 22, 24, 27

Hope
Christmas, Propers I and II
After Epiphany 6
Lent 2

Holy Week—Tu, F, S
Easter Day
Ascension Day
Pentecost
After Pentecost
Propers 5, 7, 10, 11, 14, 18, 21,
    22, 24, 25, 26, 28
All Saints' Day

Hosanna
Palm Sunday

Hostility
Holy Week—W

Humanity
After Pentecost
Propers 18, 22

Humility
After Epiphany 1
Palm Sunday
After Pentecost
Propers 13, 25

Hunger
Advent 4
January 1—New Year
After Pentecost
Propers 13, 28, 26

Hypocrisy
After Pentecost
Propers 20, 22

Image of God
After Pentecost
Propers 17, 18

Impatience
Lent 4

Iniquity
Lent 5

After Pentecost
Propers 4, 14

Injustice
After Pentecost
Proper 18

Integrity
After Pentecost
Propers 21, 22

Jealousy
After Pentecost
Propers 10, 12

Jesus Christ
Christmas, Propers II and III
January 1—Holy Name
After Christmas 2
Epiphany
After Epiphany 1, Last
Lent 2, 4, 6—Passion, Palm
Easter Day, 3, 4, 6, 7
Ascension Day
Trinity Sunday
After Pentecost
Propers 4, 5, 10, 11, 12, 13, 16,
    17, 19, 20, 22, 23, 24, 26,
    27, 29
All Saints' Day

Joy
Advent 1
Christmas, Propers I, II,
    and III
After Christmas 2
After Epiphany 6, Last
Ash Wednesday
Lent 4, 5
Easter Day 3, 6, 7
Ascension Day
Pentecost
Trinity Sunday
After Pentecost

Propers 9, 10, 12, 13, 16, 17, 18,
19, 24, 25, 26, 27, 28, 29
Thanksgiving Day

Judgment
Christmas, Proper III
Holy Week—S
Easter 5, 6
After Pentecost
Propers 10, 13, 18, 20, 22, 23

Justice
Epiphany
After Pentecost
Propers 11, 13, 26, 29

Justified
Christmas, Proper II

Kindness
After Pentecost
Proper 7

Know(n), Knowledge
After Epiphany 2, 9
After Pentecost
Propers 12, 19, 20, 24, 25

Last Supper
Holy Week—Th

Lead(ing)
After Epiphany 2

Learning
Lent 1
Easter 7
After Pentecost
Propers 16, 18, 19, 24, 25, 28, 29

Life
Christmas, Proper III
After Christmas 1, 2
January 1—New Year

After Epiphany 6
Holy Week—M, W
Easter Day 2, 3, 4, 5, 7
After Pentecost
Propers 4, 14, 16, 23, 24,
27, 29
All Saints' Day

Lift (Up)
Advent 2
Lent 5
Pentecost
After Pentecost
Proper 26
All Saints' Day

Light
Christmas, Propers II and III
After Christmas 1, 2
Epiphany
After Epiphany 1, 9, Last
Lent 4, 6, Palm
Holy Week—M, Tu, F
Easter 2, 7
After Pentecost
Propers 4, 17, 24, 29

Listen
After Epiphany 1, 3, 6
After Pentecost
Propers 4, 7, 17, 18, 19, 20,
23, 26

Living Bread
After Pentecost
Proper 15

Living Water
After Pentecost
Propers 20

Loneliness
After Pentecost
Proper 12

Loss
After Pentecost
Propers 14, 25
All Saints' Day

Love
Lent 4, 5, 6—Passion
Holy Week—M, Th, F
Easter 5, 7
Pentecost
After Pentecost
Propers 17, 18, 19, 26, 28, 29

Love of Neighbor
January 1—Holy Name
After Epiphany 2, 6
Holy Week—Th, F, S
Easter 5, 6
After Pentecost
Propers 7, 9, 10, 12, 13, 15, 27, 18, 24, 26, 28

Love of Self
January 1—Holy Name
Holy Week—Th
After Pentecost
Propers 17, 26

Love to God
Easter 5
After Pentecost
Propers 17, 24, 26

Loyal(ties)
After Pentecost
Proper 17, 26

Manger
Christmas, Proper II
January 1—Holy Name

Marvel(ous)
Palm Sunday
Easter 6

After Pentecost
Proper 24

Meditation
After Pentecost
Propers 19, 20

Mercy
After Epiphany 8
Ash Wednesday
Lent 1, 4, 5
Holy Week—F, S
Easter 4
After Pentecost
Propers 7, 11, 12, 13, 15, 16, 20, 23, 25

Message (Messenger)
After Epiphany 2, 3, 5
After Pentecost
Proper 18

Ministry
After Epiphany 8
Lent 5, 6—Passion
Easter 7
After Pentecost
Propers 7, 13, 16, 18, 20, 22, 24, 27, 29
All Saints' Day

Mission
Easter 7
After Pentecost
Propers 10, 16, 20, 24
All Saints' Day

Mountain(top)(s)
Easter Evening
All Saints' Day

Mourning
Epiphany 6

Mystery
Easter 3
After Pentecost
Propers 16, 24

Name
January 1—Holy Name
After Epiphany 5, 6, 7
Lent 2
Palm Sunday
Easter Day
After Pentecost
Propers 4, 16

Need(y)
Epiphany
Easter 2
After Pentecost
Propers 7, 11, 13, 14, 18, 20,
    23, 28
Thanksgiving Day

Neighbors
Lent 6—Passion
After Pentecost
Propers 14, 17 23, 24

New Covenant
Holy Week—Th

New Creation
After Christmas 1
After Epiphany 1

New Day, Year
January 1—New Year
After Epiphany 7
Holy Week—M

New Heaven, Earth
Advent 2
January 1—New Year
All Saints' Day

New Life
Christmas, Proper II
After Christmas 2
After Epiphany—Last
Lent 5, 6—Passion
Holy Week—M
Easter Day 2, 3
Pentecost
All Saints' Day

New Possibilities
Pentecost
After Pentecost
Proper 12

New Song
Easter 6

New Spirit
After Pentecost
Proper 13

Obedience
Advent 4
Lent 5
Easter 4, 6

Open(ness)
Easter Evening
After Pentecost
Propers 7, 12, 16, 20, 29
All Saints' Day

Opportunity
After Pentecost
Propers 14, 15, 24

Oppression
Epiphany
After Pentecost
Propers 7, 21

Outreach
After Pentecost

Prayer(s)
Advent 1
After Christmas 1
After Epiphany, Last
Ash Wednesday
Lent 2, 5
Easter 4, Ascension, 7
Pentecost
After Pentecost
Propers 16, 20, 21, 24, 25, 27, 28
Thanksgiving Day

Preparation
Advent 2, 2
After Pentecost
Proper 18

Pride
After Epiphany 1
Ascension Day
After Pentecost
Propers 17, 28, 29

Priesthood
After Pentecost
Proper 24

Privilege
After Pentecost
Proper 4

Problems
After Pentecost
Proper 7

Promise(s)
Easter 5
After Pentecost
Propers 7, 11, 17, 23

Prophets
After Epiphany 4, Last
After Pentecost
Propers 9, 11, 13, 22

Proverb(s)
After Pentecost
Propers 15, 18, 20

Purity
Easter 3
After Pentecost
Proper 20

Race
Holy Week—W

Radiance
After Christmas 2

Reach
After Epiphany 3
After Pentecost
Proper 14

Rebellion
After Pentecost
Proper 4

Rebirth
Trinity Sunday
After Pentecost
Proper 24

Reconciliation
Easter 3
After Pentecost
Propers 11, 22, 29

Redemption
Christmas, Proper II
Lent 4, 5
Easter 3
After Pentecost
Propers 10, 14, 15, 16, 25

Refuge
After Pentecost
Propers 12, 25

Rejoicing
Advent 4
Christmas, Proper I
Epiphany
Lent 4
Holy Week—W
Easter Day
After Pentecost
Propers 27, 28, 29
All Saints' Day
Thanksgiving Day

Relationships
After Pentecost
Propers 13, 14, 15, 16, 19, 20, 22,
23, 26, 27, 28

Religion
After Pentecost
Proper 17

Remembrance
After Epiphany 1
Holy Week—Th
Easter 3
After Pentecost
Propers 15, 28

Renew(al)
Advent 3
After Epiphany 5
Easter 2
Pentecost
Trinity Sunday
After Pentecost
Propers 5, 11, 14, 20

Repentance
Advent 2
After Epiphany 3
Easter 3
After Pentecost
Propers 4, 12, 17, 25

Reproof
After Pentecost
Proper 19

Resistance
After Pentecost
Proper 25

Resources
After Pentecost
Propers 15, 16

Responsibility
January 1—Holy Name, New
Year
After Pentecost
Propers 10, 12, 27

Responsiveness
After Pentecost
Propers 16, 18, 26, 27

Rest
Advent 4
After Pentecost
Proper 11

Restoration
After Epiphany 5
After Pentecost
Propers 12, 27

Resurrection
Easter Day, Evening, 2, 7

Return
Ash Wednesday

Revelation
Christmas, Proper I
Epiphany
Ascension Day
After Pentecost
Proper 22

Reverence
Lent 5

Rewards
After Pentecost
Proper 24

Rich(es)
After Epiphany 1
Lent 4
Easter 2
After Pentecost
Propers 12, 15

Righteous(ness)
Advent 2
Epiphany, Proper II
After Epiphany 1
Epiphany
After Epiphany 4
Holy Week—S
Easter 6, 7
After Pentecost
Propers 11, 17, 19, 20, 21, 25, 26
Thanksgiving Day

Risen
Easter Day, Evening

Risk
Lent 5
Easter 4, 5, 6
After Pentecost
Proper 19

Rock
Advent 4
Holy Week—Tu
After Pentecost
Proper 11

Sabbath Times
After Epiphany 9

After Pentecost
Proper 4

Sacrifice
After Epiphany 1
Ash Wednesday
Lent 2, 4, 6—Passion
Palm Sunday
Holy Week—M, W, Th
Easter 2, 3, 4
After Pentecost
Propers 14, 15, 20, 25, 28
All Saints' Day

Saints'
Epiphany
After Pentecost
Propers 11, 12, 13, 16

Salvation
Advent 2, 3
Christmas, Propers II and III
After Epiphany 1, 2
After Epiphany 3, Last
Ash Wednesday
Lent 4, 5
Easter Evening, 2
After Pentecost
Propers 7, 10, 11, 13, 16, 24, 27

Scattered
Advent 4

Season(s)
January 1—New Year's Day

Secret(s)
Ash Wednesday
After Pentecost
Proper 4

Self-Centeredness
Advent 1
Pentecost

After Epiphany 9
Trinity Sunday

Society
After Epiphany 2

Sorrow
Lent 6—Passion
Holy Week—S
After Pentecost
Proper 21

Soul(s)
After Pentecost
Propers 5, 11, 18, 19, 26 28

Spirit
Advent 4
After Christmas 1
Ash Wednesday
Holy Week—M
Pentecost
Trinity Sunday
After Pentecost
Propers 13, 20, 24, 27
All Saints' Day

Spiritual Blessings, Growth, Hunger
Advent 4
Lent 5
Ascension Day
After Pentecost
Propers 10, 11, 16

Star(s)
Epiphany
After Pentecost
Proper 24

Steadfast Love
Advent 2, 4
Christmas, Proper III
After Epiphany 8

Ash Wednesday
Lent 1, 3, 4, 5
Palm Sunday
Holy Week—S
Easter Day, 6
After Pentecost
Propers 5, 7, 9, 11, 12, 13, 14, 15, 22
All Saints' Day

Stewardship
Advent 4
Easter 4
After Pentecost
Proper 17

Storms
After Pentecost
Propers 7, 12

Story
Easter 7

Strangers
Easter Evening
After Pentecost
Propers 11, 16, 18, 26

Strength
Advent 3, 4
After Epiphany 1, 5, 6
Lent 4, 6—Passion
Holy Week—Tu
Easter 2
Trinity Sunday
After Pentecost
Propers 5, 9, 12, 16, 18, 20, 23, 24, 25, 26, 27, 28

Stumbling
Holy Week—Tu
After Pentecost
Propers 21, 25

Suffering
    January 1—New Year
    Lent 5, 6—Passion
    Holy Week—S
    Easter 3
    Trinity Sunday
    After Pentecost
    Proper 21, 23
    All Saints' Day

Surprise
    Easter Evening, 3, 6
    After Pentecost
    Proper 23

Tasks
    January 1—New Year

Teach(ers) (ing)
    Lent 1, 6—Passion
    Holy Week—Th
    Easter Day
    Ascension Day
    After Pentecost
    Propers 13, 14, 17, 19, 20, 22,
        23, 28

Tears
    Easter Evening
    After Pentecost
    Propers 24, 25
    All Saints' Day

Temple
    Proper 8
    Propers 5, 11

Temptation
    Lent 1
    Easter 5
    After Pentecost
    Propers 23, 24

Testify, Testimony
    Easter 7

    After Pentecost
    Propers 28, 29

Thankfulness
    Advent 3, 4
    After Epiphany 9
    After Pentecost
    Propers 5, 12, 14, 15, 18, 19,
        26, 27

Thanks(giving)
    After Epiphany 4, 6
    Lent 4
    Palm Sunday
    Holy Week—Th
    Easter 4 6
    Pentecost
    After Pentecost
    Propers 5, 15, 17, 22, 23,
        24, 28

Thirst
    After Pentecost
    Propers 13, 21

Thoughts
    After Epiphany 2
    After Pentecost
    Propers 10, 11, 12, 23, 26, 28

Time(s)
    January 1—Holy Name, New
        Year
    After Epiphany 3
    Ash Wednesday
    Ascension Day
    After Pentecost
    Propers 9, 22, 23, 24, 26, 27
    All Saints' Day

Together
    Holy Week—W
    Easter 7
    Pentecost

After Pentecost
Propers 5, 15, 17, 27

Tongues
Holy Week—W
Pentecost
After Pentecost
Propers 17, 29

Touch
After Epiphany 5, 6
After Pentecost
Propers 4, 11, 19, 22, 23
All Saints' Day

Transformation
Christmas, Proper I
After Epiphany 2, Last
Easter Evening
After Pentecost
Propers 18, 19, 23, 25
All Saints' Day

Transgressions
Lent 5
Holy Week—F

Treachery
After Pentecost
Proper 12

Treasures
Ash Wednesday
After Pentecost
Propers 19, 23

Trouble(s)
Lent 4
Holy Week—Tu, S
After Pentecost
Propers 7, 25, 28

Trumpet
Ash Wednesday

Trust
Christmas, Proper I
After Epiphany 3, 8
Lent 1, 2
Holy Week—Tu, S
Easter 2, 3, 4, 5, 6, 7
After Pentecost
Propers 7, 11, 12, 13, 14, 16, 18,
19, 20, 22 24 26, 27 29
Thanksgiving Day

Truth
Christmas, Proper III
January 1—Holy Name
After Christmas 2
Epiphany
After Epiphany 3, 4
Lent 1, 4, 5
Holy Week—Tu
Easter Evening, 3, 4, 6, 7
Pentecost
After Pentecost
Propers 9, 10, 13, 14, 16, 17, 19,
21, 25, 27, 28, 29
All Saints' Day

Understanding
After Epiphany 2, 4, 5
After Pentecost
Propers 15, 16, 17, 18, 23, 24,
25, 26

Unity
Holy Week—F
Easter 2, 7
After Pentecost
Propers 5, 11, 13, 18, 22

Universe
After Epiphany 5

Uprightness
After Pentecost
Propers 15, 17

Valley
  Easter 4
  Pentecost
  After Pentecost
  Proper 15

Value(s)
  January 1—New Year
  After Christmas 2
  Lent 5
  Ascension Day
  After Pentecost
  Propers 11, 23, 27, 29

Vanity
  Holy Week—Tu
  After Pentecost
  Proper 27

Veiled
  After Epiphany, Last

Victory
  Christmas, Proper III
  Easter Day, 6
  After Pentecost
  Proper 9

Vine and Branches
  Easter 5

Violence
  Passion Sunday
  Holy Week—F
  After Pentecost
  Proper 17

Vision
  Christmas, Proper III
  Pentecost
  Trinity Sunday
  After Pentecost
  Propers 10, 22, 25
  All Saints' Day

Voice(s)
  Advent 3
  After Epiphany 2
  Lent 5
  Holy Week—Th
  Easter 4, 6
  Trinity Sunday
  After Pentecost
  Propers 4, 7, 14, 15, 23

Vows
  Holy Week—Th
  After Pentecost
  Proper 4

Waiting
  Advent 2
  Ascension Day
  After Pentecost
  Propers 5, 27

Walk
  Easter Evening
  After Pentecost
  Propers 16, 22

Warning
  After Epiphany 3

Washing
  Lent 5
  After Pentecost
  Propers 13, 22

Watchfulness
  Advent 1
  After Pentecost
  Propers 14, 27

Water
  Christmas, Proper II
  Easter 4, 7
  After Pentecost
  Proper 21

Waywardness
After Pentecost
Propers 18, 29, 24

Weakness
Holy Week—Tu, F
Pentecost
After Pentecost
Propers 7, 9, 12, 23

Wealth
After Pentecost
Propers 19, 23

Weary
After Epiphany 5, 7
Holy Week—W
After Pentecost
Proper 21

Welcome
After Pentecost
Propers 16, 20, 22, 24, 27
All Saints' Day

Wholeness
After Epiphany 6, 9
Lent 4, 5
Easter 3, 4
After Pentecost
Propers 10, 11, 17, 18, 20, 27
All Saints' Day

Wickedness
Easter 7
After Pentecost
Propers 16, 17, 25

Willfulness
After Pentecost
Proper 15

Wind
Pentecost

Trinity Sunday
After Pentecost
Proper 7

Wisdom
After Christmas 1
After Epiphany 4
Lent 4, 5
Holy Week—Tu
Ascension Day
After Pentecost
Propers 7, 10, 15, 17, 19, 20, 24

Witness
After Christmas 2
After Epiphany 4
Lent 6—Passion
Holy Week—W
Easter Day, Evening, 5, 7
Ascension Day
Trinity Sunday
After Pentecost
Propers 9, 17, 19, 23, 25, 27, 28, 29

Wonder
Christmas, Proper I
Easter 3
After Pentecost
Propers 19, 25, 27
Thanksgiving Day

Wonderful Counselor
Christmas, Proper I

Word(s)
Advent 3
After Christmas 2
After Epiphany 2, 3, 4, 6
Lent 3, 4
Holy Week—F
Easter Evening, 5
After Pentecost

Propers 4, 5, 13, 14, 19, 22, 23, 24, 27, 29
All Saints' Day

Word(s)
After Epiphany 4
Lent 4
After Pentecost
Propers 17, 24, 27

World
After Epiphany 3
Lent 3, 4
Easter 6, 7
After Pentecost
Propers 17, 18, 29, 24, 29

Worry
Advent 3
Thanksgiving Day

Worship
After Epiphany 4
Lent 2, 4

Holy Week—F
Easter 5
Trinity Sunday
After Pentecost
Propers 4, 12, 15, 17, 18, 21, 22, 24, 26, 27, 28
All Saints' Day

Worth(iness)
Advent 3
After Epiphany 5
After Pentecost
Propers 13, 22, 24, 25, 26

Wrong
After Pentecost
Propers 13, 25, 28

Yeast
Easter Evening

About the Author

Lavon (Burrichter) Bayler is no stranger to worship planners, having authored five previous books of lectionary-based resources: *Fresh Winds of the Spirit* (1986), *Whispers of God* (1987), *Refreshing Rains of the Living Word* (1988), *Fresh Winds of the Spirit, Book 2* (1992), and *Gathered by Love* (1994). Revisions in the *Revised Common Lectionary* have prompted this new volume.

Lavon works as minister of the Fox Valley Association, Illinois Conference, United Church of Christ. She spent twenty years in parish ministry before joining the conference staff seventeen years ago. She resources and counsels pastors and congregations, assists pastoral search committees, and administers her association of fifty-two churches, often appearing in one of their pulpits on Sunday morning or on other special occasions. She has led numerous retreats, workshops, and seminars on a variety of topics.

Lavon and her husband, Bob, have three adult sons, a daughter-in-law, a granddaughter, and a grandson.

Printed in the United States
42931LVS00004B/157-276